THINKING *poetry*

by lynn keller

THINKING *poetry*

READINGS IN CONTEMPORARY
WOMEN'S EXPLORATORY POETICS

UNIVERSITY OF IOWA PRESS

iowa city

University of Iowa Press, Iowa City 52242
Copyright © 2010 by the University of
    Iowa Press
www.uiowapress.org
Printed in the United States of America

Design by Teresa W. Wingfield

The University of Iowa Press is a member of
Green Press Initiative and is committed to
preserving natural resources.

Printed on acid-free paper

Library of Congress
Cataloging-in-Publication Data

Keller, Lynn, 1952–
Thinking poetry: readings in contemporary
women's exploratory poetics / by Lynn Keller.
p.   cm.
Includes bibliographical references and index.
ISBN-13: 978-1-58729-867-7 (cloth)
ISBN-10: 1-58729-867-8 (cloth)
1. American poetry—Women authors—History
and criticism.   2. Women and literature—
United States—History—21st century.
3. American poetry—21st century—History
and criticism.   4. Experimental poetry,
American—History and criticism.   I. Title.
PS151.K453 2010
811'.54099287—dc22   2009040741

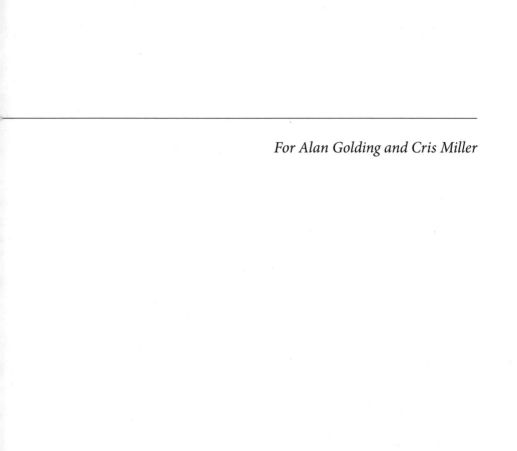

For Alan Golding and Cris Miller

CONTENTS

ACKNOWLEDGMENTS
AND PERMISSIONS

AS I REACH THE FINAL STAGES of preparing this manuscript, I am acutely aware that writing a book of literary criticism is a collaborative enterprise, one that builds not only on the thinking of one's teachers and the writing of other scholars, but also on the contributions of a network of colleagues and friends, to all of whom I am deeply grateful. I wish to acknowledge first my debts to the poets whose work is discussed in the pages to follow—Alice Fulton, Myung Mi Kim, Joan Retallack, Cole Swensen, Rosmarie Waldrop, Susan Wheeler, and C.D. Wright—each of whom provided invaluable assistance supporting my attempts to do some justice to her work.

A senior fellowship at the Institute for Research in the Humanities at the University of Wisconsin–Madison provided time in which to develop this study in the early stages of its writing, as well as sharp audiences to push my thinking. Mike Shank and David Schalkwyk offered particularly helpful suggestions, while David Sorkin's invitation to give a public lecture on my work provided a valuable impetus to conceptualize the larger picture into which its parts fit.

So many people have responded to drafts or discussed with me ideas that play into this book that I could not possibly list them all. I particularly wish to acknowledge Charles Altieri, Susan Bernstein, Elisabeth Frost, Alan Golding, Jenny Goodman, Joseph Jonghyun Jeon, Linda Kinnahan, Cristanne Miller, Dee (Adalaide) Morris, Marjorie Perloff, Eric Rothstein, Laura Sims, Ron Wallace, and David Zimmerman. Many of these are personal friends who have with remarkable generosity read more than one chapter, or even several drafts of a single chapter. I owe thanks, too, to my wonderful graduate students at the University of Wisconsin–Madison, who have repeatedly brought me to fresh perceptions of this poetry. In the final months prior to going to press, it was my good fortune to have the immensely capable assistance of one of these students, Lisa Hollenbach. Joe Parsons at the University of Iowa Press has been a superb editor and a delight to work with. My thanks to him and to Holly Carver for their faith in my work, and to all those who have helped produce this book, including Karen Copp, Karin Horler, Allison Thomas Means, and Charlotte Wright. Most of all, I am profoundly grateful to Jim Weber for his unflagging personal support.

My thanks to the anonymous readers for the University of Iowa Press for their thoughtful attention to this manuscript. I am grateful also to the editors of the scholarly journals in which earlier versions of some of these chapters appeared, and to the anonymous readers for those journals. A version of the chapter on the work of Retallack and Waldrop appeared in the special issue of *Contemporary Literature* on poetry of the 1990s edited by Thomas Gardner, and the chapter on Swensen appeared in that journal as well. *American Literature* published earlier incarnations of the chapters on Fulton and on Wheeler, and the chapter on Wright had its first appearance in *Arizona Quarterly*.

In the late 1970s, when we were graduate students at the University of Chicago, Alan Golding, Cris Miller, and I began meeting regularly in a basement coffee house to discuss volumes of contemporary poetry. I have been thinking about poetry—and much else—in their good company throughout the years since. One could have no finer interlocutors or more generous friends; this book is dedicated to them.

EMILY DICKINSON: *To hear an oriole sing* (J526/F402) from *The Poems of Emily Dickinson*, Thomas H. Johnson, ed., Cambridge, Massachusetts: Belknap Press of Harvard University Press, copyright © 1951, 1955, 1979, 1983 by the President and Fellows of Harvard College. Reprinted by permission of the publishers and the Trustees of Amherst College.

ALICE FULTON: Lines from "Volunteers," "Wonder Bread," "= =," "Fuzzy Feelings," "Mail," "Splice: A Grotesque," and "A New Release" from *Sensual Math* by Alice Fulton, copyright © 1995 by Alice Fulton. Reprinted by permission of W. W. Norton & Company, Inc.

MYUNG MI KIM: Excerpts from "Exordium," "317," "Vocalise," and "Works" originally appeared in *Commons*, published by University of California Press, copyright © 2002 by Regents of the University of California. Reprinted by permission of the publisher. Excerpts from *River Antes*, copyright © 2006 by the author. Reprinted by permission of Atticus/Finch Chapbooks.

JOAN RETALLACK: Excerpts from "Icarus FFFFFalling" from *AFTERRIM-AGES*, copyright © 2005 by the author. Reprinted by permission of Wesleyan University Press.

COLE SWENSEN: Excerpts from *Try*, copyright © 1999 by the author. Reprinted by permission of University of Iowa Press.

ROSMARIE WALDROP: Excerpts from "Lawn of Excluded Middle" from *Curves to the Apple*, copyright © 1993 by the author. Reprinted by permission of New Directions Publishing Corp.

SUSAN WHEELER: Excerpts from "One," "Forty-eight," "Twenty-six," and "Thirty-four" originally appeared in *Source Codes*, published by Salt Publishing, copyright © 2001 by the author. Reprinted by permission of the publisher.

C.D. WRIGHT: Excerpt from "The Lesson" from *Further Adventures with You*, copyright © 1986 by the author. Reprinted by permission of Carnegie Mellon University Press, www.cmu.edu/universitypress. Excerpts from "Just Whistle" in *Steal Away: Selected and New Poems*, copyright © 2002 by the author. Reprinted by permission of Copper Canyon Press, www.coppercanyonpress.org.

THINKING *poetry*

one

THINKING POETRY

An Introduction

We are currently living in a moment of extraordinary complexity when systems and structures that have long organized life are changing at an unprecedented rate. Such rapid and pervasive change creates the need to develop new ways of understanding the world and of interpreting our experience.
—MARK C. TAYLOR, *The Moment of Complexity: Emerging Network Culture*

The kind of agency that has a chance of mattering in today's world can thrive *only* in a culture of acknowledged complexity. . . . The more complex things are, the less certain the outcome but also the more room for the play of the mind, for inventing ourselves out of the mess.
—JOAN RETALLACK, *The Poethical Wager*

If poetry reaches the point which chess has reached, where the decisive, profound, and elegant combinations lie within the scope only of masters, and are appreciable only to competent and trained players, that will seem to many people a sorry state of affairs, and to some people a consequence simply of the sinfulness of poets; but it will not in the least mean that poetry is, as they say, *dead*; rather the reverse. It is when poetry becomes altogether too easy, too accessible, runs down to a few derivative formulae and caters to low tastes and lazy minds—it is then that the life of the art is in danger.
—HOWARD NEMEROV, *Reflexions on Poetry and Poetics*

THIS BOOK IS DEVOTED TO poetry that is complex in the thinking it enacts and, correspondingly, in its compositional strategies. My most cherished hope is that its publication might heighten readers' appreciation of the value of a literature of complexity. Most of the chapters included here, along with some of the poems they discuss, were first drafted during the presidency of

1

George W. Bush, whose administration demonstrated with depressing regularity that ours is a culture dangerously attracted to simplicity: to simple ideas of good and evil, to belief in simple solutions, to a self-absorbed faith in our nation's simple rightness. This has no doubt been true at least since the Cold War, but it was frighteningly apparent during the composition of this book—although the final stages of reflection on the individual parts and the whole they create have occurred when the new Obama administration is attempting to embrace the complex challenges confronting us. One of the greatest responsibilities of intellectuals and of artists today may be to reveal the truth of complexity; ours is an astonishingly complex world, in which right and wrong are intricately interwoven, in which difficult problems require multifaceted, inventive solutions that may well involve material sacrifice and uncomfortable change.

What I am calling *exploratory poems* do not aspire to be comfortable or comforting, but, importantly, their opacities are not gratuitous. As Susan Howe puts it, such poems "are the impossibility of plainness rendered in plainest form" (*The Midnight* 64). The women who create the exploratory work examined here are convinced that poetry, like philosophy or political theory, enacts a significant intellectual engagement with the most important and challenging issues faced by contemporary Americans. The concepts and terminology I have developed to capture at once the complexities of their work and ways to think fruitfully about those complexities—such as "contracts of (contracted) intelligibility" (chapter 2), "pattern-bounded unpredictability" (chapter 4), or "iconoplasm" (chapter 6)—are intended to illuminate as well the poetry of numerous other writers who also are seeking ways to give sufficient but not falsifying form to ongoing, often chaotic discovery.

Within the sphere of literary criticism, this book joins existing efforts to foster recognition that Language poetry is not the only form of contemporary poetic linguistic experimentation and that female poets are playing a key role in expanding the possibilities for alternative poetic practices. That such a project can take its current form as an array of close readings, rather than requiring a focused polemic, reveals a good deal about recent developments in the U.S. poetry scene as well as changes in the state of poetry criticism over the past fifteen years.

In the 1990s, the dominant critical model (predictably outmoded, being much more accurate as a characterization of U.S. poetry a decade earlier) portrayed the poetry scene as divided into two or three sharply opposed camps. The three-camp model included the "mainstream" poets, whose practice was dominated by the personal, expressive, usually free verse lyric; the "New Formalists," who were interested in revitalizing regular poetic form and meter; and the "Language poets," who were committed to linguistic innovation prompted in part by poststructuralist ideas of language's constitutive—as opposed to expressive—role and by an awareness of the ideological dimensions of the formal resources of language.[1] The more widely invoked two-camp model simply set mainstream against Language writing. Although by the mid-1990s both monolithic categories were obvious reductions, this model retained enough credibility to be the basis of major critical studies at least as late as Christopher Beach's *Poetic Culture*, from 1999.

Discussion of experimental poetry and poetics from the mid-1980s to at least the mid-1990s in both literary and scholarly venues tended to recognize only one kind of linguistically innovative poetry practice, that identified with Language poetry.[2] And, because so much of the published theorizing for that group had been done by men—Charles Bernstein, Ron Silliman, Steve McCaffery, and Barrett Watten, among others—critical attention to Language writing tended to focus on the work, often especially the essays, of male poets. By 1995, a critical literature was only beginning to emerge on the work of Lyn Hejinian and Susan Howe, with some initial attention also to Leslie Scalapino, Rae Armantrout, Carla Harryman, and a few other women closely associated with the Language community. Even now, my focus on women writers remains a necessary compensation for a continuing gender imbalance in contemporary criticism. For in fact, experimentation by female poets was not only extensive but was taking a range of forms, and those undertaking such exploration had more and less tenuous links to Language writing.

In the 1980s and 1990s both male and female writers were experimenting in diverse ways, but numerous women writers in particular were dissatisfied with the models offered both by "official verse culture" and by Language writing. Their story has been well told by others,[3] but a quick recounting is relevant here. As early as 1982, the notes that Kathleen Fraser produced to conclude the anthology of Language writing assembled by Ron Silliman in *Ironwood* acknowledged an ambivalence she and some other experimentally inclined women poets felt about Language writing, both as a social phenomenon and as a set of principles, a poetics. In part, these women were wary because the dominant theorists within the group were men, while their own feminist perspectives left them unwilling to assume that what currently seemed needed by male writers was needed by female ones as well. Fraser explained that the Language poets' "esthetic distaste for self-referentiality and/or *evident* personal investment in one's subject immediately introduces a series of prohibiting factors. For a writer whose awareness has been tuned by a growing need to claim her own history and voice/s, such as Feminism provides, Language Writing's concerns are often *experienced* (if not intended) as directives she cannot afford" ("Partial Local Coherence" 137).[4] Writing a few years later, in 1985, Fraser recalled the feeling of double marginality she had experienced in the 1970s, when she found herself uncomfortable with the expectations of not only the Language community but the women's writing community as well. The dominant strain of American feminism at the time, focusing on the politics of poetic content, called for "the immediately accessible language of personal experience" and regarded the poem "as a place for self-expression, for giving a true account, for venting rage, and for embracing sexual love of women" (Fraser, *Translating* 31–32). Fraser's sense of having no outlets led her, in collaboration with several other women, to found the feminist experimentalist journal *HOW(ever)*, which appeared between 1983 and 1992 and which looked back especially to precedents offered by the female experimental modernists. In the years since, a growing number of women poets have felt empowered to experiment in gender-conscious ways.

As Jed Rasula noted in 2004, "[I]t takes a generation (at least) to overcome a dominant paradigm" so that "a real diversity of style and idiom among women writers has only recently become evident on a widespread scale" (*Syncopations* 10). We are now a generation past Fraser's launching of *HOW(ever)*; its second-generation embodiment exists on the Internet as the vibrant electronic journal *HOW2*. And, with the Language writers now a senior generation among experimentalists, recognition that Language poetry is not the only form of contemporary poetic exploration and innovation in the United States is growing, partly thanks to the publication of such anthologies as Mary Margaret Sloan's *Moving Borders: Three Decades of Innovative Writing by Women* in 1998; Claudia Rankine and Juliana Spahr's *American Women Poets in the 21st Century: Where Lyric Meets Language* in 2002 and its sequel, edited by Claudia Rankine and Lisa Sewell, *American Poets in the 21st Century: The New Poetics*, in 2007; Aldon Lynn Nielsen and Lauri Ramey's *Every Goodbye Ain't Gone: An Anthology of Innovative Poetry by African Americans* in 2006; and, most recently, Cole Swensen and David St. John's *American Hybrid* and Reginald Shepherd's *Lyric Postmodernisms: An Anthology of Contemporary Innovative Poetries* (both 2008).

As Rasula observes, "[T]he legacy of language poetry has been disseminated into the environment of poetic innovation at large" (*Syncopations* 18), and, importantly, "it seems to have nourished poetic practice in markedly nondenominational ways" (24).[5] One no longer needs to argue to gain recognition for diverse experimental practices; it is now apparent that poets at the beginning of the twenty-first century experience far less programmatic affinities and rigid boundaries than were evident a quarter century ago, while institutional factors make it relatively easy for poets to diverge from received models of either experimental or nonexperimental practice and still gain an audience (granted that the audience for any written poetry in the United States now is small). Those who have no interest in producing expressive personal lyric are nonetheless able to publish with reputable university and mainstream presses, while radically experimental writers are beginning to teach in AWP (Association of Writers and Writing Programs) writing programs and to appear on the boards of such normative institutions as the Academy of American Poets.[6] Journals such as *Fence*, founded in 1998, and *Fulcrum*, launched in 2000, have set out deliberately to build bridges between what would formerly have been opposed camps. (Avant-gardists have not necessarily welcomed this development.[7]) It's no longer easy to say what typifies the "mainstream," as a good deal of recent work from establishment venues has begun to demonstrate skepticism about the coherent subjectivity that had previously controlled mainstream first-person narratives and seems interested in more than direct personal statement; approaches language as a nontransparent medium of generating and constructing, rather than recording or representing, experience; and no longer attempts to convey the illusion of naturalness on which the recently dominant "scenic mode" of writing depended.[8]

   In addition to opening the field and prompting other forms of experimentalism (in part by nurturing another generation of innovators determined not simply to mimic their elders), Language writing itself has been evolving in response to changed political, institutional, and aesthetic circumstances. Thus, Marjorie Perloff, the most influential critic to champion Language writing, when collecting her 1999 essay "Language Poetry and the Lyric Subject: Ron Silliman's Albany, Susan Howe's Buffalo" a few years after it was written, observed, "Rereading the essay in 2003, I have a strong sense of the difference four years has already made in the poetic formations in question" (*Differentials* 129). The essay itself addresses a set of changes Perloff discerned within Language writing in 1999: one of that movement's "cardinal principles" had been "the dismissal of 'voice' as the foundational principle of lyric poetry" (129), but when the "exploratory poetries associated with the Language movement are more than twenty years old" (132), Perloff finds it necessary to "reconsider the role of the subject in Language poetry" (134). While acknowledging that the poets affiliated with Language writing have no more interest at the turn of the century than they ever did in what she calls "the closural first-person metaphoric model of mainstream poetry" (141), Perloff nonetheless discerns in the poems she examines individual signatures "as unique and 'personal' as any we have in poetry today" (151). Her primary point is that the time has come when it is useful for critics "to look at special cases *within* the Language movement and related alternative poetries rather than at the group phenomenon" (153). Yet the essay also indicates that experimental poets' own assessments of the place of the author, of agency and identity, have changed over the past quarter century—and that their poetic practices have evolved accordingly. Indeed, Linda A. Kinnahan has pointed out that in calling for a reconsideration of the subject's role in experimental writing, "In effect, [Perloff] is echoing, although in different terms, an imperative articulated at least from the early nineties by feminist critics and poets . . . who have wrestled with [Language poetry's] 'given' of subject banishment," finding it an inappropriately "closed model for reading a range of works positioning themselves differently in relation to the masculine, white, and Western model of subjectivity that underlies the 'transcendental ego' cast off by avant-garde poetries" (*Lyric Interventions* 12).[9]

Now, nearing the end of the first decade of the twenty-first century, most readers and critics interested in contemporary poetry recognize not only that poetic practices are evolving at a pace with which criticism can only stumblingly keep up, but also that there are a range of what Fraser has termed "uncommon language[s]" being used today, varied approaches to experimentation often indebted to Language writing but not necessarily closely tied to it. (Tellingly, her phrase, transcribed in an interview with emphasis as "*uncom*-mon," both evokes and rejects Adrienne Rich's "dream of a common language," placing the poetics that most interest Fraser in relation to mainstream feminism yet deliberately moving in other directions [Fraser, "Interview" 18].) That many of those doing particularly interesting work are women is also widely acknowledged, and there exists a significant body of criticism that assumes female poets may differ from male poets in the approaches they take to experimentation, perhaps especially as their explorations investigate subjectivity. My interest in fostering fuller appreciation of the present diversity of poetic practice can now appropriately take the form of a loosely linked series of chapters that attend to compelling individual oeuvres or single books, what Perloff calls "special cases."

The particular "uncommon languages" selected for focus here do, however, collectively illuminate a specific period of transition from a polarized poetry scene to a more open and polyvocal one. The title of a 1999 conference, "Where Lyric Meets Language," suggested that the new diversification of poetry was occurring at the intersection of lyric and Language poetry.[10] That formulation encouraged perception of current practices as negotiated in the terrain between the extreme positions of the two recently dominant camps, or as a cross or synthesis between them. The two already mentioned anthologies published in 2008, Swensen and St. John's *American Hybrid* and Shepherd's *Lyric Postmodernisms*, reinforce such perceptions, presenting what Swensen describes as "a combinatory new" "that hybridize[s] core attributes of previous 'camps' in diverse and unprecedented ways" (xxi, xvii) or Shepherd describes as "work [that] combines lyricism and avant-garde experimentation in a new synthesis" (xi).[11] Increasingly common, formulations like Shepherd's suggest a problematically tidy model in which a thesis and antithesis—lyric and Language, or mainstream and experimental—are now being succeeded by a synthesis. They tend to erase awareness of the messier processes of literary history—specifically, awareness that the mainstream/Language binary was from the outset being complicated or even collapsed from within, particularly by women writers.[12] The poets from a particular generation and a half whose work is examined here enable a more nuanced historical view, since they were managing to create positions between or outside the two dominant camps when the binary was still very much in place. Their work reminds us that deconstruction of the historically powerful lyric/Language polarity was an always already available option or set of options—indeed, as the origins of *HOW(ever)* make clear, it was perceived by some women as a necessity—although such explorations were far less acknowledged and less accepted than a "third way" or "third space" is for young writers today.

The works examined in this book have received little critical attention, though their creators, all of whom are now at least in their fifties, are widely respected.[13] These poets—Alice Fulton, Myung Mi Kim, Joan Retallack, Cole Swensen, Rosmarie Waldrop, Susan Wheeler, and C.D. Wright[14]—have all received some mainstream recognition in the form of major awards or publication with established presses, and some of them move in overlapping literary circles. (For instance, Wright and Waldrop run innovative small presses in Providence, Rhode Island; Retallack and Waldrop have known one another for decades; Wright and Kim spent formative years in the Bay Area in contact with Language writers.) Despite these commonalities, they provide diverse examples of current exploratory writing, ranging from experimentation within relatively conventional free verse forms to radically open, thoroughly disjunctive writing, from texts expanding current uses of visual elements and page space, to those in which multilingualism or digital technology provide arenas for innovation, from revitalized forms of ekphrasis to fresh approaches to pop culture. For these singular writers, publishing in the same kinds of presses or receiving the same kinds of awards has not been associated with either a shared feminist enterprise, a common aesthetic, or notions of a writing community like that nurtured by the Language writers.[15]

Nonetheless, the volumes to be discussed here have some general but significant traits in common, beyond being published in a fifteen-year period beginning in the early 1990s. First, all of them demonstrate a desire on the part of their creators to manipulate language in uncommon ways so as to significantly "stretch the boundaries of the sayable" (Swensen, "Against the Limits" 630), and they therefore fit into a permeable category for which Perloff's term "exploratory" provides an apt label. Second, they are created by women who write as Americans with a feminist consciousness nurtured by second-wave feminism. Even Rosmarie Waldrop and Myung Mi Kim, who immigrated to this country and did not speak English as their first language, write from within the context of the cultural and social milieu of the United States, though as reluctant insiders to America's history of racial oppression and international domination. Thus, all respond to global issues, including feminist concerns, with keen awareness of the limitations, shames, and burdens, as well as the freedoms and privileges that follow from their position as Americans near the turn of the twenty-first century. Third, as noted in my opening, these works are intellectually ambitious, reflecting their creators' belief that poetry should address and resonate with the most current scientific, social, and philosophical understandings of the world's workings. These broad commonalities warrant some elaboration, beginning with the poetry's attempt to expand the boundaries of linguistic and literary convention.

Sometimes the work discussed here transgresses the very limits of intelligibility, for "[t]he realm of the unintelligible is the permanent frontier," Joan Retallack observes, "—that which lies outside the scope of the culturally preconceived" (*Poethical Wager* 111–12). Sometimes its experiments are much less radically disruptive. Either way, the poetry pushes beyond what is readily grasped, familiar. This work is "innovative" in being boldly creative and defamiliarizing, but neither its techniques nor the ideas shaping its strategies need be truly new. As Retallack puts it, explaining how a new sense of pattern emerges from the teeming multiplicity, the mess of contemporary living, "Of course *new* never means ex nihilo. It means *ex perturbatio, ex confusio rerum*" (*Poethical Wager* 30). Perloff stands on solid ground when arguing as she has in another recent book, *21st-Century Modernism: The "New" Poetics* (published in 2002), that even the most radical contemporary avant-gardists, rather than doing something "new," are in fact recovering modernist insights and exploring resources of language tapped, abortedly, by the early modernists. The radical and utopian aspirations of first-stage modernism, Perloff claims, were cut off by World War I and repressed during the decades of totalitarian threat that culminated in World War II and the Cold War, so that only now are the lessons of early modernism really being put into practice. She is certainly correct that the premises even of early Language writing were not as new or as extreme as both its proponents and opponents claimed, since those premises recalled earlier theories of Jakobson, the Russian formalists, Bakhtin, and Wittgenstein, along with more contemporary theories of French poststructuralists (*Differentials* 159).

Indeed, the very sense of needing to respond to a historical moment of complexity with new, complex, and often difficult modes of representation currently evident among exploratory artists and intellectuals echoes high modernist views. Thus, there are marked similarities between Mark Taylor's statement in the first epigraph above, from 2002, concerning the need to respond to a period of "extraordinary complexity" and rapid change with "new ways of . . . interpreting our experience" (Taylor 19) and this statement by T. S. Eliot from 1921: "[I]t appears likely that poets in our civilization, as it exists at present, must be *difficult*. Our civilization comprehends great variety and complexity, and this variety and complexity, playing upon a refined sensibility, must produce various and complex results" (Eliot 65). Recent concern with finding linguistic forms adequate to convey a perception of increased complexity of human experience may itself be understood as part of the legacy of modernism.

So novelty per se is not my concern here. Indeed, the drive for novelty for its own sake generates a good deal of poetry today that is either empty nonsense pretentiously presented or conventional work in a costume of radical chic, its closed structure and tidy take-home messages disguised with a veneer of fashionable disjunction and abstraction. In contrast, the work analyzed in the chapters to follow convinces me that it reflects some kind of impassioned imperative to go beyond the limits of familiar language use, to develop—again, Fraser's term— "uncommon languages," a phrase suggesting more than lexical unusualness. Its explorations seem unrelated to the trendiness of the stylistic devices and techniques associated with experimentalism in the post-Language scene; rather, such writing involves innovation as Rasula defines it: "a necessary response to force of circumstance in which the apparent utility of the medium is insufficient" (*Syncopations* 38).

Since one's gender may be a significant circumstance affecting one's perception of the utility of common language, it is perhaps not surprising that many of the most visible and compelling experimentally inclined/exploratory poets writing today are women. Rachel Blau DuPlessis argues that precisely because of the socially charged life of words, if poetry is to disrupt the social structures that have oppressed women, it "has to be allowed to depoeticize itself and enact a rejection of the cultural character of its own idiom" (*Pink Guitar* 144). That "turning away from poetry as already written" requires precisely the kinds of rupture and re-vision of linguistic and literary convention that characterize exploratory writing (151). To the extent that women have occupied at least ambiguously (non)hegemonic positions, contemporary women writers may be particularly ready to step outside the dominant conventions.

This has not always been the case, just as it often has not been true for other marginalized groups, including racial minorities. One explanation for the recent emergence of female experimentalists is that experimental practice, which pushes to extremes the "*heterogeneousness* to meaning and signification" characteristic of poetic language (Kristeva 133), has long involved traits associated with the feminine (as in Julia Kristeva's semiotic), but only recently have women "finally" grown "powerful enough sociopolitically to undertake the risks of this feminine challenge in their own texts" (Retallack, *Poethical Wager* 113). If, as Rae Armantrout speculates may be the case, experimentalism and feminism are "natural allies" (since women as outsiders are "well positioned to appreciate the constructedness of the identity that is based on identification" and to challenge poetic conventions such as the "unified Voice"), perhaps the expanded field of feminist experimentalism simply reflects the permeation of feminist perspectives through literary America (48, 40). Or perhaps, in the aftermath of the second wave of feminism with its prescriptive sense of what the poem should be and do, women are less invested in specific forms of gender empowerment (this is Rasula's claim), even while they remain wary of the conventions entangled with social structures that so long excluded or oppressed them.[16] Whatever the reasons, an impressive number of women poets is contributing to a richly varied body of exploratory poetry that is now being published, many of them operating without the structuring context of group identities and manifestos. I have focused my attention on books by a handful of the best known of these, poets born between the late 1930s and the late 1950s whose work I admire.

The poets discussed in the chapters to follow vary considerably in the extent to which feminist thinking comes to the fore in their work, though all write self-consciously as women; all are keenly aware of women's historical oppression as one of numerous social issues that concern them; all are interested in a thorough rethinking of the role of the feminine in culture and in helping release masculine and feminine from the limits of an oppositional sexual politics. These concerns take different forms in their distinct oeuvres, as is evident if one compares two books from the same year (1995), Alice Fulton's *Sensual Math* and Joan Retallack's *AFTERRIMAGES*. Some readers might question my decision even to include Fulton in a book on experimental writing, arguing that although the unusual intellectual energy and the linguistic heterogeneity of Fulton's work are undeniable, her poetry remains too carefully controlled in its meaning and effects to "count" as genuinely exploratory. In her composition Fulton does not approach the radical indeterminacy of Retallack's chance procedures in the poem "AFTERRIMAGES," and although her dense, often punning wordplay generates genuine polysemy, it does not have the openness created by Retallack's extreme disjunctions. Yet, as chapter 4 reveals, Retallack's particular selection of texts on which to enact those procedures clearly indicates that her disruptions of conventional order are, like Fulton's, significantly motivated by a desire to disrupt ideas of gender that have held Western culture in thrall for centuries. Playing with contradictory clues to create voices and characters who occupy an unsettling and unsettled space between masculine and feminine, Fulton unhinges many nearly unconscious but powerful assumptions about gender, while the invented punctuation mark she calls the bride (after the recessive threads in lace) is one strategy in her effort "to change background into foreground and associate women with the power of negative space" ("The Wick That Is the White"). That Fulton's work is less radically experimental than Retallack's does not mean the exploratory dimensions of her poetry are insignificant. Moreover, it is precisely by appreciating the feminist aspects of her poetics that one perceives the full inventiveness of her work, its rejection of the poetics of both then-dominant camps, and its challenges to the literary and social status quo.

Fulton has been awarded coveted poetry prizes and fellowships, as have Cole Swensen and Susan Wheeler. Both Fulton and C.D. Wright have been recipients of the MacArthur "genius" fellowships, and most of the poets here have had at least some of their books published by major university presses or widely known literary presses. Clearly, alternative practices no longer exclude one from the markers of "mainstream" institutional success (although such success doesn't necessarily translate into critical attention). Yet even if formal experimentalism that might be attributed to the disseminated legacy of Language writing is no longer confined to the margins of the literary scene, it still generates some strong hostility, and I think Rasula is right when he attributes this to its intellectual character:

> The issues that continue to emanate from language poetry are not formal. Formalism is a straw dog. The real dirty word in the American poetry clubhouse is *intellectual*. The fitful absorption of modernism into Anglo-American letters was prelude to a lurking and easily revived anti-intellectualism. Resentful accusations of "difficulty" in poetry, commonly associated with modernism, usually mean that the reader (critic) doesn't want poetry to think. This attitude consigns the poet to a kind of hotel-bar, cocktail-hour pianism, a strictly decorative role. It does not proscribe thoughts from the poem, but asks that the thoughts be familiar enough so as not to disturb the atmosphere—that is, the idle chatter, the drinks, the flirting. Difficulty returned to poetry with a vengeance in the context of Black Mountain, but not always in the obvious terms of intellectualism. (*Syncopations* 19–20)

Rasula goes on to discuss the importance of "'theory' in the scholastic sense" (20), the poststructuralist theory associated with the French intellectual scene of the 1970s and '80s, as a source for the intellectualism of Language poetry.[17] Indeed, in their collectively authored "Aesthetic Tendency and the Politics of Poetry: A Manifesto" (1988), Ron Silliman, Carla Harryman, Lyn Hejinian, Steve Benson, Bob Perelman, and Barrett Watten—all members of the Language community—refuse to separate critical and creative practice, asserting that "theory has opened up a speculative vocabulary that permits critical discussion of the work toward other ends than quasi-religious communion [which they attribute to the "'expressivist' personal lyric"]. It has connected writing with broader realms of intellectual discourse and has staked out a space for creative writers as equals with serious thinkers in other areas" (269).

Rasula's claims about resentment of intellectual difficulty are readily supported, for instance, by a review essay that appeared in the *New Republic* in 2002, two years before his essay "Women, Innovation, and 'Improbable Evidence,'" from which I quoted above, was collected in *Syncopations*.[18] It is worth quoting Adam Kirsch at length, as he takes the opportunity of reviewing C.D. Wright's selected poems to meditate on what he calls "poetic courtesy":

> The courteous poet meets his ideal reader on conditions of equality. He approaches language as a medium of communication, which must be brought to a height of precision and eloquence to move and to delight the reader. As a result, care is taken to bring the poem into the open region shared by reader and writer, where it can be delivered with artistic generosity. Concretely, this means that the courteous poet will try to make clear the situation of the poem, its basic grammar and concepts, and its emotional atmosphere. Reference and allusion will be used to deepen understanding, on the assumption that reader and writer share a common literary tradition. Formally, such a poet will naturally gravitate toward meter and rhyme, which knit the poem to the traditions of English verse and provide a pattern to guide the reader's expectations. This emphatically does not mean that the experience offered by the poem will be inoffensively "pleasant"; it means simply that the poet's knowledge—even of extremity, perplexity, tragedy—will be made coherently available to the reader, so that it can be genuinely shared.
>
> For the discourteous poet, by contrast, novelty and complexity are the fundamental values, both because they provide aesthetic pleasure and because they differentiate the poet from his peers. The implied reader does not need to be invited or seduced into the poem; his presence is assumed, or ignored. As a result, no effort is made to avoid confusion about the subject or situation of the poem; confusion may actually be invited. If actual experience is the spur for the writing, the finished poem will not reveal what event or feeling brought it into being; often the implication of incommunicability is an important part of the poem. Reference and allusion tend to be idiosyncratic and alienating, and form is conceived intellectually and theoretically rather than discursively or musically.
>
> . . . Both types of poet have produced work of the first rank—the history of Modernist poetry shows the tremendous power, under the right circumstances, of discourtesy. Yet the balance today has swung so far in the direction of discourtesy—it is the standard mode of writing and consider-

ing poetry in those precincts where poetry survives—that a cautionary and probing criticism of this practice of writing seems necessary. (32–33)

Kirsch goes on to state that extreme discourtesy is evident in "poems in which the action, the situation, the grammar, and the purpose are deeply obscure" (34). C.D. Wright—one of whose books I examine in the pages that follow— is, for Kirsch, "one of the most influential of the discourteous poets," and he uses her career as his cautionary example of a poet gone astray (32). As Kirsch sees it, she has, for instance, lost sight of "the function of allusion, which is a courtesy: allusion exists to remind the reader of precedents and to establish an orientation for reading" (35).[19]

Leaving aside the inaccuracies in his characterizations of the writing he considers "discourteous," what I find striking about this review are its underlying condescension toward the poetry reader's intelligence and its implicit assumptions that neither the poet, the poem, nor the reader is or should be engaged in intellectual pursuits. For Kirsch, the poet is spurred to write by knowledge of states like "extremity, perplexity, tragedy" or by feeling, not by intellectual curiosity, intellectual debate, or intellectual excitement. The assumed reader—apparently a being of little imagination, and one who takes no pleasure in being challenged or led toward new knowledge, emerging political or intellectual perspectives, or even fresh forms of aural stimulation—wants everything either to be spelled out or to point back to what is already familiar. (In Rasula's terms, the poem's thoughts must be entertaining and uncomplicated enough for cocktail party conversation.[20])

Today's experimentally inclined writers—including C.D. Wright, though she has characterized herself as not avant-garde, "just ornery" (letter, 28 Feb. 1999)—have quite different ideas than Kirsch about what constitutes treating the reader as an equal and about poetry's aims and responsibilities. It is a commonplace in the poets' statements of Language poetics that their polysemous writing invites the reader's participation as "co-producer" of the text. To cite two of the numerous possible examples: Steve McCaffery explains in "The Death of the Subject" (1980) that, in Language-centered writing, "the text becomes the communal space of a labour, initiated by the writer and extended by the second writer (the reader). So we break, finally, the divisive structure of the conventional reading process. The old duality of reader-writer collapses into the one compound function, and the two actions are permitted to become a simultaneous experience within the activity of the engager." Similarly, Lyn Hejinian, in her well-known essay from the early 1980s, "Rejection of Closure," asserts that the "open text" (as opposed to the "closed text," in which all the elements are directed toward a single reading) invites the reader's "participation, rejects the authority of the writer over the reader and thus, by analogy, the authority implicit in other (social, economic, cultural) hierarchies" (*Language of Inquiry* 43). One might well argue that the poets producing linguistically innovative writing approach the reader with the utmost respect and courtesy by assuming a relationship of intellectual equality and exploratory community. This attitude is also maintained by post-Language writers of various exploratory stripes.

A well-known example of work whose opacity Kirsch would presumably find discourteous, but which I would argue extends to the reader a respectful yet playful invitation to learn and grow, would be Harryette Mullen's *Muse & Drudge*. In a valuable interview with Calvin Bedient, Mullen explains that she grew up ignorant of much of the cultural material the book's quatrains contain. In the religious and proper African American family in which she was raised, the blues, for instance, was considered "gut-bucket, lowdown music." Later Mullen "collected ['her'] culture" from books, from the media, from college classes, and from other kinds of experience. She elaborates, "When you asked 'How do you know all this stuff?' it's because I've been searching. We feel incomplete, and we search to make ourselves, our knowledge, more complete" (Mullen, "Solo Mysterioso Blues" 669). *Muse & Drudge* performs "very hard-won knowledge," but Mullen also asserts, "I figure that once I get it, it's mine, regardless of how I got it" (669). The same applies to her readers, who are invited by the poetry to expand their own cultural vocabulary. Though she deliberately "compress[es] information in these quatrains" (668), Mullen is not lording her knowledge over her readers. Anyone can enjoy the music of the text, and she provides plenty of repetition of key themes and related phrases so that any attentive reader will be able to discern the work's concern with race- and gender-based oppression, its celebration of female sexuality and African American creativity, its enactment of cultural hybridization. At the same time, she does assert, "If readers spent time, there is information about Afro-diasporic culture that is collected in these fragments. Each one of the fragments could lead you into another area of study" (668). Those who make the effort to learn more will hear more.

Consider, for instance, the quatrain "edge against a wall / wearing your colors / soulfully worn out / stylishly distressed" (*Muse & Drudge* 5). Two of the most obvious echoes, "up against the wall, motherfucker" and "stylishly dressed," emphasize the bravado, the aggressive confidence, the violence stereotypically associated with urban African Americans. The phrase "wearing your colors" evokes the seductive methods of salesmanship associated with American consumerism (are your colors warm or cool, the salesperson at the cosmetics counter asks), which constructs the image of those "stylishly distressed." Mullen's modifications of the standard phrases suggest another story if one knows that African American gang members wear their colors to display their allegiance. That it is gang members who "edge" against the wall, as if fearful or furtive, suggests their confidence is more show than substance, thanks to the skin colors that they always "wear out," in the sense of wear on the outside, and that put them at a disadvantage in white-dominated America. Some readers will miss the echo in "soulfully worn out" of a line attributed to civil rights pioneer Rosa Parks: "My feet are tired but my soul is rested." But their comprehension will be assisted by Mullen's having played with that line a couple of pages earlier in a context that links the phrase to the civil rights movement. The relevant quatrain, though directly quoting Langston Hughes, invokes Martin Luther King's "I Have a Dream" speech, which most Americans do know, to suggest that few advances have come since the civil rights movement of the 1960s: "I dream a world / and then what / my soul is resting / but my feet are tired" (3). Linked to this earlier quatrain, the one about gangs can more readily be heard encouraging readers to understand both the stylish display and the violent crime of African American youth as evidence of their spiritual exhaustion and distress in a society that still defers fulfillment of their dreams. Mullen's heterogeneously allusive, polysemous, but not "discourteous" or exclusionary lines cultivate an intellectually alert readership interested in thinking about the linguistic or extralinguistic residues of America's troubled racial history and compassionately aware of the multiple social forces shaping the behaviors on which negative stereotypes may be based.

The process of interpreting this text is a highly individual one, dependent upon each reader's prior knowledge as well as her or his willingness to seek out more knowledge. Ideally, the reader will be inspired to do the same kind of work Mullen did, poring over books on African American vernacular such as Clarence Major's *Juba to Jive* or Geneva Smitherman's *Black Talk*, and even pursuing some of the "areas of study" the vernacular phrases point to—seeking out what's known about the Middle Passage, the conditions of slave life, the relation between Yoruba religion and voodoo practices, or the civil rights struggles of the 1960s. "[C]arve out your niche / reconfigure the hybrid," Mullen urges (60). One reader's "reconfiguration" of the text joins her to Mullen and to a community of readers who are open to learning from *Muse & Drudge* to relinquish limiting preconceptions about black writing and black identity, a community of "stray companion[s]" who emerge from the "ludic routines" of this text bonded by a politicized appreciation of the rich syncretism of African American culture (80, 49).

A great range of exploratory women writers are motivated by a search for knowledge comparable to Mullen's, what Hejinian in "The Rejection of Closure" calls a "'rage to know'" (*Language of Inquiry* 52; she is apparently quoting from Goethe's *Faust*, but perhaps also playing upon Wallace Stevens's "rage to order"). For some, that quest for knowledge through language takes forms that parallel the scholar's. Probably the best-known example of this would be Susan Howe (like Mullen, a poet not treated in the chapters that follow): rebelliously immersing herself in history as a field once forbidden to her as a woman by her historian father and the patriarchy he represented, Howe has turned to the world's great libraries as the forbidden wilderness that invites her excursions. She is—using the terms in which she describes Coleridge—a "cormorant of libraries, [who] dives *deep* in books as if they were a sea" (*Birth-mark* 32), and what she plucks from libraries' oceanic waters are fragmentary traces of particular historical incidents and "passionate enunciation(s)" that have been erased, veiled, or misrepresented in received historiography (81). As she describes it in an interview, the method that supports her often iconoclastic intellectual quest is one that Kirsch would deplore: "I start in a place with fragments, lines and marks, stops and gaps, and then I have more ordered sections, and then things break up again" (*Birth-mark* 166). Yet both the unpredictability of such composition and the disjunctive complexity of its results are absolutely necessary to the project. For many of today's exploratory writers, as for Howe, poetry is valued as a process of discovery that has a distinctly intellectual cast.

The work of Cole Swensen, who, like Mullen, is significantly younger than Howe and not closely identified with the Language movement as Howe frequently is, exemplifies a position typical of the "uncommon languages" explored here: less invested in speaking absences within archives than Howe or in a politicized reading of poetic form than Hejinian, Swensen shares with both—and with all the other poets whose work is examined in this book—an understanding of her art that links the process of composing poetry with investigative thinking. She approaches poetry as a "way of getting into interesting subjects much more deeply" ("Interview" 81). The "post-Language" (84) techniques she employs are crucial to this intellectual adventure: "[T]hose fractures crack subject matter open . . . juxtapositions and broken syntax open a subject to a different kind of view. Through the cracks, we can see aspects that have not yet been articulated and can get intimations of what those articulations might be. Broken language is often not in the process of breaking further down, but of building up, heading toward fuller expressions, heading toward articulations that have not been previously achieved" (85). As in Howe's work, in much of Swensen's poetry manipulation of page space is a key resource for trying to "stretch the boundaries of the sayable" (Swensen, "Against the Limits" 630). This increased emphasis on poetry as a visual form—which figures in some way in every chapter but will be most central in that on Myung Mi Kim—seems particularly important to women writers at this moment in literary history.[21] In having written about that deployment of space in terms of "fractal form," Swensen has underscored the connection between this interest in the resources of page space and a desire widely evident among exploratory women poets—demonstrated in this collection by Fulton, Retallack, and Waldrop, as well as Swensen—to align their work with insights from contemporary science.[22]

Joan Retallack has articulated what is at stake in this attitude via the punning metaphor of the "know ledge" (*Poethical Wager* 63), a precarious space of uncertainty and forward-directed, ethically intellectual quest. She speaks of "an ethos of knowing as transitive, paradoxical, revelatory act—knowing in the form of poetry" that depends on a difficult-to-maintain attention (69). Once again, this vision is best conveyed by a lengthy quotation:

> The language of knowing (as distinct from believing, and remembering) is tied to what we care about *now* and intend to value in the future. One does not know outdated science, one knows (now) "about" it. That the word *now* inhabits the English word *know* seems a sweet accident. The ancient etymology (Indo-European root) of *know* is tied to sensory data, what is perceived in the continuous present of the senses. . . . Out of which flows a poethics of knowing: Curiosity, the desire to k'now our cognitive future tense—what may be present but unaccounted for in our moving principles. . . . Curiosity, a discipline of attention turned toward humorous shifts in perspective, those that might give us a chance to find newly productive silences in the noise of culture. On the know ledge, on the verge of awareness, in the mIdst of unintelligIbility, there's room for accident and possibility: in medias race of the orderly fall of atoms, there comes the Eve of the swerve. (*Poethical Wager* 72)

A passage like this—by the end of which language seems on the verge of explosion, propelled by the energy of the puns, shifting spellings, true and false etymologies, conceptual swerves, and new coinages—perhaps conveys the difference between the kind of thinking enacted by the work discussed here and the kind of thinking found in less exploratory work. It would be absurd to suggest that those poets whose allegiance lies with traditional forms of verse or the conventional stances of expressive personal lyric are unthinking or uninterested in ideas. Although reviews like Kirsch's might not acknowledge it, a good deal of mainstream work derives from research into historical subjects (often imaginatively creating voices of another historical moment or situation); reflects on challenging works of art; invokes recent scientific theories; provides well-informed responses to urgent issues like nuclear threat, climate change, or current international conflicts; or intelligently considers such social issues as poverty, immigration, gender inequity, and racial injustice. Moreover, it seems to me that very little poetry actually fits Hejinian's definition of closure, according to which "all the elements of the work are directed toward a single reading of it," since poetic language has long been regarded as a suggestive rather than exact medium, susceptible to more than one interpretation; a certain degree of interpretive openness characterizes the genre (*Language of Inquiry* 42). Nonetheless, I find a significant difference in intellectual character between the more closed writing and the exploratory work discussed here, which positions itself in more precarious spaces of more complex speculation and intellection—on the know ledge. This difference derives in large part from an extension of the premise that separated the New American poets from the mainstream of the 1960s, having to do with the centrality of process to artistic creation. The New Americans were interested in the poem as the space of experience itself—as is evident, for instance, in Robert Creeley's frequent allusion to Jackson Pollock's expression "when I am in my painting"—rather than the record of experience. Similarly, the later alternative poets in this book approach the page as the space not of thought but of thinking, not of knowledge achieved prior to writing—even if they have worked to acquire knowledge in order to compose the poem—but of knowing immediately enabled by what is happening to language and ideas on the page. The difference of the exploratory work also reflects an unapologetic and fearless intellectualism.

What drew me to the particular writers whose work is analyzed here has everything to do with the way their work thinks and its ever-active demands that I as a reader be thinking as well. These poets have been my intellectual guides and teachers in ways that make me endlessly grateful. I am not referring simply to my having had to gain more knowledge to read them well, though it is certainly true that to come to terms with their work I read Wittgenstein and poststructural theorists, stretched my mind around chaos theory, learned about the history of landscape painting or of Hangul, and so forth. At least a few of today's nonalternative poets might have required a comparable amount of learning. But these poets' bold exploratory approaches to language and to poetry as process unfolding in page space—filled with humor and playfulness, fierce political and spiritual conviction, extraordinary music—have pushed me to consider, unthink, and rethink the limits and powers of language, and the relations between language and gender, and between language and our larger social realities, as no conventional articulation could. In part because I am conscious of being one of the first to examine these poems carefully in print, my approach to this work has been to read *with* rather than *against* the grain, hoping to elucidate the poetry in terms close to those the poets would themselves use. The chapters that follow will demonstrate varied reading strategies that can make encountering the initially off-putting difficulties of today's exploratory poetries an inspiring, often joyful, adventure; significant effort is required, but the journey is exhilarating, and unexpected vistas are a frequent reward.

Both because I wish to suggest the range of poetic exploration that now exists alongside Language writing and because of my interest in the multiple forms of influence Language writing has exerted on recent experimental practice, in selecting the poets I treat in these chapters, I deliberately did not choose any who were core figures in what are now regarded as the key Language scenes in New York and San Francisco in the 1970s and early 1980s. All the poets on which I focus, however, have been significantly affected by Language writing. Although her profound engagement with the theories of John Cage sets her apart, Joan Retallack was active in the experimental scene in Washington DC, that Ann Vickery has argued in *Leaving Lines of Gender* should be recognized as a third center for the development of Language poetics. Rosmarie Waldrop is of an older generation than the Language writers and her interest in linguistic experimentation predates theirs,[23] but the Waldrops' Burning Deck Press has for decades been a crucial venue for Language and Language-influenced writing. C.D. Wright, while thoroughly grounded in her Arkansas roots, was involved in the Language scene during formative years in San Francisco; and Myung Mi Kim, though significantly younger, was supported by what remained of the Bay Area Language community as part of the broader San Francisco–based alternative poetry scene in the 1990s. Alice Fulton, Cole Swensen, and Susan Wheeler—all born in the 1950s and slightly too young to have been participants in the early development of Language writing—have been variously influenced by Language poetics and by their own engagements in many of the same intellectual currents that stirred up the Language experiments.

The chapters that follow are organized chronologically according to the publication dates of the volumes on which they focus: C.D. Wright's *Just Whistle*, from 1993, is the subject of chapter 2; Alice Fulton's *Sensual Math*, published in 1995, is examined in chapter 3; chapter 4, the only chapter to consider the work of two poets, examines volumes from the same years as those already discussed: Rosmarie Waldrop's *Lawn of Excluded Middle*, from 1993, and Joan Retallack's *AFTERRIMAGES*, from 1995. Cole Swensen's *Try*, published in 1999, is the focus of chapter 5. The last two chapters treat works from the first decade of the twenty-first century: Susan Wheeler's *Source Codes*, from 2001, in chapter 6; and Myung Mi Kim's *Commons*, published in 2002, and *River Antes*, a chapbook from 2006, in chapter 7. This order roughly corresponds with that of the chapters' original composition. Read sequentially, they will reflect some of the evolution of the poetic and critical scenes sketched in the foregoing pages.

This book provides evidence of the dissemination of the Language legacy that Rasula identified. At the same time, it keeps in view the impulse to diverge from Language writing or, sometimes, to locate an exploratory space between Language writing and mainstream lyric that has been operating since the mid-1980s, when the Language avant-garde came into view of the larger poetic and academic communities.[24] Most importantly, I hope it demonstrates the intellectual, aesthetic, and political vision, the astonishing vitality and varied *jouissance*, of the exploratory poetry currently being produced by women in the United States. Even more than other forms of intellectual speculation such as philosophy or political theory, poetics can delight in risk taking, pushing to the dizzying brink of Retallack's know ledge, and that is key to the distinctive pleasures this thinking poetry can provide.

two

INK OF EYES AND VEINS
AND PHONEMES

C.D. Wright's Eclectic Poetics

SINCE THE MID-1980S, C.D. Wright has positioned herself as an eclectic artist, free to draw upon the resources even of "antithetical poetries." Her 1987 essay "Op-Ed" provides a typical assertion of her aesthetic credo:

I believe in a hardheaded art, an unremitting, unrepentant practice of one's own faith in the word in one's own obstinate terms. I believe the word was made good from the start, that it remains so to this second. I believe words are golden as goodness is golden. Even the humble word *brush* gives off a scratch of light. There is not much poetry from which I feel barred, whether it is arcane or open in the extreme. I attempt to run the gamut because I am pulled by the extremes. I believe the word used wrongly distorts the world. I hold to hard distinctions of right and wrong. Also I think that antithetical poetries can and should co-exist without crippling one another. They not only serve to define their other to a much more exacting degree than would be possible in the absence of one or the other; they insure the persistence of heterogeneous (albeit discouragingly small) constituencies. While I am not always equal to it, I appreciate the fray. . . . Important, I believe, to resist finality in one's own work while assiduously working toward its complete-ness. Detrimental, I think, the dread of being passed on the left as is the deluded and furthermore trivializing notion of one's own work being in advance over any thing or any one. Truthfulness is crucial. (*Cooling Time* 3)[1]

Even as Wright suggests some value in preserving the boundaries that are reflected in different reading constituencies, she presents herself as an artist who can "run the gamut" of aesthetic possibilities. Her assertions of indi-vidualism and her moral grounding in good and evil, right and wrong, align her with premodern traditions. Yet her openness to "arcane" writing and her resistance to "closure"—the term that appeared in place of "finality" in the early versions of "Op-Ed," perhaps echoing Lyn Hejinian's 1984 essay "Rejection of Closure"—ally Wright with postmodern experimentalist proponents of open forms. At the same time, Wright's critique leveled against those claiming to make an advance precludes affiliation with any self-styled vanguard, perhaps particularly with the mainly *left*ist Language writers.

Wright attributes the mixture constituting her own poetics to the varied geographical circumstances of her career. Having grown up in the strongly Christian society of the Ozark Mountains (though not in a particularly religious household) and having launched her poetic development from the narrative and vernacular traditions of the rural "upper south," in 1979 she moved to San Francisco, where she lived into the early '80s. At that fertile time for Language writing, when the Bay Area Language community was fully energized but still a genuinely marginal avant-garde virtually unknown in the academic world and unrecognized in mainstream publishing venues or poetry institutions, Wright worked at one of Language writing's generative sites, the Poetry Center of San Francisco State. Although she kept to "the sidelines," she was "stimulated" by the fractious debates taking place; Wright read work being produced by Ron Silliman, Lyn Hejinian, Carla Harryman, and others we now label Language writers and incorporated aspects of their aesthetics into her own ("Looking").

Eclecticism per se is hardly controversial in postmodern culture, yet when its mix has involved drawing directly upon Language writing, hackles have risen, both inside and outside the Language community. Hostile responses were particularly vehement in the 1990s, when hybrid poetries began to be increasingly visible. Thus, following a talk Wright gave on her poetics at Breadloaf in the summer of 1997, mainstream poet Edward Hirsch attacked her for quoting from writers affiliated with the Language group when such writers, he claimed, belonged to a "cult" who would assert "the exclusivity of their truth claim" and deny the legitimacy of her own inclusive aesthetics.[2] Though hardly a "cult," Language writers have experimented in carefully theorized ways that reflect particular understandings—often associated with poststructuralism—of the construction of the self and the world through language, the imbrication of ideology and language, the materiality of the signifier, and the political significance of disrupting linguistic conventions. Consequently, they have been skeptical about the intellectual soundness of work that selectively appropriates disruptive techniques (and in the 1990s, young writers especially were starting to produce a good deal of such work) as if these were a means of spicing up otherwise conventional writing, without participating in the critique those techniques have been employed to enact.[3] In this climate of mutual suspicion, C.D. Wright's poetry demonstrates the possibility of generating a coherent aesthetic derived partially from Language writing that opens fresh possibilities for innovation and that possesses a political and artistic integrity distinct from, though often in harmony with, the integrity of Language poetry.[4]

Wright is by no means alone in this achievement. Harryette Mullen, for instance, is a parallel figure in that her work similarly underwent a transformation prompted by her (slightly later) contact with Language writing, even as she, too, maintained a principled resistance to some aspects of Language poetics. One aim of this book is to highlight some of the varied ways in which Language poetry has proven influential, and to do so in a historically informed way. Now, nearing the end of the first decade of the twenty-first century, emerging practices are commonly seen as moving beyond the opposition between Language poetry and personal lyric. The current acceptance of "hybrid" poetics should not, however, obscure the innovative force of the groundbreaking explorations conducted by poets like Wright, who were deliberately complicating that binary when the divide was fiercely maintained on both sides and when such transgressive, combinatory alternatives—if they were noticed at all—tended to generate substantial resistance.

C.D. Wright's generalizations about poetry in "A Taxable Matter" (published in *Field* in 1989) allow insight into how she absorbed the practices and principles of the Bay Area Language writers who interested her into the linguistic and social perspectives she carried from Arkansas:

> It is poetry that remarks on the barely perceptible disappearances from our world such as the sleeping porch or the root cellar (Grandmother Collins maintains the last root cellar in our family; who values their life would rather take a chance with a twister than descend the mossy steps, much less sample the roots hanging for generations by their screaming ganglia). And its barely perceptible appearances. In the book length poem *Tjanting*, Ron Silliman jerks us into critical awareness by creating syntactical disturbances with cultural ephemera calling up everything in our "two-ply kingdom" from "baskets to hold wire garlic. . . . A little swoop cesnas by" to "'Eraserhead saved my life,' said the woman with blue hair." It is left to poets to point out the shining particulars in our blunted lives like the strands of blue lights Cotter, Ark., drapes every haunting Christmas from one empty storefront to the storefront across the street for eight unoccupied blocks. And it falls to poetry to keep the rain-pitted face of love from leaving us forever. (25–26)

Wright's talk of disappearances and appearances here suggests she is responding to Silliman's essay "Disappearance of the Word, Appearance of the World" (first published in 1977). Decrying "the subjection of writing (and through writing, language) to the social dynamics of capitalism," he contends that words have become commodities, "torn from any tangible connection [as mark, as sound] to their human makers" (Silliman, *New Sentence* 8); "language itself appears to become transparent, a mere vessel for the transfer of ostensibly autonymous [*sic*] referents" (11). Poetry can counter this capitalist transformation, manifest especially in the "optical illusion" of novelistic realism and the conduit notion of communication that follow from it: "the poem returns us to the very social function of art as such" (17). In "A Taxable Matter" Wright, who identifies poetry as "tribal" and poets as "the griots of the tribe—the ones who see that the word does not break faith with the body," reinforces Silliman's emphasis on the social responsibilities borne by poetry in a world gone seriously astray. In this pathologically money-driven nation—"What America cannot sell it can barely stomach"—poetry battles commercial advertising in a contest where "[a]t the very least, the secular soul of the species is at stake" (24–25). The consciousness-raising Wright calls for, the careful attention to appearances, explicitly includes the "syntactic disturbances" Silliman employs in *Tjanting*. Through her allusions to this Language writer's essay and poetry, then, Wright invokes their shared commitment to poetry's transformative possibilities of deformation and of reconnection with material realities.[5]

Yet the "shining particulars" that catch Wright's eye—the Christmas lights strung in a particular dying Arkansas town—stand apart from the urban mass culture that Silliman tends to present. Interpolated between Arkansas memories in "A Taxable Matter," that "two-ply kingdom" seems less devouringly omnipresent than it does in Silliman's texts. The sweeping structures of capitalist hegemony invoked in his essay's Marxist social critique seem at least partially askew from the quirky social particulars Wright observes in what Flannery O'Connor called a "Christ-haunted" region (44).[6]

The "haunting" grotesquerie of Wright's specific, eccentric geographical frame of reference offers additional ways of generating "critical awareness" besides the Language writers' imposition of extreme verbal "disturbance" and disjunction. In "A Taxable Matter" Silliman's techniques emerge merely as one notable strategy, particularly suited for countering the consciousness-blunting forces of consumer culture. Meanwhile, in Wright's own presentation of barely perceptible appearances and disappearances, the descriptive conventions of realism—problematic for Silliman, since they can easily obscure the materiality of the word—remain largely intact.[7] Again, Wright's geographical history may explain why. She comes from a place of remarkable "cultural independence." In the introduction to her collection of Arkansas writers, *The Lost Roads Project*, she proudly offers *arkansas* as a verb for the action of writers who "precisely and uncommonly expressed" Arkansas culture: "I arkansas. Others I have known, or have had the honor to meet in print, arkansas also. It is neither a hieratic nor a hermetic tongue, but it is almost distinct. The inexorable course of cultural assimilation and the willful course of historical amnesia put the distinction at risk. Because I consider assimilation and amnesia artistic violations, I will try to emblazon the differences expressed here on the bark of the trees yet standing" (1). The subtitle of Wright's collection, *A Walk-in Book of Arkansas*, itself suggests that one can counter the culture of rapid drive-through convenience and consumption not just by the de- or re-formation of verbal sameness but by the *preservation* of difference, verbal and otherwise.[8]

The poetry that C.D. Wright composed before her encounter with the Bay Area literary scene explored extensively the social and linguistic resources of the particular hill society she came from. What Jenny Goodman has aptly termed the "hard-bitten" cast of Wright's vernacular ("Politics" 41) is apparent, for instance, in the opening lines of the first poem in her 1977 chapbook, *Room Rented by a Single Woman*:

As long as my butt's still behind me
I might as well
sing about the slaughter of innocents
give me the whole road
I pay the most tax
and put the lid on them garbage cans
the flies'll be pouring in here
(13)

Many of the poems in this collection are terse vernacular monologues or clipped, ominous third-person portraits revealing the desperations and brutalities of ordinary small-town lives. "Room Rented by a Single Woman in Van Buren, Arkansas," for instance, the monologue of one woman renting a room to another, concludes:

I moved in on her close I knowed
She couldn't see
I passed my emery board in front of her face
She couldn't see shit
I could feel her breasts
Giving in like snow under a boot.
(22)

In "Hills," the essay that opens her 1986 collection, *Further Adventures with You*, Wright reflects on the artistic importance of her roots and how her move to San Francisco, with its very different social, political, and intellectual urgencies, affected their poetic manifestation:

> When I began to write seriously I wrote strictly dialect with aberrant spelling, subject-verb disagreements . . . I wrote blue tick hounds accompanied by untunable git-tars and ocarinas. . . . Until recently my writing has continued to reflect the pitch of that speech. Now that I can recognize it from the outside, I can reproduce it at will, but am no longer committed to pursuing a course whereby my language is rife with *idiom Ozarkia*. I mean I can only yammer and yarn my way through so many hundred of lines, living as I do between the Wisconsin Street Housing Project and the San Jose Freeway, in a flat that oversees the shipyards of Bethlehem Steel. It is a warboat they are assembling at the water's edge, a far cry from midwifery in Leslie or Evening Shade. (11, first ellipsis in the original)

Elsewhere in "Hills" she asserts, "I aim to carry the smoked ham of my voice to Beulahland. I do not intend to write as though I had not gotten wind of 'this here' or 'that there' semiotic theory, regardless of which if any one theory, prevails" (11). While Wright saw her move to San Francisco as releasing her from the danger of provinciality, it did not deprive her of the resources of a distinctive lexicon, oddly twisted characters, and unsettling stories. She could, then, enter into the urban intellectuals' defamiliarizing project without having to rely exclusively on their methodologies.

Even so, some poems in *Further Adventures* strongly suggest the influence of Silliman's "new sentence" employed in works like *Tjanting* (1981). Here, for instance, is a passage from "The Lesson":

> Your bed is good and hard. The fruit is cool and dark. People are friendly here. The barman has information to burn. If the moon becomes too much you can close this gown. From the gallery you see the big lights of our Holy Father's summer place, and the flower farms. The lake turns purple from the fertilizer. It is so lovely, it is a pity the fish have to go belly up. The other woman kept a boa for a pet. When her children came she would listen and alternately glow. Leave your soiled things where you will. Service is complete. You enjoy typing, I can tell. If you wake up bleeding from the mouth, use the spider's web as a styptic. Would your hair be red everywhere. She was what you call a bottle blond. Not a true blond. In the beginning she was fervent, more fervent, most fervent. Try staying in the vocative case. That window has been painted shut. The radio is for your listening and dancing pleasure. Do

you cotton to Dixieland. Excuse my little joke. You will have to share a toilet with a man who plucks his eyebrows. Allow me. (39)

"The Lesson" gains considerable clarity if understood as the monologue of a boardinghouse owner introducing a new patron to the room she will occupy and occasionally referring to the room's previous occupant. This passage remains distinct from Language writing in that it seems less a torquing (Silliman's term) of conventional language than a revelation of the bizarre in "ordinary" speech acts.[9] Still, striking disjunctions between and within sentences call to mind Silliman's characterization of the "new sentence" (from 1979, the year Wright arrived in San Francisco): the limited use of syllogistic movement keeps the reader's attention "at or very close to the level of language, that is, most often at the sentence level or below" (i.e., smaller units than the sentence) (*New Sentence* 91). In "The Lesson," Wright's calling attention to the difficulty of sustaining the vocative case, her playing with grammatical degree in a modifier, her using the unexpected "gown" in place of the sound-similar "curtain," her use of formulaic idioms like "allow me"—that is, her several ways of focusing the reader's attention on language—signal her affinity with Language poetics.

The qualified or partial nature of Wright's absorption of the techniques of Language writing can be attributed not only to the stubborn peculiarities of her regional background, but also to her feminist consciousness. Kathleen Fraser, who was teaching at San Francisco State when Wright worked as office manager of the Poetry Center from 1979 to 1982, addresses this subject in "Partial Local Coherence: Some Notes on Language Writing," her essay that concludes "REALISM: An Anthology of 'Language' Writing," assembled by Ron Silliman for *Ironwood* (1982).[10] Fraser notes widespread ambivalence about Language writing among experimentally inclined women writers, who, newly aware of the male perspective of the literature they have been taught, now "struggle for access to their own experience" ("Partial" 136):

[T]here is an understandable wariness in simply following the diagrams of the new formalists [i.e., the Language writers] who are, once again, male-dominant in their theoretical documents. It would seem more urgent and more interesting, really, for many women writers, to first attend our own buried history and its unearthing. . . . While the structural preoccupations of language-centered theory and practices are both stimulating and, at times, concretely useful in this enterprise [of speaking "from our own fragmented experience of the world in the most accurate voices we can discover"], their esthetic distaste for self-referentiality and/or *evident* personal investment in one's subject immediately introduces a series of prohibiting factors. For a writer whose awareness has been tuned by a growing need to claim her own history and voice/s, such as Feminism provides, Language Writing's concerns are often *experienced* (if not intended) as directives she cannot afford. ("Partial" 137, emphasis in the original)[11]

Fraser means by "self-referentiality" not the text's referring to itself but the writer referring to her self—a perceived necessity for many women at that historical moment, even in the face of poststructuralism's emphasis (crucial to Language writing) on the discursive construction of the self and its critique of the self imagined as a unified subject located outside the text. Wright seems to have been among those feeling such a necessity, for, as Goodman has noted, Wright's mid-1980s collection *Further Adventures with You* "departs from her earlier work most noticeably in its personal tone," in the "decreased distance between poet and speaker" (Goodman, "C. D. Wright" 331).[12]

Wright, being less interested than Fraser in experimental modernism and poststructuralist feminism, would not have shared Fraser's exact perspective on poetic innovation.[13] But both of them, writing self-consciously as women when the possibilities and responsibilities of women's writing were expanding dramatically, found received conventions and existing groups inadequate to their needs. Invested in language as a means of resistance to much that they had inherited and as a means of discovering much that they now needed, such experimentally inclined women were "reinventing the givens of poetry" (Fraser, *Translating* 142). They were not interested in reproducing the kind of personal lyric that had become the sanctioned form for feminist expression. But they were equally uninterested in the exclusivity they associated with what they perceived as the male-dominated Language scene. Besides interrogating the restrictions and resources of language itself, they had intensely personal experiences to explore, stories to tell or histories to recover, and issues to raise that might be served by their drawing upon some elements of personal lyric and upon some mainstream conventions of intelligibility.

By the early 1990s, when significant numbers of AWP writers first began to take an interest in Language experimentalism, Wright's idiosyncratic aesthetic was well developed; her language-based experimentalism had grown more pronounced than in the '80s—her diction more jarringly heterogeneous, her syntactic disjunctions more extreme—even as her own "*evident* personal investment" and autobiographical material became more apparent. She continued to combine a griot's commitment to communication that will draw people together with a highly politicized desire to "challeng[e] the pugnacious privileges and prerogatives of power," in the inherited structures of language as well as the social structures of the world (Wright, "Adamantine"

57). Analysis of her powerful book-length poem *Just Whistle* (1993) will demonstrate how Wright in her mature work has successfully grafted elements from multiple genres and traditions to produce an innovative literary hybrid profoundly indebted to the insights and techniques of Language writing as well as to possibilities adhering in more conventional senses of subject matter and theme that Language writing rejects.[14] In the work's hybridity, its aesthetic eclecticism, lies its most daring experiment, one that sustains a complex project of challenging mind/body dualism and reconceptualizating the body. This hybridity is sustained, I will argue, by an implicit contract with the reader that promises a certain intelligibility and coherence derived from familiar literary conventions while at the same time continually straining against that intelligibility and defying the conventions that encode it.

In *Just Whistle*, Wright's long-standing attraction to narrative takes a form that fits Marjorie Perloff's characterization of "postmodern" storytelling (first published in 1982): "the lyric of the solitary self, engaged in the ceaseless longing for disclosure, may well be giving way to a more communal poetry. . . in which narrative once again becomes the locus for *gnosis*" (*Dance of the Intellect* 170).[15] "[W]hen story reappears in postmodern poetry, it is no longer the full-fledged *mythos* of Aristotle, the 'specific syntactic shape' Robert Scholes speaks of, but a point of reference, a way of alluding, a source . . . of parody. To tell a story is to find a way—sometimes the only way—of *knowing* one's world. But since, in the view of many of our poets, as in the view of comparable fiction writers, the world just doesn't—indeed shouldn't—make sense, the *gnosis* which is narration remains fragmentary. By frustrating our desire for closure . . . such 'stories' foreground the narrative codes themselves and call them into question" (*Dance of the Intellect* 161). The story *Just Whistle* presents is fragmentary and dislocated; in as well as through the gaps and cracks in its structure, Wright seeks knowledge and understanding. Yet she does not skew or multiply her stories, as Language writers would, to the point where readers must perform what Barrett Watten terms "nonnarrative reading[s]" (*Constructivist Moment* 203). Wright's formal eclecticism enables her to depend on narrative intelligibility for much of the communicative and political efficacy of her work, even while—in a different sort of political gesture—she challenges and distorts narrative conventions.

The events in *Just Whistle* are narrated as happening to generalized entities: two bodies. These bodies have thoughts and emotions, yet the text avoids the language of personhood, insists on their status as bodies, and assigns them no gendered pronouns. The body is "it," whether the presumably female "body in panties" or the "priapic" body of a man. Wright's persistent reference to people as pronominally neutered bodies indicates an unwillingness to accept a Cartesian sense of human intellect or spirit as distinct from, merely housed in, the body. This linguistic contortion also enacts a determination not to replicate received assumptions about the significance to identity of gender or sex. The gnosis Wright seeks here concerns the human condition of embodiment, though with significant attention to the gender expectations linked to the female body and to the sex-specific experience of the body's giving birth.

Wright's aims may be illuminated by the work of feminist theorist Elizabeth Grosz, who refigures the body so that it becomes central, not peripheral, to subjectivity in *Volatile Bodies: Toward a Corporeal Feminism*.[16] Grosz proposes to take the body as a point of mediation between what's perceived as internal and external, and therefore as the point from which to rethink not only the oppositions of mind/body and inside/outside, but also of public/private, self/other, cultural/natural, and so on (20). Wanting to replace the dualistic and hierarchical models of the relation between (conventionally feminine) body and (conventionally masculine) mind, Grosz seeks to invert the primacy of a psychical interiority by demonstrating its necessary dependence on a corporeal exteriority (xii). Rather than dividing the subject into mutually exclusive categories of mind and body, she proposes an embodied subjectivity or a psychical corporeality. She offers the Möbius strip as one model for this understanding: "It enables subjectivity to be understood not as the combination of a psychical depth and a corporeal superficiality but as a surface whose inscriptions and rotations in three-dimensional space produce all the effects of depth. It enables subjectivity to be understood as fully material and for materiality to be extended and to include and explain the operations of language, desire, and significance" (210). Although the figure of the Möbius strip is not invoked in Wright's recent work, Grosz's description of the understanding it "enables" clearly pertains.

The story traced in *Just Whistle* begins with a sleeping body awakened by the "closed set of words, *I wish you wouldn't wear your panties to bed*" (*Steal Away* 102).[17] This complaint is a wounding experience for the body addressed, an "unmistakable run in the heretofore seamless nights" prompting anguished awareness of emotional and physical distances that have come between the two lovers (105). The alienation between the lovers and the pain of the body in panties increase as the pantied one broods. The excruciating wound of this divide is reenacted, with some key differences, when midway through the book that body experiences labor and a traumatic birth with massive hemorrhaging. That body's subsequent recovery of health is accompanied by a healing between the lovers (now parents) as well. These events prompt the book's meditations—in oblique, cryptic, and disjointed form—on gender roles, on sex and sexual dependency, on the body and its mortality, on partnership and love.

The particularized details through which this tale of an intimate relation-ship unfolds seem on the one hand to suggest a specific biography, or indeed autobiography. The memories of a lover who committed suicide could well pertain to Wright's early mentor Frank Stanford, the birth might be that of C.D. Wright's son, and the struggles depicted might have occurred in her marriage to Forrest Gander. But the text conveys no "longing for disclosure" (Perloff's phrase) by the solitary self. In contrast to the established poetic mode of personal revelation, a central point seems to be that much we hold as private is in fact common (recall Wright's characterization of poet as griot of the tribe). Our sense of privacy is exposed as motivated more by a desire "better to disguise [the body's] beastliness" than by respect for the unique individual (111).

Similarly, consumer culture's titillating images of sexuality as private exot-icism and of the female body as erotic object—images like those of lingerie-clad female bodies in *Victoria's Secret* catalogs—are resisted by Wright's way of presenting the body in panties. Even if the hair on its legs is specified as "long and gold" and its height as five and a half feet, this body remains an entirely typical unglamorous object or set of processes, sloughing off cells, dropping hairs, and oozing liquids. The undergarment it wears is equally unaestheticized: "the panties, which the body had not really noticed so used was the body to the cloth, the plight of their facticity, the elastic in the legs and the waist not being felt, the discoloration having blended them perfectly with the flesh, no line or hair, neotenous, and there being very little moisture, except for the thinnest issue of piss" (105). Wright underscores materiality in ways that discourage fetishizing and commodifying the body, especially the female body, that demystify our common—that is, both ordinary and shared— physical "facticity."

Wright's depersonalizing and ungendering reference to her story's actors as bodies, a practice that heightens readers' awareness of (violated) conven-tions of reference and characterization, is one of several devices that call attention to narrative codes—and to related social codes. Other realist narra-tive conventions brought into focus and challenged in the story-telling of *Just Whistle* include those of point of view and explanatory metaphor.[18] Wright's locating the center of consciousness in or close to the notably concretized perceptions of the pantied body (Grosz's "embodied subjectivity or psychical corporeality") dramatically exaggerates the difficulty of distinguishing literal from figurative and of then interpreting the figurative. For instance, "hinged" denotes sitting in *Just Whistle*. By convention, hinge is a metaphoric vehicle, but Wright's physicalized perspective makes us aware we'd more accurately identify sitting as the abstraction that stands in for the literal reality of being bent at the hips, "[t]he body on its hinges" (115).

The second piece in *Just Whistle* demonstrates the interpretive complications that emerge from this kind of perspective sustained over extended passages of the text, now involving more internal sights/sites.[19] This piece builds directly upon the closing phrases of the first one, where the body, "having slept, as if in a boat," finds itself—after the remark about wearing panties to bed—"oarless, unmoored, sand pouring out of a canvas bag" (102). A fairly conventional image of self-contained drifting, suggesting isolation and loss of control, is yoked with a less conventional image conveying a violation of formal integrity, a loss of wholeness. These relatively straightforward figures become more baffling as they are extended in the second piece (quoted here in its entirety), where they seem at once more literal and more allegorical:

SAND SEEPING FROM CAVITIES NO LONGER MOIST, not removing
the panties, but making every effort to conform to the hull among scales,
and leaves from overhanging willows, weepers, older than them even, wept,
wounded into dormancy, unable to plug the wound, water deeper than night,
the lewd, newly enlivened wound, night deeper than water, wound older than
the body's marrow, older than its rocks, dogs glomming along the unstable
rocks of its words, stirred up by days, sunblare, dreaded as the vulture dreads
its own shadow; then, a slightly taller body waving from the shoreline with
an armadillo on its shoulder, waving wildly as if for the pantied body to pull
to rocky shore and share the armadillo, as if they had not crowed the night
before (103; almost all the untitled pages begin with words in capital letters)

Reading metaphorically, one might paraphrase the first lines as follows: feeling like something dead and inanimate rather than a living being, this person attempts to adapt to its situation of wounded isolation (figured in the boat hull littered with fish scales and leaves), gives way to its seemingly boundless pain, and weeps. But how is this newly enlivened wound "older than the body's marrow"? Indeed, are sonorous patterns like "night, the lewd, newly enlivened wound" generated by their music more than their sense? And what are the body's "rocks," or the "rocks of its words"? One would associate rocks with the shore, but aren't we to imagine this body as if floating on a boat? Such metaphorical inconsistency is not customary in realist narrative. And are these dogs literal household pets drawn to their sobbing owner? Or are they, more figuratively understood, what is "stirred up" and "dreaded"—or do those modifiers apply to the unstable rocks? Reference is ambiguous, distinctions between internal and external blur. Without resolving toward any single interpretation, the story continues: in a cinematic mini-narrative the other body tries to entice the weeping wounded one out of its withdrawn state with the prospect of shared pleasure. This scene with the wildly gesticulating figure and the armadillo is incongruous to the point of comedy; unconventional tonal inconsistencies, present perhaps since the first "closed set of words," gain prominence. Narrative elements of this scene, too, are baffling: what are we to make of the two having "crowed"? The verb resists interpretation either in relation to the literal narrative (about panties in bed) or its figurative rendering (involving a boat, deep waters, rocky shores). *Crow* will accumulate meanings in subsequent passages, but here we might guess it refers to an ugly squawking quarrel, or perhaps to a cry uttered during sex.

Using techniques that are far more prevalent in Language writing than in conventional storytelling or conventional lyric—marked tonal inconsistencies, indeterminate references, playing off literal against figurative meanings, syntactic disjunction or ambiguity—Wright opens possibilities for multiple exegeses. Like the Language writers, she resists producing a "closed set of words" and thereby heightens her readers' consciousness of all the choices made in constructing an interpretation. If at the end of the passage just analyzed we assume that the narrative perspective approximates that of the pantied body (as seems plausible throughout much of the book), it would seem that the couple's recent crowing bears a significance for the pantied body that it apparently lacks for the slightly taller body. If we further assume a tone of scornful disbelief in "as if they had not crowed . . . ," we can understand the pantied one angrily to reject the taller one's invitation. Narrative coherence emerges from such interpretive assumptions. Wright does not compel us to resist them, but her metaphorical obliquities and her surprising nonmetaphorical accuracies demand that we remain conscious of the assumptions we make, and presumably of the biases that underlie them.

Further linking her practice with those of the Language writers, Wright employs several lexical techniques that focus attention on the operation of language and on words themselves. Just as the narrative veers between direct accessibility or literal denotation and highly coded, oblique, or figurative presentation, the diction shifts startlingly from the abstruse to the vernacular. Wright frequently incorporates isolated arcane or specialized terms— "seiche," "teratogenic," "haulm," "neotenous," "limerance," "nulliparous," "flensed," and others—sometimes where a common synonym might have served. At the same time, some simple terms that routinely denote common objects or acts—such as "crow," "whistle," "armadillo," or "boat"—function as complex, possibly mutating abstractions. Consider, for instance, the following passage from the third piece, in which the pantied body recalls previous lovers; Wright's handling of language here mutes the possibility of the reader's voyeuristic involvement in material that could well figure in a confessional poem:[20] "the memory fulgurant, sheet lightning of other bodies, of the one that did not have a book in its house, the one that kept running to the pot, the one that admitted it loved the boat, the body stayed because it loved the boat, the impartial body, the inseminator, the second inseminator, the one over which the body had cut itself, just whistle cuts, the one that did not end after the aspirin incident but only much later during the war" (104). Three defamiliarizing techniques here are worth commenting upon as typical of *Just Whistle*: interpolation of arcane words, occurrences of destabilizing repetition, and syntactically wrenching usages or coinages. *Fulgurant* (or *fulgurating*), a recurrent term in the book, exemplifies the first of these. If, as is likely, the reader does not know the word's meaning, she or he can choose either to interrupt the imaginative act of reading and consult a dictionary or to continue on, freshly conscious of the gaps in his or her understanding and of multiple possibilities of meaning to be held in play as he or she proceeds. Either way, what Silliman calls the "illusion of realism" has been disrupted (*New Sentence* 12). The reader encounters a further challenge with the reappearance—exemplifying the second technique—of "the boat": does the word function as it seemed to in the second section, as a figure for individual isolation? Or can more than one body be in the same boat, so to speak, and love it there? Although the term seems to have acquired meaning beyond its ordinary denotations, it cannot be assigned a fixed symbolic function. Lyn Hejinian's comments on how repetition functions in "open texts" pertain: "Repetition, conventionally used to unify a text or harmonize its parts, as if returning melody to the tonic, instead, in these works ... challenges our inclination to isolate, identify, and limit the burden of meaning given to an event (the sentence or line). Here, where certain phrases recur in the work, recontextualized and with new emphasis, repetition disrupts the initial apparent meaning scheme. The initial reading is adjusted; meaning is set in motion, emended and extended, and the rewriting that repetition becomes postpones completion of the thought indefinitely" (*Language of Inquiry* 44). Because many of the recurrent words and phrases in *Just Whistle* are tied to the governing narrative and its thematic concerns in discernable ways (and the narrative itself may be read as following the essentially linear dramatic structure of the development and resolution of a crisis), repetition serves more of a unifying function here than it does in, say, Hejinian's *My Life*. Nonetheless, repetition in *Just Whistle* complicates rather than stabilizes meaning; recurrence of textual elements in different contexts requires continual adjustment of one's understanding of earlier passages and thereby necessitates nonlinear processing of the text.[21]

The curious phrase "just whistle cuts" demonstrates the third lexical technique. Because it is the book's title, one tends to hear "just whistle" as a phrasal unit—one that may evoke the saying "just whistle and I'll come running," allude to Lauren Bacall's suggestive remark to Humphrey Bogart in

To Have and Have Not, or echo *The King and I*'s "Just Whistle a Happy Tune."
But what would just-whistle cuts be? Cuts inflicted by what is supposed to
bring closeness or confidence or by what is supposed to be a carefree state?
Thinking of Bacall/Bogart, might we understand them as cuts inflicted in the
erotically charged battle of the sexes? Alternatively, we might hear "just" as
modifying "whistle cuts"—merely whistle cuts—a clearer phrase except that
it's not obvious how or why one would get cut on a whistle. Perhaps, though,
the whistle is not the object inflicting cuts (as paper inflicts paper cuts) but
one's response to a cut; might a whistle cut be a sufficiently minor wound
such that one would sharply exhale through pursed lips rather than cry out
when it occurred? In the passage, might this refer to a halfhearted attempt at
wrist-slitting? Single lexical elements keep rendering the terrain of this passage unstable and difficult to negotiate, although mapping its overall configu-
ration (as a recollection of previous lovers) is relatively easy. Even with that
overarching narrative coherence, the shifts in levels of diction as well as the
unexpected concrete terms function as the disjunctions in Language writing often do: they interfere with realism's illusion of linguistic and phenom-
enological transparency, its simplification of our polyvalent and confusing
experience. As I will demonstrate shortly, in *Just Whistle* the simplifications
at issue especially involve easy divisions of gender, too ready distinctions by
sex, and dissociations of mind or spirit from body.

Conventions disrupted in *Just Whistle* include not only those of narrative,
lexicon, and syntax but those of genre as well. Passages of legal or academic
discourse (e.g., "[t]he body is a suspect / in the offense of crow. It has the right
/ to remain naked" [121], "[a]ccording to the author of *Points / for a Compass Rose*" [122]) are paratactically arrayed beside graceful lyricism, while the
eroded bodies of Deborah Luster's photos emerge startlingly between pages
of Wright's text in the original edition. The text of *Just Whistle* is in Wright's
view *poetry*—that "[a]damantine" material she envisions in its ideal form as
"[b]rilliant," "[i]mpenetrable," and entirely "utopian" ("Adamantine" 55, 58,
57). Nonetheless, the majority of the book's pages appear as prose (more evidently so in the Kelsey Street edition), though their syntactic density—phrases
piling upon one another, often without forming grammatical sentences—is
more characteristic of free verse.[22] The inappropriateness of distinguishing
poetic from prose genres on the basis of margin use is suggested by the variety
of forms Wright devises within these two visual categories. A number of the
sections in which text in the original printing runs to right-justified margins
achieve an intensity associated with lyric by being built entirely of brief linguistic units separated by a repeated punctuation mark (a series of commas,
periods, semicolons, or colons). Some sections intersperse grammatical sentences with these shorter units: for example, "This includes the pool painter

whose hands are perpetually blue. Aquatic. Transbluent. One hand signs the blued canvas of our body. Other hands. Cigaretted. Hired hands" (112). In others, syntax unfolds and expands without ever reaching a full stop. Each of the sections employing the margins and spacing we associate with poetry uses page space and lineation differently, except for the closing trio of pieces that rearrange the same five words in three centered and triple-spaced lines.

Wright's unorthodox understanding of generic divisions may draw upon Language theory; Silliman, for instance, conceives of his work using the "new sentence" as poetry because that generic label identifies a long tradition of using defamiliarizing techniques (rhyme, meter, assonance, alliteration, etc.) that heighten awareness of the materiality of language. Yet Wright also makes prose/poetry distinctions that Language writers like Silliman would not make, for instance when she approvingly repeats Mary Hunter Austin's designation of prose as the medium of communication and poetry as the mode of communion ("Infamous Liberties" 1).[23] Just as Wright's book-length poem attends to sexual difference while it highlights ways in which conventional thinking about gender exaggerates biological difference (and thereby unnecessarily restricts women), so Wright's approach to genre in the 1990s allows for distinctions between poetry and prose but encourages an inclusive approach to poetry that will maximize its freedom.

In Wright's recent poetry, as in the Language poetry of Silliman, Hejinian, and others, defamiliarizing techniques serve to challenge myths of uniquely private experience existing prior to language ("the ink completes [rather than records] the feeling" [Wright, *Tremble* 4]), so as to highlight commodification of the body and language in contemporary society and emphatically to resist such commodification. These are profound affinities, at once aesthetic, intellectual, and political. But, as Wright's previously quoted pronouncements have demonstrated, she is committed to other perspectives besides language-centered ones. Charles Altieri provides one way of conceptualizing the difference between her poetry and Language writing when he observes, speaking of the theory articulated by Language poets, that "we find radical poetics stressing the negative work of resistance or turning for its positive claims to a version of compositional dynamics in which the pleasures of the material text are asked to carry the axiological burdens that for [Charles] Olson extended into the ways in which texts could model and partially transform human agency" ("Some Problems" 182). Language writing works largely within the formalist traditions of modernist poetics, and "this fealty exacts a substantial price in what we can claim as the 'content,' and hence as the cultural force made available by works of art" (182). Less purely a formalist, while passionately committed to expanding the cultural and political force of poetry, Wright is less interested in making the work's qualities as compositional, discursive, or material object (and the social or political implications thereof) the content of her poems than are the Language poets Altieri discusses. Instead, she remains attached to some conventional notions of content and subject matter, though with a heightened awareness of the dangerous seductions of absorption into a text's representational field.

The most fundamental concern of *Just Whistle*—its content, if you will—is the body: not just linguistic representation and construction of the body, but embodiment and the limits, needs, and powers of the body itself. (This emphasis is reinforced by Wright's collaboration with visual artist Deborah Luster, who created for this text photographs of women's bodies "gnawed and wounded," "transformed by the bleach and etch process called mordancage" [*Just Whistle* 55]). The material body, controversial among feminists, is problematic terrain for poststructuralist poetic experimentalists. For, to the extent that such experimentalists rely on poststructuralist understandings of the signifying systems of language, their writing tends to take as its content what is discursively constructed or the process of such construction, even as it highlights the material aspects of words. While gender is one such construction, the body, at least in some ways, is not. I suspect that Wright would differ with Hejinian, who, in arguing that "[l]anguage generates its own characteristics in the human psychological and spiritual conditions," asserts, "[i]ndeed, [language] nearly *is* our psychological condition" (49). However great Wright's interest in language as a determinant of perception and social identity, *Just Whistle* would seem to indicate that ultimately *the body* nearly *is* our psychological condition. Wright's way of exploring that condition and testing the limits imposed by biology, moreover, requires holding in tension varied forms and degrees of intelligibility. She relies on conventional structures of intelligibility, even if they are attenuated, with far more consistency than Language writers do.[24]

One of the impulses behind *Just Whistle* seems to be an effort to distinguish the threshold where sexual difference comes into play as necessarily significant, not as gender constructions might suggest, but as biological facts or material specificities determine.[25] In this context, Wright investigates how the commonalities between male and female bodies may be respected or extended (and stereotypical assumptions about gender obstructed) through linguistic experiment, and she explores the significance of the childbearing experience unique to the female body. Often she pushes to extremes the ungendering of her poem's bodies. Her ability to do so in ways that communicate to her reader specific ideas about conventions of gender, and about where those conventions leave off and physical facts take over, depends on preserving certain kinds of conventional coherence that establish what I would call a *contract of intelligibility* with her reader. More precisely, it is a *contract of (contracted) intelligibility* in that certain conventions of intelligibility operate, though within a context of purposeful obscurity. The promise of a single overarching narrative, for instance, prompts readers to assume that the interactions throughout this work are between a woman and a man who have been lovers; having provided enough narrative coherence for her readers to persist in that assumption, Wright then deliberately—and instructively—makes it difficult to tell one actor from the other. The eighth section, for example, begins: "THE ONE WATCHING THE OTHER ONE a long time before it got up, the one shoving a pillow under the plums of the other, the one not removing the panties even *in situ*." Only in the third phrase are we certain who acts (or refuses to act). "[T]hen *ex nihilo* the one who was asked not to wear the panties to bed was told to go check on the dogs" (109). We now infer that the one watching and getting up must be the pantied one, since logic dictates that the one in bed would be telling the one out of bed to check on the dogs. It could well be that every time "the one" appears in these lines, the phrase refers to the woman. If so, plums would not be, as one might have expected, the woman's breasts; countering gender stereotypes, this fruit metaphor would apply to some part of the male anatomy, perhaps the testicles, though perhaps it refers to some body part such as hands that the two sexes share. Only because the character of the writing has encouraged me to assume consistent dramatis personae who maintain emotionally consistent relations with each other do I attempt logically to chart each body's words and acts, a process that heightens consciousness of how much we rely on sex or gender as defining categories of identity and how quickly we seek to differentiate individuals according to sexed characteristics or gendered behavior.

A similar contract of intelligibility operates in "A BRIEF AND BLAMELESS OUTLINE OF THE ONTOGENY OF CROW." Here Wright relies on her readers' applying the conventions of characterization through dialogue, as she stretches those conventions in order to make points about sexual and gender difference. The title promises a biologically based account of the development of "crow," a still ambiguous term that might refer to nasty quarreling, to the creation of poetry, or to sexual intercourse that lacks the loving communion Wright names "interpenetration."[26] The piece "outlines" a conversation of sorts, in which the two speakers—the pantied woman and her partner, we again assume—never address the same topic or really address each other.

Tonight one said   Bluets the other said
Goosefoot one said   Hungry the other said
Hangnail it said   Spanish bayonet it said
Daylilies it said   Hotel it said
Matches it said   Sickle Senna it said

. . . .
Morning glories said one   Money said the other
Whistle it said   Asshole it thought it said
(108)

The differences between "the one" and "the other" do not appear to rest on biology. If we posit a consistency in each character's focus while observing that in nearly every line one speaker names a plant while the other never names growing things, then we might deduce that hegemonic gender roles foster the divisions between them: the woman is involved with domestic nurture, the garden; the man is concerned with more public business of money, hotels, tickets, and the like; consequently the two cannot respectfully connect with one another. At the same time, the attenuation of dialogic cues keeps us conscious that all this may be a false narrative generated solely by our tendency to assume gender stereotypes; it may be that each speaker is sometimes interested in trees and flowers, perhaps located in their immediate surroundings, and at other moments interested in discussing other, less bucolic, matters. In that case, it might be that "crow" develops from sheer ornery individualism, and that gender and sex are equally irrelevant.

In this piece as throughout the book, Wright does not focus on anatomical difference or, as some French feminist theorists would, on differences in sexual desire or sexual pleasure between male and female bodies. She links that kind of focus to limiting gender stereotypes, emphasizing how restrictive and overdetermined our genitally focused images of (hetero)sexual encounter in fact are. For instance, she mockingly offers, perhaps as a jealous fantasy of the pantied body, the once normative urban middle-class version, complete with the sloshing of evening cocktails, observed voyeuristically through a screen: "ADVANCE OF THE DISTINCT BODIES behind the partition, the death of day, the rupture of motors, contamination of news, lightblare, sloshing sound, the time-honored tool ever alert under its suit, the long maligned tube manufacturing trouble under its folds, the frisson of their proximity, the ineluctable concussion" (120). Another piece, "In the Old Days," provides an accessible reminder of the debilitating gender expectations that accompany such anachronistic visions of male and female sexuality. In the days when women were taught to think of men as "harmful bodies"—impregnating figures of unstoppable lust—"we" women

. . . loved their smooth torsos
Like bluffs we leaped off
We loved them rough as boards
Hard as rocks we loved them

We had a voice soft and filmy as a mussel
We were like farm kittens
Each one different but the same
Our love was like the pulp
Of luscious fruit
. . . .
Who could have penetrated the fog
In such bodies in those days
(107)

Even the lineation, in respecting the breaks dictated by syntax, reflects the power of convention. The familiar hard/soft opposition links such disabling stereotypes to the culture's focus on genitalia and its glorification of the hard penis. Wright's distinctive experiments with the depiction of bodies in other sections of *Just Whistle* acquire value in the context of such ingrained polarized stereotypes. Not wanting to glorify the male tool, malign the female tube, or simply reverse the hierarchy, Wright rarely refers to any part of the anatomy that distinguishes men from women. Hands are the most frequently mentioned appendage. Other than the one mention of the "tool," there are no direct references to the penis. The occasional references to female genitalia use unconventional, unsexy terminology such as the medically correct term "vestibule."

Instead of a genital focus, right at the center of the book Wright presents something that "no one, in those days" would have let loose with: "a panegyric to its hole" (124). Again, it is important to Wright's project that her reader trust that the piece, fragmented as it is, really is to be read as a paean to the hole. The introductory context involving a suicide and "point blank range" (124) establishes that multiple kinds of holes are to be invoked here, bullet holes and death's "vast funnel of silence" among them (125). But this piece, which begins by announcing itself (with humor, but in seriousness) as spiritual doctrine—"HOLE OF HOLES"—celebrates anatomical apertures as well, from the asshole, to the vaginal opening, to the mouth that produces *o*'s and odes. Both sexes may "let loose" such a tribute, particularly since some of these holes are aural or conceptual. Yet women's bodies having one hole men lack, from which life emerges, gives the female body some primacy in this hymn of praise. In the section's conclusion, one cannot distinguish physical apertures ("original opening, whistling well, first vortex . . . insubduable opening" might all name the opening of the vaginal canal) from philosophical conventions or ultimate spiritual and moral truths ("an idea of beautiful form, original opening"). This merging is of course central to the book's "content," its insistence on embodiment as the very stuff of our intellectual, emotional, and spiritual lives: "an idea of beautiful form, original opening, whistling well, first vortex, an idea of form, a beautiful idea, a just idea of form, unplugged, reamed, scored, plundered, insubduable opening, lightsource, it opens. This changes everything" (125). Countering the tendency to identify woman with the body in a Cartesian system that opposes body to mind and spirit, passages like this confound all such divisions: the hole is the materially bounded orifice, the unbounded opening, the physical mark O, the utterly abstract idea, the lofty ideal, the object of violent abuse or rape, the site of absence, the locus of desire, and the source of plenitude. It is this confounding of divisions, this corporealizing of subjectivity that "changes everything."

Relying on repetition in its more traditional unifying function, Wright repeats many of the phrases from the panegyric to the hole in the piece in which the body gives birth—an experience that brings the (female) body close to dying, itself thought to be the most extreme physical and most extreme spiritual event we can know. Some of the details are factual data—"four fingers" denoting the width of the cervical dilation, "hair seen through the vestibule" describing the infant's head crowning—but as the body's experience of "pain without walls" becomes overwhelming, Wright progresses from more tangible images—"tremendous fall of rock . . . plummeting like a meteor"—to more abstract ones echoing "HOLE OF HOLES": "vast funnel of silence: dark parting the multiple folds about the hole: spinning into darkest surround: final vortex: plummeting into absence: from such a height: idea of beautiful form: intense monitoring of form: lights conk out as they pass: beautiful: darkness: spinning:" (134). We need the intelligibility of such thematically significant repetition if we are to appreciate fully Wright's revisionary representation of the reproductive female body as an integrated spiritual, emotional, intellectual, and material entity.

Wright's concern with the beautiful in the context of holes of course invokes a vast complex of problematic expectations for female beauty. Her unglamorizing (also undemonizing) presentation of the body has a powerful social significance, as my earlier comparison with the sexual sell of *Victoria's Secret* suggested. Unlike the representations of women's bodies on Madison Avenue and in much of Western poetic tradition, Wright's female body is not suspended in perfect youthful allure. Indeed, almost as distressing to this body as the first "closed set of words" is another introduced soon after: "*I just want you to last*" (119). However customary that desire, Wright condemns its divorce from material reality: "already the unlasting has started, ruts have formed, petechiae, bags, dents, lacunae, sloughing, discharge, rot, the blaze between the cheek and the jaw, gouged out areas, new growths, horrible excrescency, discoloration, elongated lobes, the build-up of wax, crud, the degenerate mortar of lime, hair, and dung, whilst the beckoning of the thousand-odd boats in the bay . . ." (119, ellipsis added). In this context, Wright's allusion to the thou-sand ships launched by the beautiful face of Helen, reminding us that the ideal of perfect female beauty has long been an inspirational subject for poetry, posi-tions her poem and the story it tells against that falsifying tradition. Beauty's decay is not a female tragedy but a simple universal fact: "They all rise up and leave their hairs on the pillowcase. They all enter breath's cul-de-sac in their own precious time" (118). Wright's reference to one individual as "the body" enables her to suggest through its perspective more generalized, communally shared desires: "What does the body want. . . . To meet another body coming through the haulm. Swinging its plums freely. Awhistling" (115). (Note how allusion to the old song "Comin' thro' the Rye" lends historical depth to this claim, while the unfamiliar "haulm" prevents the familiar folk material from fostering an illusion of transparency.)[27]

In this context, a phrase like "*I just want you to last,*" which encapsulates a whole tradition of love poetry men have addressed to women, signals a moral failure. For Wright is profoundly concerned with humanistic morality, and in her mind this marks a crucial divergence between her work and Language writing, or at least the theory behind it. Thus in a 1987 essay, Wright criticized on moral grounds Silliman's "irksome" dictum (that appears in *Tjanting* and in his introduction to the "REALISM" anthology) that "the most political thing you can do is face the language": "I appreciate the return of reflexiv-ity to the imaginative writer's linguistic province, but does that mean, the province of the writer is language period. What about us. What about what Agee named 'the sorrow, the effort and the ugliness of the beautiful world.' What about EVIL" ("Argument" 86). Wright goes on to explain that Silliman's emphasis on language is "too engrossed with technique. Not with authentic-ity, what Sharon Doubiago calls 'the art of seeing with one's own eyes'" (86).[28] Authenticity and witness are highly suspect notions for poststructuralist thinkers, but Wright's aesthetic combines the language-centered skepticism with faith in what she sees with her own eyes and experiences in her own female body: her poems, indebted at once to the likes of Agee, Doubiago, and Silliman, are written with "ink of eyes and veins and phonemes" (Wright, *Tremble* 4).

Thus, in *Just Whistle*, Wright uses as the frame for establishing our com-mon, easily thwarted desire to connect with another body the kind of highly fragmented, nonconfessional, communal narrative Perloff identifies with postmodern directions in poetry. But the gnosis Wright evolves from that fragmented structure posits not postmodernism's multiple permissions and perspectives but a single common law like that endorsed in Christian doc-trine (just as her language frequently echoes the Bible's): when we have met another body, it is our difficult moral obligation to accept that body, male or female, and ease its life's journey: "if a body coming through the haulm were willing to help the body scaled and riddled with mistakes, to help the crumbling, hacky, runny body, the stiff, fitful body, the dumb, anachronistic body, the teratogenic, totally gnarled, hobbled body get to the other shore" (106). This hypothesized act—suspended in the uncompleted if/then clause—is of course an act of love, and ultimately this book about the body, subtitled "A Valentine," is also a book about love, what it enables and what it requires of us. Wright draws upon both defamiliarizing and conventional techniques to renew some old, loosely Christian, messages though in forms consonant with the social and linguistic structures of our time.

One old-fashioned message here is that the sexual act can yield either betrayal or transcendence. The pieces concerning "the body [being] a suspect / in the offence of crow"—where, as I understand it, *crow* signals loveless sex, even rape, or violent assertion of power—have to do with ways in which the body's desires and pleasures may encourage brutality and interfere with our moral obligations to care for the bodies we meet (121). This, the downside of sexual desire, is the subject of the "very old and intensely sad" "ballad of sexual dependency," something we absorb early as part of childhood's lore (114). At the same time, *Just Whistle* holds out hope for a nonwounding, loving sexuality that is not driven by dependency, social conventions, or ineluctable drives, that is in some way salvational or transcendent. Thus "On the Eve of Their Mutually Assured Destruction:" imagines a sexual union in which "The body would open its legs like a book / . . . like a wine list, a mussel, wings // To be mounted without tearing" with the result that "The whole world would not be lost" (127). And a parallel piece, "On the Morn Of," imagines the body closing so as to "feast upon the marl / of the other body like a wilderness. To wit: // Its whistling world would be not harmed" (131). As if offering court testimony to argue against criminalization of the sexual body—"let the record show"—the speaker emphasizes that it makes these optimistic but (punning on plaintiff) "plaintive" claims about sexual union between a man and a woman even "in the wake of its flensing"—that is, even following violence done to the body (127). That violence to its psychic corporeality would encompass emotional/ physical woundings generated by past or present sexual relationships, including consequences such as abortion or giving birth.

Two activities especially enable this particular couple to move beyond "flensing" (to flense is to cut up and slice the fat from [a whale or seal], to flay or skin) and violence—beyond grief, isolation, punishment, cries, and so forth—to healing and possible transcendence. In the language of Christianity, two acts serve as the body's "shepherd," enabling "the angel's wee victory over the beast," and both are quite traditional sources of hope and consolation. One is singing, for which we may read poetry: "Sing. Where. Sing. Is its shepherd" (123). (Whistling, too, may be a form of singing.) The other, made possible by the sex act itself and paradoxically for the female body a source of wounds as well, is producing children. When the body that had worn panties has given birth and the baby's wet body is held up for it to see, love pours from the birthing body as blood does: "glossy god brought to the head: golden: gorgeous: great gust of love: shown to the head: gone: gushing blood:" (134). Even in the physical emergency of hemorrhaging, this body wonders "is love king: is it The One:" (134).[29] Later, in the recovery room where "the other body wipes the leavings from the swollen distended body," "the gorgeous god is set upon an aureola [that is, on her nipple, to nurse]: loveblinded: they are: in the country: it is: golden: of the blind: they are: kings" (135). Having a child prompts an emotional opening that, at least for the time being, "changes everything" within and between them.

Now figured as a flower garden where grow the species named in the dialogue tracing the ontogeny of crow, the body that gave birth experiences the growth of "a blanket of fresh, vivid, lush, optimistic green; the verdancy rising even from the foundations of its ruins . . . sickle senna grew in extraordinary regeneration . . . among distended folds and through rents in the flesh" (136). Out of this astonishing healing and rebirth (and the equally surprising proliferation of adjectives describing it) comes acceptance of the body, and of our own duplicitous relation to it:

Is it. is it.
it is. it is.
an object of worship.
graven.
an object of contempt.
craven.
asshole it thought it said.
whistle it said. just whistle.
(137)

The sexual connection is renewed, and the book ends with both lovers sleeping, as the pantied one had been as the book began. The three final pieces, each titled "They Sleep," describe the "outstretched" bodies so as to combine tenderness with suffering, violent disturbance with rest. This, *Just Whistle* proposes, is inevitably the case with our embodied lives and loves. Wright's rearrangement of the same words (first "they sleep // with tenderness, wracked // heaving // outspread" [142], then "they sleep // heaving, outspread // with tenderness // wracked" [143], and then "they sleep // outspread, heaving // wracked // with tenderness" [144]) underscores the restlessness of language, its always unfinished procedural nature, its continually unfolding options. There is no closure here; sleep, too, is a changeful state. But the sections depicting sleep—even heaving, wracked sleep—establish a strong sense of completion. The three inversions, as Kathleen Fraser notes, calm and slow the reading process, "bring[ing] us to a different emotional and musical pitch" (Wright, "Bedrock" 6), while the final word "tenderness" conveys at least temporary resolution. That such resolution seems not to depend on outmoded notions of subjectivity, romantic self-delusion, nostalgia, or sentimentality seems to me possible largely because of Wright's eclecticism and its inclusion of elements from Language writing. That is to say, such credible and therefore powerful "completeness" results from Wright's extensive exploration, within the context of intelligible personal stories and moral messages, of devices that enforce vigilance against poetry's possible false consolations.

Language poetics is travestied if approached merely as a bag of formal tricks available to add an aura of theoretical sophistication to conventional work. Such a charge might legitimately be leveled against some young writers today, who as possible members of what Calvin Bedient in 2002 dubbed the "soft avant-garde" employ a new period style that, although much indebted to Language writing, can be adopted without the writer's grappling with the dynamics of (or even reading) Language writing.[30] The very different example of C.D. Wright shows that it is possible for an individual who reads Language writing carefully and takes seriously the critique it enacts to assimilate some of that movement's outlook and techniques without disrupting conventions of intelligibility and meaning-making as radically as Language writers do. If Wright's simultaneous trust and distrust of representation risks intellectual inconsistency, perhaps Grosz's figure of the Möbius strip, at once double and single sided, can help us appreciate a version of experimentalism—an exploratory poetics—that relies as much on synthesis as on replacement.

three

THE *THEN SOME* INBETWEEN

Alice Fulton's Feminist Experimentalism

NOTES ALICE FULTON MADE while working on her fourth book of poems, *Sensual Math*, suggest some recurrent thematic preoccupations of that volume, published in 1995: *"The quality of betweenness: what comes between two quantities, objects, people. Or the nature of being between categories. Being in the Midwest. Being neither a 'language' poet nor quite in the mainstream. Being neither a* gendered *female nor a male. The horizon is a between. The priming on a canvas is. Bring in electrons as emblem for betweenness?"* ("Alice Fulton" 48). Noteworthy here is Fulton's linkage, through parataxis, of her sense of poetic outsiderhood—"being neither a 'language' poet nor quite in the mainstream"—with an assertion of distance from conventional gender configurations—"being neither a *gendered* female nor a male." For in the work of Alice Fulton, as in the work of a number of women poets during the 1990s,[1] the effort to inscribe new understandings of gender generates ways of writing that fall "between" the two most widely recognized poetic camps.[2] The language of betweenness is in some ways problematic since, in implying two poles between which some middle position is located, it reinscribes the binary that poets like Fulton are trying to escape. I adopt it in this chapter nonetheless, because it conveys how clearly divided the poetry scene of the mid-1990s appeared to be and because it captures how it felt to occupy a pioneering position like Fulton's at a moment when hybrid poetries were a nascent phenomenon. Not surprisingly, the rich pleasures of such work are most evident when one attends to its exploratory or innovative dimensions while rejecting both the expectation imposed by many of Fulton's reviewers that poetry follow "mainstream" conventions of expressive personal lyric and the assumption that genuinely "experimental," "oppositional," or "alternative" writing necessarily takes the radically disjunctive forms associated with Language writing.

The mainstream and Language categories—inevitably simplifying mono-liths—have been a particularly uneasy fit for many feminist poetries.[3] Indeed, although there have been numerous feminist practitioners within each mode, some feminists would see both the presumption of individualized speaking subjectivity in mainstream lyric of the 1980s and 1990s and its rejection in Language poetry of the same period as inverse reflections of the privilege accorded to (white) male subjectivity. Fulton's search for approaches to poetic subjectivity alternative to both models supports such a perception. By stressing her preoccupation with the power dynamics and manifold restrictions of binarized gender, I wish to call attention to ways in which her feminist experimentalism highlights, even as it destabilizes, the androcentric dimensions of the dominant categories of the closing decades of the twentieth century.

The institutional recognition accorded Fulton's work might suggest that, rather than occupying a position of "betweenness," she epitomizes the mainstream. Her first collection, *Dance Script with Electric Ballerina*, won the 1982 Associated Writing Programs Award; her second collection, *Palladium*, was selected by Mark Strand for the National Poetry Series; in 1991, following the publication by David R. Godine of *Powers of Congress*, she won a MacArthur fellowship; *Sensual Math* was published by Norton in 1995, as were *Felt* in 2001 and *Cascade Experiment: Selected Poems* in 2004. *Felt* won the Rebekah Johnson Bobbitt National Prize for Poetry from the Library of Congress; Fulton has been awarded fellowships from the Guggenheim and Ingram Merrill foundations and from the National Endowment for the Arts. Having taught for many years in the creative writing program at the University of Michigan–Ann Arbor, she now teaches at Cornell, where she herself had studied with A. R. Ammons. Yet in the 1990s, Fulton's obvious interest in language as a means of construction rather than representation and her rejection of a voice-based aesthetic, along with her delight in tonal inconsistency and semantic multiplicity, put her practice at odds with what Charles Bernstein dubbed "official verse culture" (*Poetics* 6, 46, and passim). Moreover, reviews of her work suggest that Fulton's poetry made many in the establishment uneasy. Again and again, reviewers use the word "excess" or its synonyms,[4] particularly in discussing Fulton's language, which insists on calling attention to itself as language. Critics speak nervously of energy threatening to get out of hand, of technique overwhelming subject matter. Many prefer the poems in which they feel she has "tempered [her] whimsicality and verbal pyrotechnics" (Wasserberg 2). Clearly, Fulton's poetics push conventional limits. For some this is exhilarating, but the disapproving tone of many reviews indicates how much the heterogeneity of her diction, the polysemy of her line breaks and phrasing, the multiple voices, the playful and digressive movement, and the showy mixture of high and low culture in the poetry all violate norms for contemporary lyric. The ideological biases and the constructedness of these norms (which define what is not "excessive") are masked in the critics' language of taste and decorum.

Disapproving reviewers often lash out in explicitly gendered terms. Cristanne Miller has called attention to the tendency among Fulton's critics to discuss her poems as though they exhibit the poet herself and to describe the imagined poetic body in gendered ways:

> "I"/the poem/Fulton is not just female but exaggeratedly and dismissively so. Holly Prado, for example, writes that "much of [Fulton's] poetry comes across the way a woman does who wears too much makeup: strained" (1984, 9). Calvin Bedient describes the verse in *Palladium* as "high-spirited, but a bit egoistic and noisy" and "look[s] forward to her years of middle-age sag, when her energy will be easier to bear" (1988, 143). Most recently, Mutlu Blasing writes that the "coat" of Fulton's poetry "is woven of 'consumer products' but [unlike Ashbery's] hers is a skin-tight fit" (1992, 431). Taken together, these reviews evoke an image of Fulton's poems that suggests a clichéd portrait of lower-class sexual display: wearing too much makeup and skintight clothes, and being noisy. ("'The Erogenous Cusp'" 320)

William Logan made a particularly visible contribution to this trend when reviewing *Sensual Math* in the *New York Times Book Review*; he refers to Fulton's "fussiness," her "giddy images," the "calculated cuteness of her style," and her "mincing Shirley Temple campiness, all dimples and self-congratulation" (37).

Why these *ad feminam* attacks? One answer, already suggested by Miller, is that reviewers within the poetry establishment simply assume that the speaker is the poet. In other words, the assumed norm is that of the (mainstream) expressive personal lyric. Fulton has described its conventions via a handful of "shopworn maxims": "*The language should be as much like everyday speech as possible: It must not draw attention to itself. A good poem sticks to the same tone: it does not mix levels of diction. If metered, the prosody should be fairly regular (blank verse is encouraged). Metaphors and imagery are to be added like salt and pepper—not too many, not too few. The imagery should all be drawn from the same group—that is, don't compare something to a football field in one line and a coal mine in the next*" ("Her Moment of Brocade" 21).[5] In an interview published in 1997, she elaborated, identifying mainstream poetry as "a genre of lyric poetry that's very voice-based, where the poet is speaking. There's little mixing of registers of diction as a rule, and there's a limited range of emotion. It tends to be humorless—that's one emotion that's missing, humor. Authority is not questioned, I would say. Today's generic poem seems to be the lyric-narrative; it's an emotive poetry, as lyric poetry is, and its autobiographical anecdotes foster the traditional range of emotions allowed in lyric poetry—loss, desire, mourning, grief, love" ("An Interview" 594). While Fulton's defining statements may emphasize the conventions she finds most uncongenial, her descriptions of mainstream writing are by no means idiosyncratic. There is widespread consensus that the dominant poetic near the end of the twentieth century—an outgrowth of deep image writing of the 1960s and of what Charles Altieri termed the "scenic mode" of the 1970s (*Self* 5)—depends on an aura of authenticity and earnest individual testimony; that, as much as possible, it presents the self as natural and unmediated; and that it consequently favors some version of the plain style. The diminishing hold of these norms in the mid-1990s is suggested by the changes evident in the work of such well-known mainstream figures as Jorie Graham and Caroline Forché. (As the introductory chapter indicates, after the turn of the century what typifies mainstream poetry seems much less clear.) Even so, those norms continued to dominate; it's hardly surprising, then, that reviewers who accepted such autobiographical and voice-based standards would regard a poet like Fulton, whose heterogeneous language is clearly a performance and whose ingenious figures flaunt their artifice, as a poseur lacking authenticity or integrity.

I sense another dynamic at work here as well, one tied to Fulton's often indirect way of incorporating into her writing her strongly feminist perspectives. In an essay about her volume *Powers of Congress*, she explains her approach:

> The feminist strategies of my work are embedded because I believe linguistic structures are most powerful when least evident. If we are aware of racist language, for instance, we either fight it or accept it (and are thereby in league with its assumptions). If people notice an idea, they can argue against it, thus undermining it. But a more secluded assumption won't be disabled. It will be absorbed and work its stowaway changes. The covert traces of language operate on the subconscious to affect our views. I have tried to turn this linguistic tendency against itself: Whereas concealed meanings usually enforce the status quo, I use recondite structures to say subversive things. Few readers have noticed the preoccupation with gender in my work because it's eclipsed by the poems' starring subjects. (*Feeling as a Foreign Language* 185)[6]

I would hazard that the negative critical commentary of the 1980s and 1990s registers the discomfort generated by Fulton's attempts at "stowaway changes" in her readers' assumptions about femaleness, femininity, and dualized gender.[7] Critics sense, even if change is being wrought on a less than fully conscious level, that the mind behind this work challenges received ways of thinking about gender. Thus, Joy Katz, who does note feminist dimensions to the sequence "Give," complains that it is "heavy-handedly feminist" and makes explicit her preference for the "more feminine, less theatrical Fulton" ("What Are We Doing" 310).

It may well be that the innovative dimensions of Fulton's work, the traits determining its "betweenness," have been overlooked, or seen only in terms of "excess" rather than as an alternative poetics, precisely because of the difference that results from their feminist origins—just as, to quote from Fulton's "Cascade Experiment," "thirteen species / of whiptail lizards composed entirely of females / stay undiscovered due to bias / against such things existing" (*Powers of Congress* 1–2). For despite the frequent theoretical association of the experimental with the (transgressive, open, multiple, decentered, fragmented) feminine, in the 1980s and 1990s feminist experimentalism often remained relatively invisible. As Kathleen Fraser, Marianne DeKoven, Linda Taylor (Kinnahan), and others noted, even women associated with Language writing—that is, even those recognized as experimentalists—were likely to find their writing "addressed primarily as postmodern and only secondarily (if at all) as woman-centered in both form and content" (L. Taylor 338). Those aspects of their experimentation that involve the interrelation of gender issues and language tended to be overlooked.[8] Fulton's feminist experimentalism is still less visible than theirs because her strategies emerge from a more idiosyncratic set of models and not from traditions of the modernist avant-garde. Unlike the feminist poets recognized within Language circles, Fulton never demonstrated any particular interest in the tradition of Ezra Pound, Louis Zukofsky, George Oppen, and Charles Olson, while the Williams who influences her work has been processed through Ammons's writing. Although she does share with many Language writers a profound sense of debt to Emily Dickinson's poetry, she is not drawn to the examples offered by Gertrude Stein, Mina Loy, Laura Riding, or H.D.; among female modernists, only Marianne Moore may have influenced her writing.[9] Poststructuralist theory, especially feminist poststructuralism, has certainly influenced Fulton's poetics, but she has not adopted its discourses in her poetry or played out its implications in the same disjunctive and deliberately deforming ways that Language-affiliated writers have. Instead, she looks primarily to the theories of contemporary science—especially quantum physics and complexity theory—for means of reflecting current intellectual perspectives.[10] This distinction, too, has impeded recognition of her experimentalism, since it has meant that key postmodern dimensions of her work are as likely to be unrecognized as the woman-centered ones. As I will demonstrate, the postmodern trait that *is* recognized—her incorporation of pop and mass culture—is often devalued as frivolous display (Katz: "Fulton skims the froth of camp and slang" [316]) rather than read as serious creative engagement with contemporary social and cultural conditions.

To substantiate these claims, I turn now to *Sensual Math*. Here one encounters Fulton's characteristically dazzling rebuttal to the earnest plain style conventional to personal lyric of the 1970s through the 1990s. She combines in deliberately unsettling—and often deliciously funny—ways a multiplicity of styles, tones, and registers linked to various genres and diverse cultural contexts, so that the reader is kept constantly aware of the play of language and never allowed to rest in the fiction of unmediated personal expression. The breaks between Fulton's frequently enjambed lines generate puns or semantic ambiguities that further foreground the processes of language and interpretive choice. Two sample passages can give some sense of the wildly shifting levels of diction, the verbal games and pregnant line breaks, the aural variety and extravagance typical of Fulton's anti-plain style. The first, from Fulton's sequence "reimagining" the myth of Daphne and Apollo, concludes Daphne's depiction of her suitor in metamorphosis:

> and his scent—the exsanguinated scent
>   of godly flesh—the rank smell
>   of hound begins to foul it,
> surprising him, still clinging to eminence
>   as he naturalizes, pure splice,
>
>   hymn to hound—raptor to roadrunner—blurring
>   before firming up—
>
>   as witness, I am midwife
>   to the pulse, the composite
>   pelt and feathers, the nascent maybe
>   monstrous innovation of
> a god with a gift in his teeth,
>   who bows
> until his mouth is thrust between his legs,
>   wags his tail and stammers—
> "Hey Talltits, I ain't stealing what you own"—
> (*Sensual Math* 90–91)

Here the linguistic leaps—among arcane polysyllables, the vernacular of health clubs, academic jargon, names from Saturday morning cartoons, and oxymoronic curiosities like "pure splice"—are as dramatic as the god's physical transformation. The second passage employs a more meditative mode:

Do women need fuzzy feelings?
A man asked in the waiting room's
frayed *Glamour*. Do they need simulated intrigue
dinners, candlehours, cuddle-wuddle
teddy bears and wittle tittie tats?
Anything with ribbons on it,
an earthtone rainbow baby angel goose and floral bed.
Do women need texture and men
need sex? "To stick it through
the uprights," this guy said.

Scientists think the universe was smooth before it loomed
itself into a jacquard
of defects known as textures.
A texture is not localized.
It's an overall sensation, like being

enthralled or born, in love or mourning, growing
at the speed of light and leaving
its distinctive signoff on
the sky.
(59–60)

We would be mistaken in reading this second passage (or the entire poem) as either a wholehearted endorsement or an unqualified critique of the view expressed by the man writing in the "women's" magazine.[11] Here, as in so much of Fulton's work, the reader finds no easily attained or stable "point of purchase," to adopt the title of a multivocal poem from *Powers of Congress*, although more than one reviewer has mistaken a particular voice for that of the author and scolded Fulton for her purported views.[12] Such responses fail to grasp the nuanced and multilayered thinking Fulton attempts not only to set forth on the page but to prompt in her readers as well.[13]

Like the Language writers, Fulton conceives of poetry as possessing larger intellectual powers and cultural responsibilities than personal expression, even though she remains comfortable, as they tend not to be, incorporating such expression into her writing.[14] Marjorie Perloff's characterization of Language writing as responding to the commodification of language by "tak[ing] on the very public discourses that seem so threatening and explor[ing] their poetic potential," while recognizing that even the most "personal" statements "are already coded by the historical and social context in which they function," applies to Fulton's poetry as well (*Dance of the Intellect* 234). But because Fulton's way of taking on these discourses does not follow the Language model, her work remains largely unrecognized within "experimentalist" circles. Jed Rasula, who is strongly allied with Language experimentalism but remains a more eclectic poetry reader than many Language writers, goes only so far as to list Fulton's *Powers of Congress* among a handful of books by middle-aged workshop poets who demonstrate "a shift away from the lyric croon and the confidential talkshow patter" he sees dominating mainstream verse (*American Poetry Wax Museum* 434). The only review of her work to appear in a journal associated with Language writing—by Roberto Tejada in *Sulfur*—offers the following condescending assessment: "The language of advertising, TV and mass culture play a . . . prominent role in the writing of Alice Fulton. In this, her poetics is visibly more advanced than generally becomes the mainstream—which may lead one to suspect that perhaps even tamer sensibilities have been hip to specific developments in the North American avant-garde over the last fifteen years—and perhaps for this reason *Sensual Math* is not entirely devoid of interest" (155). The depth of Fulton's social and cultural critique and the extent to which her work thinks and theorizes are aspects of her achievement reviewers within both dominant camps seem unprepared either to recognize or to value.

"My Last TV Campaign," the more conventional of the two extended sequences in *Sensual Math*, can demonstrate Fulton's poetic "betweenness," for the sequence uses two structures fundamental to mainstream writing: an organizing plot that attains closure and a coherent, individualized speaker. Yet it does so in ways that refuse or subvert assumptions that undergird conventions of "mainstream" writing. The narrator is a retired successful advertising executive, a wisecracking wit steeped in advertising clichés, who recounts coming out of retirement in pursuit of loftier goals: "Before being tucked into oblivion, / I wanted to raise something more / than mercenary monuments / to high sales curves" (23–24). The anonymously funded campaign that this person finds irresistibly "sweet" is supposed to demonstrate

> the beauty of dissolving
> boundaries between yourself and the Martian
> at the heart of every war.
> An ad that pushed viewers to incorporate-embrace
> rather than debase-slash-erase the other
> gal-slash-guy. A commercial saying blend,
> bend, and blur, folks. It works!
> (24)

The challenge of the campaign, then, is to sell a set of values rather than a material product—values quite different from the glorification of material consumption encouraged by the usual product advertisements. Still within the poem's first section, "The Profit in the Sell," the speaker explains how he or she happened upon the gimmick for the advertisement in a Discovery Network special on orchids. The show offered an example in species evolution of a particular species enhancing its chances of survival by assuming the character of its other:

> This orchid fashioned itself
> into a female bee, or you
> could say, a commercial
> for that creature.
> By dressing up and passing
> as a dummy luscious *she,*
> the bee orchid pulled in more
> pollinators and survived more
>
> flagrantly.
> (24–25)

Creation itself, the speaker observes, is a form of cross-dressing. By the end of the sequence's first section, the speaker is keyed up to celebrate the example of these "carnal flowers / that overstepped their bounds / to complete themselves" (25). During the remaining four sections the speaker considers several ideas for the ad's scenario and settles on a ludicrous-sounding one that involves actors posing as BEFORE and AFTER orchids with "Mr. Darwin" orchestrating their transformation from "quintessential wallflowers" to seductive creatures "rushed by bees" (43). Although the advertiser's colleagues only mock the project, the speaker remains euphoric, thrilled to be making a living "marveling / at polyphonic flowers" (47). The campaign fails, however, and in the sequence's brief final section the speaker contemplates the gap between his or her own biases and those of the culture at large that accounts for the failure.

Though accurate, this précis distorts the character of the poem not only because this unlikely "plot" unfolds obliquely with lots of verbal clowning and pizzazz but also because the narrative is not the poem's heart. Rather, the plot is an entertaining pretense for exploring issues such as authenticity, imitation, the boundaries between self and other, and the extent to which such boundaries are necessary or unavoidable. Thus, the section of the sequence titled "Passport," which occupies eight of its twenty-six pages and describes the relationship between the speaker's mother and Rudolf Valentino, does not advance the plot at all. But the actor who was "king of / costume, gesture, the skin // of drama" and who performed in "plots feverish // with disguise" provides another demonstration of the seductive power of imitation and liminality (34). Moreover, this particular demonstration enables Fulton to shift the poem's emphasis to the role of the female audience by attending to the enraptured mother who played the Wurlitzer accompaniment at local screenings of Valentino's silent films. Without her imaginative investment and the sound she added to his films—however formulaic the emotional character of her repertoire—"The Great Lover" would have been nothing (38). In her handling of the Valentino material Fulton is adopting a strategy she has noted in Dickinson's poetry, of "def[ying] notions of otherness by reminding us that all components are mutually dependent and equally important to the whole" (*Feeling as a Foreign Language* 148). Similarly, Fulton approaches narrative structure itself in such a way that all that is Other to the seemingly central narrative proves just as important as that narrative to the sequence as a whole.

Thus, although Fulton in "My Last TV Campaign" does not disrupt narrative and resist closure in the ways that Language writers do, she nonetheless rejects conventional linearity: the extravagant music and the semantic multiplicity of her language, along with her proliferating figures, repeatedly overwhelm the story, as the poem's energy continually surges toward new tangents. Narratives multiply and mimic one another, and what they provide is a means of lending the pleasures of concretion (as well as comedy) to Fulton's consideration of abstractions. Indeed, this combination is one of the goals suggested by the title phrase, "sensual math." Narrative for Fulton, then, is primarily another version of costume—not essentialized or naturalized but valued as a means for a poem to survive "flagrantly."

And what about Fulton's handling of the speaker's subjectivity? To what extent does Fulton's sequence attempt, as the voice-based mainstream lyric does, the illusion of a "real" person? We learn in the course of the poem that the advertising executive has pollen allergies, wears a wedding band, drinks martinis, drives a Legend, watches TV, sometimes listens to Bach, and has sufficient interest in home decoration to take in the "Showcase of Homes" tour (39). So the speaker is precisely positioned in social class and lifestyle. In addition, there are moments that convey sensibility, as when the advertiser scornfully distances himself or herself from "cohorts" who circulate crude jokes about orchids that want to get laid yet consider the speaker's "cross-dressing orchids . . . crass" (45). There are even moments of lyric epiphany, as in the brief section "Volunteers," in which the advertiser recalls the profound joy of listening to Bach's fugues, providing in the process an emotional grounding for her or his campaign's intellectual message, a powerful hymn to evolution as an unending fugue in which the speaker's voice participates and before which he or she can marvel. Clearly, Fulton is not so concerned as Language writers are with fracturing conventional subjectivity.

Yet the speaker's language is so heterogeneous in its figures and so lavishly orchestrated in its sound patterns that the text could never be mistaken for speech or spontaneous meditation. Here, for instance, is the gorgeous opening of "Volunteers":

> But I remember best the radiance escaping
> from the tape as I drove home
> each day. Skeins of Bach
> crossbreeding in the air.
> The instrument's strings
> mingling like a chromosome's
> toward coronation. Music forming crown
> knots and cascades.
> To improvise, anticipate and risk—
> equilibrium's like kissing
>
> your own hand in comparison.
> (46)

"Volunteers" is the section of "My Last TV Campaign" that most resembles the conventional lyric (though Fulton confounds stereotypes in attributing such spiritual depth not to a poet-speaker but to an advertising executive), yet even here Fulton diverges from the mainstream illusion of natural speech by insistently foregrounding craft and linguistic surface: the prominent pattern of dominant vowels—long *a* sounds, then long *o*'s, then short *i*'s—suggests the introduction of the first three voices in a fugue, providing formal analogue to the section's proposition that "evolution is a fugue / without finale" (46). Elsewhere in the sequence, because the speaker thinks so much in slogans and prefabricated phrases, he or she seems largely a product of the language of advertising. Even the character's moment of creative revelation emerges in the secondhand language of advertising: "Why not say it with flowers?" (43). The reader, registering the speaker's language not as personal voice but as a formal reinforcement of theme and a product of commodity culture, is compelled to recognize that there is no authentically personal language. Unlike the writers who are recognized as "alternative," Fulton does not demand thorough estrangement from romantic imaginings of uniquely sensitive individuals whose private perceptions and emotions lend radiance to their language. Nonetheless, she does challenge mainstream understandings of personal identity.

The aspect of subjectivity on which Fulton focuses her cultural critique and her experimental energies is the construction of gender identity. Again, the "Passport" section of "My Last TV Campaign" is instructive in that Valentino, the ultimate in masculine allure, is also a cross-dressing feminized figure. Extrapolating from the lesson of the orchids, we understand that Rudy's imitation of the other sex is key to his seductive power. But more fundamentally, this Valentino challenges the male/female binary so essential to our culture's notions of identity. The sequence's advertiser speaker fits conventional male/female divisions even less neatly. For, extending an experimental technique she has "embedded" in her work before, Fulton has deliberately "ungendered" every detail related to the speaker, so that neither cultural conventions nor physical traits confer a determinate gender or sex ("Interview" 590).[15] The speaker's androgyny serves thematically to reinforce the ad campaign's focus on the dissolution of binaries. More radically, Fulton's strategy opens up the possibility of indeterminate, hybrid, or changing gender positions not conventionally recognized.

At the very least, Fulton's evident ungendering forces us to consider the implications of reading the character as either a man or a woman. If we find ourselves thinking of the character as a man, we recognize that this is only because a man is far more likely to attain that level of power within the advertising world. If we read the character as a figure for the female artist, then we gain insight into the obstacles women confront in their aspirations to create or to bring about cultural change. The sequence's final section, "Wonder Bread," through its obvious echoes of Dickinson, suggests most clearly that the forces the advertiser is up against in the TV campaign are those confronted by women who do not follow the prescribed gender patterns, who are "culturally incorrect" (*Sensual Math* 12). The epigraph from Dickinson's "Master Letters" links the often misunderstood nineteenth-century poet with the speaker, in that both send messages that speak in ways their contemporaries can't process: "*You asked me what my flowers said—then they were disobedient—I gave them messages.*" The speaker's opening lines invert Dickinson's inebriate of air to convey disgust at her or his audience: "What eucharist of air and bland // was this nation raised on? No one understood / my funny flowers." The speaker grants the absurdity of those flowers, but the lines "Snips of sugar. Snails with spice. / Puppy dogs. Tales. Everything. // Nice!" seem to attribute the ineffectiveness of the television orchids to something else: to the unorthodoxy of their gender-blending, their transgression of culturally imposed divisions—their betweenness. The speaker's musings further suggest that his or her admiration for nature—something he or she failed to sell to American audiences—resists precisely those patriarchal power structures that nursery rhymes and other authorized "tales" of gender support. Here the speaker's iconoclasm goes beyond even Dickinson's, as the advertiser praises "the absence of a Master":

Was it that I liked

the absence of a Master
neuron in the brain—

the absence of a Master
cell in embryos—

the nothing in the way of
center that would hold?

What causes less comfort
than wonder?

What—does not console?
(48–49)

The speaker's "likes" distance him or her from both phallocentric order and the current version of Romanticism's heart-soothing lyric. Indeed, the passage, which defies Yeats's nostalgia for a (patriarchal) center in "The Second Coming," connects reliance on patriarchal authority with reliance on the authoritative version of lyric. For mainstream lyric both occupies the cultural "center" and enacts a consoling centering of one's self in the contained representation of one's experience. Rejection of the Master, Fulton's lines suggest, necessarily entails rejection of the cultural vehicles that convey the Master's ideology.

Fulton's most readily perceived experiment in this volume, her invention of the punctuation mark she calls the bride, manifests just such a rejection of patriarchal authority. Fulton introduces this deliberately gendered, gynocentric mark in a poem titled "= =," whose very reflexivity removes Fulton's practice from mainstream lyric. While the sign does not appear until the middle of the volume, Fulton has all along been preparing us to understand it, and to understand it multiply.[16] The poem "= =" begins:

It might mean immersion, that sign
    I've used as title, the sign I call a bride
after the recessive threads in lace = =

                the stitches forming deferential
                        space around the firm design.
                                It's the unconsidered

        mortar between the silo's bricks = = never admired
                                when we admire
        the holdfast of the tiles (their copper of a robin's
                breast abstracted into flat).

                        It's a seam made to show,
        the deckle edge = = constructivist touch.
        (56)

The first proposition, "It might mean immersion," harks back to the opening poem, "The Priming Is a Negligee," whose meditation on the spaces and layers between substances, people, and words that paradoxically allow contact between them (as mortar does in the passage just quoted) includes the following: "For immersion see / 'passion between.' See / opposite of serene" (3–4). Use of the term "immersion," then, signals that impassioned, willed connection figures importantly among the meanings of the bride mark. The instructive weaving of motifs through which Fulton expands our understanding of the bride continues in "Drills," the poem immediately preceding "= =," in which immersion (in a language, in suffering) is linked to understanding, but understanding that is unbearable, that dissolves the self.[17] Immersion pushes the limits of the imagination—and so does the bride as it challenges our bounded understandings of gender.

The poem "= =" is particularly useful here because it reveals the bride mark's contribution to both kinds of (overlapping) betweenness—poetic and gendered—highlighted at the opening of this chapter. The poem explains the mark in terms that emphasize a poetic aim Fulton shares with Language writers: to denaturalize language use in general and poetry in particular. Her unfamiliar punctuation mark heightens our awareness of all punctuation and how it works. This in turn makes us more conscious of poetic devices, keeping our attention on the material linguistic surface immediately before us. As Fulton rhymingly asserts: "The natural is what // poetry contests. Why else the line = = why stanza = = why / meter and the rest" (57).[18] The lines that immediately follow—"Like wheels on snow // that leave a wake = = that tread in white / without dilapidating / mystery = =" allude to Dickinson's "I cannot dance upon my Toes," which backhandedly calls attention to the commonalities between Dickinson's writing and the most stylized and blatantly unnatural art forms, ballet and opera (57).

Fulton's alluding to a female poet who dressed in what may be construed as bridal white and employed thoroughly unconventional punctuation contributes also to her feminist aim of opening possibilities between gender binaries.[19] For the mark that says "equals, equals" fosters awareness of how pervasively hierarchical constructions of gender difference shape our experience, precisely to subvert such hierarchical binarism and revalue the "feminine." The terms in which Fulton describes the bride mark speak both to the historical oppression of women and to the distinctive forms that female power has taken in response to that oppression. Linked by both its visual appearance and its name to a background stitch in the traditionally female art of lace making, this mark reflects many of the traditional effacing expectations of women's behavior: it is "deferential," "reticent," the negative space that acts as defining foil to masculine achievement. Yet, as "a seam made to show," this gendered mark gives the female a presence impossible to ignore. And Fulton announces its valuable potentialities: such a mark "might make visible the acoustic signals / of things about to flame. It might // let thermal expansion be syntactical" (56). It might "add stretch" (56). The poem's final lines, in which the bride mark is identified as "the wick that is // the white between the ink" (57), suggest that such feminine structures open possibilities for interpersonal communication, enlightenment, connection, community.

As I read *Sensual Math*, this typographic symbol is one means by which Fulton attempts to further poetry's contribution to a profound social restructuring not based on hierarchy. This is what I understand, for instance, when mention of reticence in "= =" recalls "A Little Heart to Heart with the Horizon," in which the horizon is addressed half seriously as a model for global harmony; the horizon's "reticence . . . serene / lowness" is precisely what permits a sense of commonality and equality with others, what binds such polarities as "body and clouds," what ultimately makes love possible (10–11). This meditation on horizons leads in turn to the poem called "Immersion," which begins,

> Let it be horizon levitating on horizon
> with sunrise at the center = =
> the double equal that means more
> than equal to = = within.
> (66)

Another reflexive consideration of the bride sign, "Immersion" makes clear the mark's significance specifically for female artists. Passages that describe women working "by night" in various media, managing to defy the obligations and disempowering expectations that impede them, appear like mortar inset between the stanzaic tiles that explain the double equal. That symbol, in its open-endedness and mysterious possibility, comes to suggest all that might yet emerge as women seize the equality that will allow them an immersion in artistic production as thorough as men's.

What stands in the way of that equality preoccupies Fulton in the volume's other extended poem, to which I now turn. "Give: A Sequence Reimagining Daphne and Apollo" lends itself to a consideration of how Fulton's integration of high and low culture—specifically her use of pop cultural material—contributes to her explorations of the possibilities for a feminist aesthetic of betweenness.

In this multilayered, polyphonic work, Fulton revamps Ovid's tale by representing Apollo partly in terms of Frank Sinatra and by depicting Cupid—the rival musician who, when scolded for stealing Apollo's song "My Way," vengefully initiates Apollo's unrequited lust—partially as Elvis Presley. (Elvis did in fact record "My Way," Sinatra's signature hit of the late 1960s.) Daphne's earth goddess mother is, among other things, a black singer with "a saurian voice"—most immediately Big Mama (Willie Mae) Thornton, whose "Hound Dog" was one of the songs that "made the King rich," although her own recording did not "cross over" (92). Thus, Fulton recasts the ancient myth of attempted rape in terms of the popular music industry—the competing performers, the song lyrics, the racial inequities—of midcentury America.

Perhaps sharing Fredric Jameson's sense that the mixture of high and low art characteristic of postmodernism can yield only "blank parody" (17), many of Fulton's (late modernist?) reviewers fail to recognize that she has serious points to make in using this pop cultural material. Sandra Gilbert sees the poem only as a "dazzlingly brilliant stand-up comedy riff on myth" and warns, "seriously, folks, wisecracks can only take a wood nymph or a poet so far" (297, 298). Similarly, David Slavitt introduces *Sensual Math* as "a breezy kind of book" and questions how well it will wear. Having identified Fulton as a practitioner of light verse, he quotes the following passage from "Give":

> Phoebus Apollo favored snapbrim hats,
>
> alligator shoes and sharkskin
> suits from Sy Devore's Hollywood men's store. In battle,
> stripped to the mail
> he wore beneath and crowned with light, he glowed like a
> refinery
> turning crude into product, roaring Doric columns of flame. "I
> make everything
> and make it into everything else," he liked to claim. He took

pride
in how cultured he was, a musician of pansexual magnitude
with his suave
ballads of desire.
(*Sensual Math* 75–76)

Slavitt then concludes the review by commenting: "On first take, those Sy Devore suits are cheeky enough. But what will I think of them in six months? (Maybe that's why I don't shop at such places.) I don't mean to suggest that there isn't a place for kitsch and poshlost in a culture where these are assaulting us everywhere. But there must be some other response to dreck than to wallow in it and declare that it smells sweet" (28). True, Fulton is a long way from the hostility and disgust toward mass culture, and the pretense of separation from it, that typifies the literature of high modernism and that survives in parts of contemporary poetry's mainstream. But she is equally far from an uncritical embrace of either mass or popular culture, both of which play crucial roles in maintaining normative gender categories and sustaining the oppression of women. Although popular culture is playfully invoked and sometimes granted a compelling fluency and panache in Fulton's poetry, most often it dramatizes retrograde forces that impede the kinds of change Fulton seeks. At the same time, as my analysis of "Give" will demonstrate, Fulton hopefully suggests that pop culture's unapologetic investment in imitation and duplication may paradoxically render it a fruitful ground for innovation in poetry—for unsettling, disequilibrating invention in between categories.

Let me, then, offer an alternative reading of the function of those Sy Devore suits. For decades they were essential to the public image of Frank Sinatra, and his setting a fashion trend is a reminder of the power the recording industry wields in shaping the public's desires. Sinatra, whose "suave / ballads of desire" caused unprecedented mass hysteria among America's youth, virtually defined the libidinal fantasies of at least one generation, and, far from being a fleeting fashion, he demonstrated an astonishing ability to hold on to his star status, even into old age and partial dementia. The lasting grip that such images have on the popular imagination is, I believe, one of the fundamental points Fulton is making: her revisionary mythography insists that Sinatra and the other pop stars who have been almost deified in American mass culture perpetuate virtually the same ideology of male sexual predation that Ovid depicted in his divine Apollo. And her mention of the mail Apollo wears beneath his Sy Devore suit reminds readers of the power and protective armor, the often invisible advantages, borne by the male. Rendering Apollo in terms of Sinatra is not, then, an outlandish gimmick, however much fun Fulton may have playing with the rendition; rather, in one dimension at least, it is a straightforward statement about how little has really changed, about the frightening cultural persistence of ideologies of gender, sexuality, and romance that have trapped women for centuries.

Fulton also emphasizes this continuity by invoking ancient customs that ritualize women's oppression and pointing to their historical survival. The section "Take: A Roman Wedding" describes wedding customs mentioned by Ovid but elaborates with allusions that evoke more recent representations of marriage or rape (the two are not always distinguishable): the "[p]ipes and timbrels" on Keats's urn and the "[t]high or breast?" of Yeats's Zeus and Leda (84). At the poem's close, Fulton notes that the whitethorn tree that provided the wedding torch in ancient Rome "still grows," if in slightly modified form: "The organza branches // of today's hybrids—though susceptible / to fire-blight— / are entirely free / of nettles" (85). For a brief moment—the suspension of a line break—it appears that dramatic change has occurred and today's brides may be "entirely free." But no, only the more obvious brutality of a bride's seizure has been removed. As with the shift from vinyl recordings to compact discs, it's the same phenomenon only in a refined technology.

This is not to say that Fulton's reimagination of past events in terms of recent ones, or her explanation of current customs in terms of past ones, simply universalizes the situation of Western women across the centuries. Awareness of historical particularity guides Fulton's selection of pop cultural material. The specific songs and celebrities she invokes flourished in decades when gender codifications in the United States were especially rigid, when myths of heterosexual romance and of women's fulfillment in subservient love were particularly powerful. With this material—material no longer current yet as enduring as the tabloids' never-dead Elvis—Fulton points to a specific era as having codified particularly influential manifestations of the oppressions women still confront, though in less blatant forms, in the 1990s when she writes "Give." The early and midcareer years of Sinatra and the period of Elvis's rise—roughly the mid-1940s through the '60s—were the heyday of the ideology Betty Friedan labeled the "feminine mystique." This mystique defined women almost exclusively in terms of their reproductive and sexual capacities within marriage. The era's mainstream music ("turning crude [that is, crude thinking] into [commercial] product") inculcated those views, presenting women primarily as the objects of male desire, locating a woman's purpose and fulfillment in heterosexual romance and in holding on to her man.

With poignancy as well as mocking humor, Fulton in "Give" highlights the grotesqueness of these enduring assumptions that were so glaringly evident in U.S. society after World War II. Daphne—a feral figure, part Annie Oakley, associated with the electron (recall: for Fulton an emblem of betweenness), with lesbianism, with what physicists term "dark matter," and with negative space—is someone who cannot or will not comply with dominant expectations of the feminine. Without being a figure of gender indeterminacy, like the advertising executive, Daphne occupies a space between conventional gender categories. Her special gift is not reproduction; indeed, in her flight from Apollo, she is attempting to evade marriage and childbearing more than rape. The special power she does possess might be conventionally coded masculine: it is a scientifically precise insight, the ability to "see right through" opaque materials. When used to see through words, this ability is socially subversive:

> her gift for visualizing the inner

chambers
of words was most impressive. She'd tell of *wedlock's* wall
that was a shroud
of pink, its wall that was a picket fence, the one of chainlink
and one
that was all strings. While Apollo hardened with love for her,
Daphne
stripped the euphemism from the pith. *Love* was nothing
but a suite
of polished steel: mirrors breeding mirrors in successions
of forever, his
name amplified through sons of sons and coats of arms,
her limbs
spidering, her mind changed to moss and symbol
(81)

Woman reduced to symbol of nature in service of man's narcissistic self-replication—Fulton's Daphne wants none of it. (And the pronounced artifice of Fulton's alternating long and short lines, defying conventions of blank verse and breath unit, reminds us of the poet's homologous rejection of the "natural.") An elusive free spirit aligned with the presymbolic, Daphne adores "the wilderness between territory and names" but loves no man (79). When Apollo invokes the ideology of the feminine mystique in order to seduce her, she is horrified. His speech—here, interspersed with Daphne's thoughts—is crude vernacular because Cupid's magic makes him use a debased language that gives the lie to his former pretensions to cultural sophistication. Rhythmic patterns that echo Cupid/Elvis's songs reinforce the chilling comedy of his presumptuous claim:

"Hey Talltits, I ain't stealing what you own"—
                    and I realize he thinks that—
"Just a bit-a bit-a honey
            that you have on loan" —what I'm living in,
                    the dark matter of myself—
                                        is his.
(91)

Yet, importantly, the popular music industry of midcentury America has its own marginal voices that offer alternative perspectives. In her mother's African American rhythm and blues, Daphne has access to a critique of Apollo's view of woman as merely a body whose possession is man's sexual right. Daphne recalls how her Big Mama, before shouting her hit that made Elvis rich, would tell it like it is. She would

            say—"Now I'm gone

to do my *own* self song" and sing
                the lyrics he'd omitted—
        "Want to steal my power, want to steal
my soul—you ain't lookin' for a woman,
        you is lookin' for a hole—"
(92)

But this mother is dead, killed by Apollo so that he could steal her oracle; she survives only as a voice within Daphne's head and as a list of albums and record labels Daphne can chant as a mantra to sustain her resistance to Apollo's bullying. "Who can she turn to, the monastic, almost / abstract Daphne?" the poem asks (98). She "winds up" pleading for help from her father, the river god, and he "makes her / into nature": "With no one to turn to— / she turns to a tree" (99). Reading all this as an analysis of the resources offered within popular music, we might say that Fulton acknowledges via the black female singer that popular culture has its own valuable countercultures. But these margins have little power against the dominant ideology and the commercial power structure that supports it—at least until we respond to Big Mama's plea and "Turn—her [and with her, marginalized groups or cultures more generally]—loose—" (96).

The possibilities for such a release emerge, somewhat ambiguously, in the final parts of this polysemous and multivalent poem. In the sections that deal with Daphne after her metamorphosis, Fulton less frequently invokes the comic incongruity of gods as drooling crooners—comedy that in the poem's early sections cracks the veneer of solemnity with which we tend to approach classical myth and challenges us to see it anew in our time. All along, Daphne has been depicted in a more lyrical and sophisticated language than the caricatured male gods. Their vernacular bluster rarely sounds in the concluding sections, which, with gentler humor and penetrating grace, render the odd liminal states both of Daphne within the laurel and of the laurel that spirals obliquely, "turning against" the woman's body it has been forced to contain. As Fulton attends less to the musical stars of the past, she uses the dynamics and terminology of the music industry—where new hits can rise rapidly, and new styles of music evolve—to speculate about the future's possibilities. In so doing she suggests some liberating potential within popular culture and popular music, if only because the music industry's relentless reinvention of itself—its insistence on novelty (even if that means only new packaging for old materials), its omnivorous appetite for whatever can be appropriated from high or low cultural sites, its continual development of new styles, new stars, and "new releases"—involves an investment in process that could yield genuine change.

If one takes as the culmination of Daphne's fate the metamorphosis Ovid recorded, then Daphne's attempt to escape the trap of woman as reproductive, sexual body has failed utterly; it has only led to an even more constricted state of woman-as-nature, "captured" within the material substance of a tree. Moreover, in Fulton's version, this has occurred despite the arrival of 1970s feminism (before her transformation, Apollo pleads with her, "be a Natural-Girl, / not a hairy Ladies-Libber" [93]). But Fulton goes beyond the chronological and psychological limits of Ovid's imagining, thereby raising the possibility that in the future Daphne might gain release. The metaphor of the recording industry's "new release" proves central to the poem's meditation on—or intimation of—the possibility of profound change for women.

"She'll get out of this one somehow," the tree asserts, referring to their "weird wedding," their collision "full of give" (100). This faith is not based on history, certainly. For despite her struggles to escape, Daphne has remained trapped for many centuries, and according to the tree, she has only grown more frivolous and babyish over time. The tree's faith in her eventual triumph probably derives, then, from witnessing the endurance of Daphne's will to resist. Indeed, the final section, titled "A New Release," while it recounts a memory from her pre-laurel state, seems to present Daphne's recognition of her own psychological resources. As Daphne replays her memories, she recognizes how she always "must have" seen and heard things differently from those around her. The new recording Daphne recalls playing announced the same old message—"'Wear My Ring around Your Neck,' the latest / hoodlum Cupid sang" (112). But, seeing that she (or woman generally) is "bent / out of shape in [the record's] reflections," she shifted her attention away from those distorted images (111). Examining not the reflections but the record's material surface, she saw the profound blacknesses of its grain; she wondered at "how music lurked in negative / space / that looked so unassuming" and marveled that "the missing / had volition" (112). Although what she attended to involves on the literal level the production of sound from the record, now its figurative relevance to herself is obvious, suggesting an enhanced appreciation of herself—the negatively charged electron, the dark-skinned daughter, the missing huntress, the person who is "neither a *gendered* female nor a male." The blackness traditionally so devalued in our racist culture and our everyday language assumes value here, and Daphne—the unconventional feminine—with it. A sense of empowered will and potential song emerges along with Daphne's remembered and renewed desire to "be the singer rather than the wearer of the ring" (112).

If there is hope for more material release, it emerges somewhat tentatively at the close, in the sound of saws that may cut down her tree. Here is the passage, Daphne's words that conclude the sequence:

To this day,
rodents gnawing at the wooden walls remind me of the rasp

of dust
before a cut. A cut. That's what we called a song.
And handsaws—
harvesting the forest in the distance where I live—
sound
like the end: the rhythmic scribble of stylus against
label
when everybody's left. Everybody's gone
to bed.
And the record turns and turns into
the night.
(112–13)

If indeed an end approaches, will it be some final termination or the end of imprisonment and a new beginning? Is the record simply revolving, or is there some revolutionary change taking place? Fulton has testified that this ambiguity is deliberate: she wanted to suggest that the record keeps on revolving and also that it is transformed into the night ("Interview" 592–93).

Since Daphne throughout the poem has been a figure of night and "dark matter," this turning into night need not be read as a movement toward oblivion. It may signal a power shift away from Apollo's brash light toward the dark recesses, the "negative space" of the female. This cut may be Daphne's song, just as the stylus scribbling against the label may be Daphne's own pen, writing tirelessly against the categories, the fixed labels (woman/man, nature/culture) that have so long restricted us.

In a 1989 essay on Dickinson's current standing, Fulton quotes poem 526, which begins:

> To hear an Oriole sing
> May be a common thing—
> Or only a divine.
>
> It is not of the Bird
> Who sings the same, unheard,
> As unto Crowd—
>
> The Fashion of the Ear
> Attireth that it hear
> In Dun, or fair—
> (*Feeling as a Foreign Language* 130)

Fulton then observes, "[A] poet's reception depends upon 'The Fashion of the Ear'" (130). That is certainly true of the reception accorded Fulton—a reception that may well tell us more about the readers of contemporary American poetry and about the U.S. poetry scene of the 1990s than about her work. It reveals a widespread resistance to kinds of mixing that one might have thought would be readily accepted in this postmodernist era: mixing of realms of reference (pop with high culture, contemporary with ancient), of genres (lyric and elegy with parody and satire), of registers, of tones, and so on. It reveals within the mainstream reviewing venues of the 1990s an acrophobic discomfort with a high degree of indeterminacy and plurality, with generic inconsistency—with work that is cerebral without being consistently meditative or serious, irreverent but not free from moralizing. It reveals within avant-garde poetry circles of the time a problematically narrow sense of what constitutes socially or aesthetically significant invention, or intervention, in language use and poetic structures. It reveals a pervasive unease with feminist thinking that is not manifest in the conventional forms of personal testimony and earnest or angry proclamation.

Fulton is very conscious of sounding somewhat out of the ear's current fashion, of functioning between or outside recognized poetics. The narrator of the prologue to "Give" has good cause to wonder of the poem's readers, "will you receive / the minus and the plus, / the—not to mention, but I must— // *then some* inbetween?" (74). Yet even if Fulton doubts that many will be able to embrace the betweennesses her work explores, one of her aesthetic aims remains to promulgate their potential—and thereby to prompt more inclusiveness in poetic fashion:

> Let's sneak one past the culture's
> fearless goalies, be neither one
> nor the other, but a third
> being, formerly thought *de trop.*
> (65)

Although Fulton's poetry does not reflect the direct influence of Language poetry as, say, C.D. Wright's does, Fulton's accurate awareness of writing in ways that position her work between Language poetics and conventional lyric makes this passage's anticipation of current "third way" rhetoric appropriate, particularly since that label seems to be shedding its initial negative connotations. Her inventive work, which stretches the linguistic, tonal, vocal, and emotional range of contemporary lyric, points ultimately to resources that lie between recognized categories, in liminal states, and at the cultural margins as offering hope for significant social as well as aesthetic change. Her double equal sign and other rejections of patriarchal binaries aim, as did her advertiser's last TV campaign, to counter the destructive othering that pervades so many aspects of our lives, including the recent poetry scene.

four

FIELDS OF PATTERN-BOUNDED UNPREDICTABILITY

Palimtexts by Rosmarie Waldrop and Joan Retallack

REFLECTING ON HER DEVELOPMENT as an experimental poet, Rosmarie Waldrop identifies as particularly formative the moment when she recognized the usefulness for her writing of "arbitrary pattern" and of a charged interaction between regulation and deviancy:

It was an important moment for me when I realized consciously that the encounter of a poem-nucleus with an arbitrary pattern (like a rhyme scheme) would tend to pull the nucleus out of its semantic field in unforeseen directions. The tension always generates great energy, not just for bridging the "gap" between original intention and the pattern, but for pushing the whole poem farther. . . . I'm spelling out what Ashbery and others have called the liberating effect of constraints. But what matters is that *any* constraint, *any* pattern can be generative in this way. It does not need to be one of the traditional forms with their heavy closure effect of regularity and recurrence. . . . [E]xtreme formalism rarely works to my satisfaction. More often I use a pattern (e.g. the grammatical structure of a given text), but *also* let the words push and pull in their own directions. Since I make the rules, I also feel free to break them. (Lehman 197)

As her reference to "Ashbery and others" acknowledges, such attitudes are by no means unique to Waldrop. Widespread use of the procedural forms Joseph Conte has identified as a distinctly postmodern poetic genre, for example, demonstrates that an interest in the interaction between imposed arbitrary constraints and generative discoveries has propelled a good deal of exploratory poetry in recent decades.

Joan Retallack, who has been influenced by John Cage's "aesthetic paradigm of deterministic randomness," is another experimentalist who sees a potential for liberatory stretch in even quite conventional formal regulations (Retallack, "Poethics" 251). But like Waldrop, Retallack articulates also the limitations she perceives in conventional formal patterns: "Any formal structure draws us outside ourselves, beyond our personal and expressive logics. Something as simple as meter, rhyme, and *abab* patterns pulls us in directions which have to do with material structures of the language, not just the ego-expressive interests of the writer. But these forms do not even begin to explore the infinite possibilities of the complex system that is a natural language and the forms that give it vitality" ("Poethics" 262).[1] Retallack goes on to introduce the Cagean strategies that she believes generate forms more appropriate to the teeming multifariousness of contemporary realities. "Chance operations and indeterminacy pull the work of the composer or writer into exploration of the kinds of events and relationships that are characteristic of richly complex systems—from the simple patterns of bone/stone or *abab* to the increased complexity of language generated by mesostic strings to the turbulent patterns of liquid, smoke, ambient noise, and high degrees of semantic and associative multiplicity" ("Poethics" 262). Sharing Cage's conviction that contemporary artists need to recover the continuity of aesthetic experience with the normal processes of living, and that these processes are wonderfully complex, Retallack believes that the artwork should be, like one's immediate experience, "a complex intersection of intention and nonintention, pattern and surprise" ("Poethics" 255). Although Waldrop is less interested in chance operations per se, what Retallack says helps account also for Waldrop's restlessness with "extreme formalism" and her tendency to complicate her own structures and break her own rules.

Seeking forms that are genuinely consonant with the present and that enable movement into the future, Waldrop and Retallack share with Cage and many other innovative artists an interest in bringing their work into line with current scientific modeling of complex systems. Thus, Waldrop links her own repeated complication of dichotomous thinking to the coexistence in modern physics of ostensibly incompatible models; the paradox of the inconsistent yet necessarily coexistent quantum and wave finds expression in her work "in the simultaneous presence of fragment and flow" ("Conversation" 373–74). She also finds in quantum physics a challenge to push poetry beyond its traditional identification with the image and into "this brave new world without images!" ("Conversation" 375). Retallack, intrigued by more recent developments in science, has produced, as I will demonstrate, verbal versions of the extremely complex fractal patterns that occur in natural phenomena. More generally, in her approach to poetic form, Retallack pursues the implications especially of chaos theory, whose "butterfly effect" (whereby a butterfly flapping its wings in China could dramatically affect the weather in New

York several months later) supports her hope that opening literary genres and generating new linguistic formulations might ultimately have significant social ramifications.

Among the social transformations both women hope to foster through their writing is the dissolution of the constraints of inherited gender categories and expectations. In ":RE:THINKING:LITERARY:FEMINISM: (three essays onto shaky grounds)" Retallack notes optimistically the convergence between current scientific thinking and the experimental literary forms associated with the feminine (though heretofore produced primarily by men). Science now, which "recogniz[es] both complexity and the constituting presence of chance in nature" (*Poethical Wager* 114), points to the relevance of those experimental literary forms that "Western culture has tended to label feminine (forms characterized by silence, empty and full; multiple, associative, nonhierarchal logics; open and materially contingent processes, etc.)" (114). Happily, this coincidence is occurring just at the moment when women finally have enough social power and cultural standing to attempt in significant numbers those "feminine" forms that push the constructed limits of intelligibility (113). Heterogeneous experimental creations that "engage the dynamics of multiplicity" and generate "a proliferation of possibility beyond invidious dualisms" (113–14)—perhaps especially those produced by women—may help us move beyond the fundamental Western binary of feminine/masculine, ultimately freeing not just women but all "the complex human" (113) to explore a world of "uncompressible possibility" (134).[2]

Just as Cage developed innovative writing from previously used language of "source texts" by Thoreau, Joyce, Wittgenstein, McLuhan, Fuller, and others, both Waldrop and Retallack draw extensively upon preexistent texts in producing their own experimental work. This reflects a belief common to all three that language is not something one possesses and makes one's own in order to express oneself; language is invariably an already used medium and is to be embraced as such, with no pretensions to originality or ownership. Neither Waldrop nor Retallack "writes through" source texts as Cage does—subjecting them to chance operations to select words that appear in mesostics. Yet, as Retallack and Waldrop write over and (collagistically) with texts in Western literary tradition, inherited linguistic formulations figure importantly among the ordering structures with and against which they, like Cage, work. Even where the source texts do not provide a formal structure— as when a new work follows "the grammatical structure of a given text"— their verbal arrangements provide a crucial set of limiting constraints that Waldrop and Retallack often deliberately encounter and transform in their writing. As Retallack puts it when describing the challenge of contemporaneity, that we "reinvent ourselves and move on," "Tradition gives us navigational coordinates, but topographies are changing even as we pick up our instruments to determine where we are, have been, might have been. . . . It's common to think of identities and traditions as useful limiting structures, points of departure from the known. But epistemological reality principles, like all others, shrivel without the dicey pleasures of interpermeability, motion, susceptibility to chance occurrences. Isn't it more fruitful to think of Identity and Tradition in ongoing, transformative conversation with a changing world? (*Poethical Wager* 97).[3]

Such a mobile "transformative conversation" with works that are part of our scribal tradition—a conversation often propelled by the conceptual structures of modern physics—will be my focus in the following consideration of the interplay between design and disorder, form and possibility in selected mid-1990s works by Waldrop and Retallack. Waldrop's *Lawn of Excluded Middle*, in interacting with the orders reflected in and generated by three male-authored texts, demonstrates with particular clarity a feminist revisionary dynamic in what I will shortly identify as palimtexts. Retallack's "AFTERRIMAGES" and "Icarus FFFFFalling" employ alternative modes of palimtextual transformation. The "dicey pleasures" of chance procedures give contemporary meanings to received texts in the former, as fractal manipulation does to the patriarchal codes and systems saturating the sources Retallack brings into play in the latter.

Waldrop calls virtually no attention within *Lawn of Excluded Middle* (1993) to that volume's extensive reliance on prior texts. The only clues lie in the ten terse entries on the volume's final page, titled "On *Lawn of Excluded Middle*." Here the names Wittgenstein and A. S. Eddington appear, but without Waldrop's indicating that she draws directly on their work in constructing her text, much less acknowledging the particular titles she draws from.[4] Presumably, this is not because she wishes to be cagey about her sources, but simply because the unidentified source texts for *Lawn* function largely as examples of the way in which the language we employ is inevitably a previously used, sedimented medium—something Waldrop has discussed in terms of palimpsest:

> The blank page is not blank. No text has one single author. Whether we are conscious of it or not, we always write on top of a PALIMPSEST.
> This is not a question of linear "influence" and not just of tradition, but of writing as a multiple dialogue with a whole net of previous and concurrent texts, traditions, schooling, the culture and language we breathe and move in, which condition us even while we help to construct them.
> Historians speak of "the conditions of occurrence;" Duncan, of the "grand collage." . . .

Many of us have foregrounded this awareness of the palimpsest as a method, using, transforming, "translating" parts of other works. ("Form and Discontent" 61)

The palimpsestic method Waldrop has chosen in *Lawn of Excluded Middle* imposes limits and shape on the ordinary "conditions of occurrence," heightening the writer's consciousness of the ever-present terms of our dialogue with the given arrangements of language. For those readers who become conscious of her use of prior texts, it foregrounds the palimpsestic nature of language and the multiple authorship of texts, while bringing into focus Waldrop's interest in compositional methods constrained by "reduced choice" or "choice at one remove" ("Rosmarie Waldrop," *L=A=N=G=U=A=G=E*; "Conversation" 348).

While employing Waldrop's term "palimpsest" for her *method* of writing a "multiple dialogue" with prior texts, I have adopted Michael Davidson's term "palimtext" for the *product* that results. Designating "a writing that displays its formations in other writings . . . an arrested moment in an ongoing process of signifying, scripting, and typing," palimtext is "a vehicle for circumventing generic categories and period styles by describing writing in its collaborative, quotidian, and intertextual forms" (Davidson 9). In identifying Waldrop's and Retallack's works as palimtexts, my intention is to convey a more dynamic, interactive intertextuality (and one less bound to historical recovery) than the fixed, chronological layering conventionally associated with palimpsests.

Three texts predominate as palimpsestic resources for *Lawn of Excluded Middle*, each representing a different intellectual discipline.[5] The one that surfaces most extensively is Wittgenstein's *Philosophical Investigations, Part I* (completed in 1945), primarily entries from number 422 on. A. S. Eddington's *The Nature of the Physical World* (1929), the published version of his Gifford Lectures of 1927, provides important conceptual material and additional language, though less language than *Philosophical Investigations*. Robert Musil's novella "The Perfecting of a Love" (1911) provides a kind of ghost plot as well as some of the imagery, atmosphere, and thematic preoccupations, but it is the most elusively present of the three texts that can be glimpsed as strata of soil nourishing Waldrop's *Lawn*.

Waldrop's decision to draw concurrently upon works of fiction, philosophy, and science may be partly explained via a passage from "Alarms & Excursions," near the close of that essay's exploration of the public and political dimensions of poetry:

So maybe our poems offer a challenge to the ruling grammar, offer some patterns of thinking and perception which might not be bad possibilities to consider. But how many readers does a small press book reach? Even if all 1000 copies of a typical press run get sold, even if they all reach readers how much effect is this book going to have on society? None, I am afraid. I suspect it takes similar patterns appearing in many disciplines at the same time. . . . For instance, many of the characteristics of innovative art which bother people to this day (discontinuity, indeterminacy, acceptance of the unescapable human reference point) were anticipated in science by the turn of the century. In contrast, the fact that they are still an irritant in art would seem to show that it takes art to make people aware of the challenge to their thinking habits or that the challenge has to come in many areas. It also gives us an inkling of how *slowly* mental habits change. (61–62)

Via the palimpsest of *Lawn*, Waldrop unobtrusively draws attention to similar intellectual developments and perceptual shifts that have occurred in separate disciplines in the modern period, presumably to reinforce the changes in thinking those works enact and examine. The authors, born in 1880 (Musil), 1882 (Eddington), and 1889 (Wittgenstein), represent a single generation and its Zeitgeist. All three invested themselves in dramatically new and iconoclastic forms of thought and/or expression—forms that test the limits of language and that remain uncomfortable for many in the supposedly postmodern era.

The net linking these three has some biographical strands.[6] Wittgenstein and Musil, having been trained as scientists (if I may count engineering, which Wittgenstein studied, as a science), might well have taken an interest in work by A. S. Eddington, a prominent English physicist and popular lecturer. Musil was among the artists who benefited from Wittgenstein's charity, though scholars think it unlikely that Wittgenstein read any of his fiction.[7] Musil, who abandoned another possible career in philosophy, might have read Wittgenstein. Yet their possible awareness of each other's thinking is not the point here. Waldrop seems to have selected the texts contributing to her palimtext primarily because each one is engaged with some of her own particular preoccupations: they play into her interest in exploring the limits of linguistic picture-making, in interrogating the relationship between mental experience and physical phenomena, and in testing everyday language as a medium for gaining access to physical experience or phenomena, including the experiences of sexuality and sexed embodiment.

To some extent, of course, Waldrop may have developed these preoccupations precisely through her reading of Wittgenstein, Musil, and Eddington. In discussing her first responses to Musil's work (when she read *The Man without Qualities* in the mid-1950s), she went beyond noting that his concept of personal identity "rang true" for her and acknowledged his methodological impact: "I was fascinated by the way the narrative calls itself into question, both thematically and by always pitting a two-dimensional grid of details against the famous 'narrative' thread. This became important for my own method of composition: the tension between clusters (lines or single words) scattered on a page and a temporal sequence" ("Rosmarie Waldrop," *Contemporary* 302–3). One could legitimately speak of Musil as an influence on Waldrop's work, though such discourse should not obscure the extent to which writings by Musil, Wittgenstein, and Eddington extended ideas that were fundamental to Waldrop's perspective even before she read them. When she speaks of the delight she experienced in finding that a "consent to emptiness" or "negative capability" characterizes modernist physics, it is clear that the field exemplifies a stance she already valued before her encounter with Eddington.[8] Similarly, having long resisted poetry's traditional identification with the image, Waldrop had independently approached (though not entirely arrived at) the challenge modern physics offers when it disconcertingly proposes a model of the world that is not amenable to representation by analogies and images, only by "mathematical formulae that defy being pictured" ("Conversation" 372). Yet even with such caveats in mind, *influence* remains too hierarchical, predictable, and unidirectional a term to capture the dynamic shaping the palimtext; *influence* cannot convey the multiple logics, the kaleidoscopic shifts, the unstable and eccentric commentaries generated by the intertextual conversations in *Lawn of Excluded Middle* or more generally in today's exploratory poetic palimtexts. While the writers Waldrop draws on in *Lawn* are certainly her intellectual allies and even her mentors, their texts become opportunities for endlessly dynamic translation and transformation.

The mobility and range of suggestion Waldrop achieves by interweaving and transforming the precedent texts invoked in *Lawn* is evident even in the final page of aphoristic notes. That page of ten explanatory or pseudo-explanatory statements, titled "On *Lawn of Excluded Middle*," suggests Waldrop's alliance with Wittgenstein by faintly echoing the structure of *Philosophical Investigations*; items that are numerically ordered stand in often disjunctive relation and forgo consistent logical sequence. Waldrop's dismissal of the law of excluded middle (the law of *tertium non datur*, according to which either *A* is *B* or *A* is *notB*—or, in her words, "that everything must be either true or false") in the first entry aligns her more directly with Wittgenstein, since both of them prefer more complex and ambiguous notions of truth and falsity to that "venerable old law of logic" (*Curves* 97).[9] The philosopher's name appears only in entry 7, which identifies his activity with Waldrop's literary practice and locates his philosophical dicta within the spatial frame she has named: "Wittgenstein makes language with its ambiguities the ground of philosophy. His games are played on the Lawn of Excluded Middle." An embrace of ambiguity provides the link to modern physics, introduced in entry 8: "The picture of the world drawn by classical physics conflicts with the picture drawn by quantum theory. As A. S. Eddington says, we use classical physics on Monday, Wednesday, Friday, and quantum theory on Tuesday, Thursday, Saturday."[10] By positioning Eddington as if he were merely someone who has presented the idea memorably ("as . . . Eddington says"), Waldrop emphasizes that her book is based on widely accepted, not eccentric, understandings. Musil's name does not appear, yet his contribution to the palimtext is suggested by item 10: "The gravity of love encompasses ambivalence." Of course, *gravity* signals the limitations of Newtonian physics, which preoccupy Eddington and appear as a recurrent motif in *Lawn*. (Indeed, item 9, "For Newton, the apple has the perplexing habit of falling. In another frame of reference, Newton is buffeted up toward the apple at rest," echoes Eddington in his chapter "A New Picture of Gravitation."[11]) At the same time, gravity in the sense of seriousness is one of the most striking traits of Musil's highly nuanced exploration of the ambivalence of love. "The Perfecting of a Love" details the inner experience of a woman bonded to her husband in nearly perfect love as she nonetheless moves with seeming inevitability toward sexual infidelity. Musil's somber tale always acknowledges the gravity of love, even while love's ironic inconsistencies are painfully evident. The same is true of Waldrop's portrayal of the interactions of a heterosexual couple in *Lawn of Excluded Middle*. This page of explanatory remarks, then, more than it identifies sources, invites readers to see Waldrop reading and writing her world through a multidimensional conversational process.

Her process of "making language think" contemporaneously requires correction and supplementation in addition to solidarity and open-ended play. The given linguistic formations exposed in *Lawn*'s palimtext are limits that, when put in place, prove generative in themselves and at the same time invite transgression and transformation. Some of this transformation results from Waldrop's adapting received linguistic patterns to her feminist perspective.[12] Of the three authors most visible in her palimtext, only Musil shares Waldrop's interest in female thought, whose stereotypical illogicality Waldrop dismisses in entry 1, while leaving open the possibility that less linear logics are suited to the feminine mind. And, as one would expect of male intellectuals of the early twentieth century, none of them shares Waldrop's desire to explore the idea, made explicit in entry 3, of "[w]omen and, more particularly, the womb, the empty center of the woman's body, the locus of fertility" as the regrettably "excluded middle." Wittgenstein and Eddington, even if they do play on the lawn of the excluded middle, continue unthinkingly to exclude the female from consciousness, writing as if the experiences of "he" were necessarily those of all humankind. (They write, that is, from an androcentric perspective that is often a source of humor in Eddington's prose, though the alternatives he posits are not gynocentric.) Even Musil, who attempts to write sympathetically from within a complex female perspective, slides into stereotypical notions of female illogicality and of female bestiality ("she was seized by a wild urge to throw herself down on this rug and kiss the repulsive traces of all those feet, exciting herself with their smell like a bitch in heat" [217]) that might easily be labeled pathological.

Examining a few sections from *Lawn of Excluded Middle* in which the palimpsest is particularly visible will demonstrate how Waldrop works "at once with and against" these three male-authored texts.[13] It will also reveal how her adoption/disruption/transformation of received linguistic orders makes a space for the nonlinear logics that have been associated with the feminine mind and for the resonant space of the female body that, as simultaneously a fertile plenitude and an empty nothingness, provides a potential ground for new writing.

The three sentences that compose the first prose poem in *Lawn of Excluded Middle* make extensive use of two Wittgenstein entries that appear in close proximity to each other. Here is Waldrop's poem:

> When I say I believe that women have a soul and that its substance contains two carbon rings the picture in the foreground makes it difficult to find its application back where the corridors get lost in ritual sacrifice and hidden bleeding. But the four points of the compass are equal on the lawn of the excluded middle where full maturity of meaning takes time the way you eat a fish, morsel by morsel, off the bone. Something that can be held in the mouth, deeply, like darkness by someone blind or the empty space I place at the center of each poem to allow penetration. (*Curves* 49)

And here are the Wittgenstein entries:

> 422. What am I believing in when I believe that men have souls? What am I believing in, when I believe that this substance contains two carbon rings? In both cases there is a picture in the foreground, but the sense lies far in the background; that is, the application of the picture is not easy to survey. (126)

> 424. The picture is *there*; and I do not dispute its *correctness*. But *what* is its application? Think of the picture of blindness as a darkness in the soul or in the head of the blind man. (126)

Another nearby remark in *Philosophical Investigations* is relevant—its detours related to Waldrop's corridors—though not visible in the palimtext:

426. A picture is conjured up which seems to fix the sense *unambiguously*. The actual use, compared with that suggested by the picture, seems like something muddied. . . . In the actual use of expressions we make detours, we go by sideroads. We see the straight highway before us, but of course we cannot use it, because it is permanently closed. (127)

Wittgenstein is puzzling out the relations among actual language games, the mental images we conjure, and what we would express, and between physical and psychological realities. So is Waldrop, but she has a particular angle, as is evident from her pointed substitution of women for men in Wittgenstein's question about the soul. The differences between her words or sentences and Wittgenstein's also indicate immediately her greater preoccupation with social inequities and stereotypes. Thus, the impediments she discerns to what Wittgenstein terms "the application of the picture" have to do with long-established biases in patriarchal culture that have led to the containment and demonization of female fecundity—for example, through virgin sacrifice or quarantine of menstruating women. Inherited assumptions about women, Waldrop implies, make it even more difficult to think clearly about women's souls than men's. With "But" Waldrop proposes a utopian alternative, a nonhierarchical space—the lawn of excluded middle—where the four points of the compass are equal, and where, with patience and an insistently sensual/corporeal attention ("the way you eat a fish, morsel by morsel"), greater understanding and meaning will emerge.

Both Wittgenstein and Waldrop reject the common assumption that the meaning of words derives from shared pictures, believing instead that experiential biases of our mental pictures are encoded in backgrounds we have so naturalized that we no longer see them. To make this point, Wittgenstein offers alternative usages to highlight how words acquire different meanings in different contexts: just as questions of spiritual belief are distinct from scientific ones, the picture of darkness conjured by the word *blindness* is not the same for a theologian considering the soul as it is for a man literally lacking eyesight. Waldrop, however, in a significant countermove, brings these differences into the same frame, as if taking the orderly design Wittgenstein has made by sorting out differences, and inserting it into a kaleidoscope where its elements collapse into more polyvalent forms. In so doing, she unsettles naturalized assumptions as Wittgenstein does, but deliberately contributes as he does not to "muddying" dichotomous or contrasting categories.[14] In her prose poem, the scientific description of materiality (two carbon atoms) applies to the woman's soul, and the experience of darkness for "someone blind" as readily exemplifies the "lawn" where "maturity of meaning" develops as does the feminizing empty space she places "at the center" of each poem. Such mergings imply that plenitude—for example, darkness for the blind—and emptiness—for example, the penetrable space—meet on this lawn. Where patriarchy's cultural traditions, including the linguistic sediment that Waldrop inherits, appropriate the procreative power of the female to an androcentric model of intellectual or aesthetic creativity, Waldrop insists that a feminine womblike space in the artwork is necessary for meaning to emerge. The discovery of meaning is figured in a "penetration" that, by its association with heterosexual intercourse, suggests the need for both masculine and feminine traits.

As already noted, it is Wittgenstein's practice to consider diverse applications in which words mean differently; 593 reads, "A main cause of philosophical disease—a one-sided diet: one nourishes one's thinking with only one kind of example" (155). Yet his examples never take into account gender difference. In contrast, the effect of differential gender expectations, either projected or internalized, on the constitution and communication of meaning is a recurrent concern in *Lawn*. Here, for example, is section 11 of "Lawn": "Whenever you're surprised that I should speak your language I am suddenly wearing too many necklaces and breasts, even though feeling does not produce what is felt, and the object of observation is something else again. Not modulating keys, not the splash that makes us take to another element, just my body alarmingly tangible, like furniture that exceeds its function, a shape I cannot get around. The way one suddenly knows the boulder in the road for a boulder, immovable, as if not always there, unmodified by inner hollows or the stray weeds and their dusty green, a solid obstacle with only trompe-l'oeil exits toward the subtler body of light accumulating in the distance" (*Curves* 54). In this prose poem the syntactic structures are more tangled, reflecting the knotted self-consciousness that unnerves the speaker. When reminded of how consistently women are seen only as sexualized and decorative bodies, the speaker cannot experience her own use of language as exciting possibility (as modulating musical keys or the splash that accompanies a transition from thin air to buoyant water). Instead, she feels entirely stuck in received expectations, with no access to the deviant or mysterious possibilities of the feminine lawn (inner hollows or stray weeds). This is a moment of backsliding into an outdated but tenacious understanding—specifically that of "the [female] body misunderstood as solid" (*Curves* 53), a belief comparable to classical physics' misconception of atomic solidity that preceded modern revelations of "the void within the atom" (Eddington 1).

Given the speaker's distressing awareness of the assumption of the male "you" that, naturally, women don't speak his language, it's not surprising that the fragment of *Philosophical Investigations* evident in the passage comes from an entry (number 596) concerning "the feeling of 'familiarity' and 'naturalness.'" In it Wittgenstein observes, "[N]ot everything which is unfamiliar to us makes an impression of unfamiliarity upon us. Here one has to consider what we call 'unfamiliar.' If a boulder lies on the road, we know it for a boulder, but perhaps not for the one which has always lain there. We recognize a man, say, as a man, but not as an acquaintance" (156). In the gender-conscious context of Waldrop's *Lawn*, a further permutation of unfamiliarity arises; a man may think he recognizes what a woman is, may think he is encountering a being comfortably familiar in its limitations and its (dichotomized) difference from him, but his feeling of familiarity is mistaken *even if*—as seems to be the case here—he is well acquainted with this particular woman.

Modern physics, breezily invoked in "the object of observation is something else again"—reinforces Waldrop's point. What is observed depends on the frame of observation. Thus, as Eddington notes, "apparent changes in the length, mass, electric and magnetic fields, period of vibration, etc." of a given object in motion are "merely a change of reckoning introduced in passing from the frame in which the object is at rest to the frame in which the observer is at rest" (62). Similarly, surprising changes in a man's perception of a woman's identity may reflect merely a shift in who is speaking and who is silent. Of particular importance in this context is the uncertainty principle, according to which we can measure the velocity of a particle *or* its position, but we cannot accurately measure both since the two measurements interfere with one another. "The principle of indeterminacy is epistemological," remarks Eddington. "It reminds us once again that the world of physics is a world contemplated from within surveyed by appliances which are part of it and subject to its laws. What the world might be deemed like if probed in some supernatural manner by appliances not furnished by itself we do not profess to know" (225). Waldrop's reference to the object of observation suggests that men or patriarchal culture generally should be similarly humble in their assertions of knowing about women.

Physics, as translated by Eddington, also provides a model that helps the speaker move beyond her sense of being blocked in her use of language or limited by her female body. In the succeeding prose poem, after presenting her anxieties in the past tense—anxieties about how commodified images of women interfere with her communicating what she intends—the speaker proposes an alternative aesthetic that obviates such fears: "I worried about the gap between expression and intent, afraid the world might see a fluorescent advertisement where I meant to show a face. Sincerity is no help once we admit to the lies we tell on nocturnal occasions, even in the solitude of our own heart, wishcraft slanting the naked figure from need to seduce to fear of possession. Far better to cultivate the gap itself with its high grass for privacy and reference gone astray. Never mind that it is not philosophy, but raw electrons jumping from orbit to orbit to ready the pit for the orchestra, scrap meanings amplifying the succession of green perspectives, moist fissures, spasms on the lips" (*Curves* 54). The lies mentioned here play upon those of Musil's protagonist, Claudine, in "The Perfecting of a Love." Having lied to her would-be seducer one evening by denying that she loves her husband, Claudine recalls the other lie she has told during her married life. It was occasioned by a solitary walk during which she had become aware that chance governs human life, that she might have adjusted herself to another man and "never have known anything of the person that one is today": "For the first time she had felt her being, down to its very foundations, as something indeterminate, had apprehended this ultimate faceless experience of herself in love as something that destroyed the very root, the absoluteness, of existence and would always have made her into a person that she called herself and who was nevertheless not different from everyone else. And it was as if she must let go, let herself sink back into the drift of things, into the realm of unfulfilled possibilities" (215). Waldrop repeats Claudine's revelation of fundamental indeterminacy, applying it to the realm of poetics: an aesthetics of sincerity (like that which underlies personal expressive lyric) rests on false premises about unique determinate identity.

Palimpsestic use of Musil's novella also contributes to Waldrop's formulation of an accommodating strategy, an acceptance of indeterminacy and disjunction. For immediately before the sexual consummation with which the novella closes, Claudine shrinks at the realization that her lover-to-be is "assuming possession of her," and as she undresses she talks about wishing she could jump back and forth across the invisible line between her and her lover or between sexual fidelity and sexual infidelity (222). Following this lead, Waldrop offers as "far better" than an aesthetics of sincerity a mode of writing (and a form of self-conception) in which something like the jumping Claudine longs for hopelessly may be not only possible but necessary. The behavior of excited electrons seems to be Waldrop's model; according to Niels Bohr's theories as Eddington explains them, "the only possible change of state is the transfer of an electron from one quantum orbit to another. Such a jump must occur whenever light is absorbed or emitted" (191). Glimpsed through the layers of palimpsest, "raw electrons jumping" point to the availability of liberating alternatives to the illusion of determinate, fixed selfhood. Comparable abrupt shifts and ruptures (syntactic, referential, and so on) are enacted in the "gap gardening" Waldrop performs within individual sentences or poems and across the spaces between poems (*Curves* 55). She also relies constantly on "scrap meanings," a phrase which, in suggesting discarded material suitable for reprocessing, aptly signals the recycling of language fragments involved in writing palimtext (54).

In the concluding lines of this poem, Waldrop celebrates what may be gained when one "cultivate[s] the gap itself," referring not just to employment of paratactic techniques but more generally to exploration of the in-between spaces dismissed in orthodox philosophy, aesthetics, or social theory and to cultivation of the fertile green lawn of the excluded middle (54). The possible benefits, presented here in utopian terms, include expanded awareness of one's environment, greater appreciation of one's body, and enhanced erotic fulfillment in one's relation to the world—the amplified "spasms on the lips" in which, recalling Irigaray, linguistic articulation and (female) orgasm merge.

The examples of palimtext I have discussed all come from the title series. This is not an arbitrary choice, for the palimpsestic character of the volume is far from uniform.[15] *Philosophical Investigations* is most frequently visible in the palimpsest of part I (the title series of 31 numbered prose poems set one per page);[16] in part II, the linguistic sediment of modern physics is more evident,[17] while Musil's novella seems most present in the first series in part II, "The Attraction of the Ground," where the I/you dynamic is most pronounced and love is a particularly central concern. Moreover, the obvious palimpsest is densest in the opening series and diminishes thereafter, as if Waldrop first worked within the constraints of that method and then increasingly transgressed them. (Of course, palimpsest remains no matter what, as a condition of all writing. As Waldrop tells Retallack in their published conversation, "the text already there is, for me, the whole past of the particular language, the whole culture, that is to say, a plenitude *almost* as large, *almost* as unlimited and full of possibilities as emptiness" [Waldrop, "Conversation" 368].) Perhaps this gradual movement away from apparent overwriting of other texts signals that Waldrop's working from a particular foundation of words already arranged together is only a temporary heuristic structure in her larger project of generating new verbal combinations.[18] Unhappy with "the way we, clamoring for sense, exclude so many unions of words from the sphere of language," she finds that the sense made by certain writers who are themselves pushing the limits of meaning provides valuable prompts for generating linguistic unions that even she might otherwise have censored (*Curves* 62). After a while, the volume's organization suggests, such aids become superfluous.

Whether or not received texts are involved, the process of generating linguistic formulations adequate to current understandings of reality navigates a precarious balance of freedom and restriction. The concluding poem in the volume (the final section in "Accelerating Frame") depicts that balancing act as "translation," in the context of negotiating the revelations of modern physics: "Finally I came to prefer the risk of falling to the arrogance of solid ground and placed myself on the thin line of translation, balancing precariously between body harnessed to slowness and categories of electric charge whizzing across fields nobody could stand on. . . . I wondered if the direction of translation should be into arithmetic or back into my native silence. Or was this a question like right or left, reversible? And could it be resolved on the nonstandard model of androgyny . . . ? Meanwhile the everyday language is using all its vigor to keep the apple in the habit of falling though the curve of the world no longer fits our flat feet and matter's become too porous to place them on" (95). Waldrop, who has extensive experience translating from several languages, has explained that she thinks of translation—one of the terms she used in describing the method of palimpsest—as "approximation rather than duplication. A re-giving of form" ("Interview" 36). She has explained that "destruction" and "betrayal" of the original are necessary for a translator to get at the "nucleus of energy" from which she or he can rebuild it. This process of deforming and reforming the linguistic arrangements she inherits generates a baffling field of possibilities, as is evident from the speaker's proliferating questions about the models and directions she might pursue. Interestingly, the course for which she notes limitations is that of "everyday language," which excludes the new and protects outmoded thought.

Waldrop's apparent distancing of her project from "everyday language" by characterizing it as regressive perhaps invites fine-tuning of Marjorie Perloff's claim that Wittgenstein's legacy for poets like Waldrop is in an "ordinary language poetics." In *Wittgenstein's Ladder*, Perloff has developed the important argument that Wittgenstein's "stringent and severe interrogation of language has provided an opening for the replacement of the 'autonomous,' self-contained, and self-expressive lyric with a more fluid poetic paradigm—a paradigm based on the recognition that the poet's most secret and profound emotions are expressed in a language that has always already belonged to the poet's culture, society, and nation" (22). Yet poets draw on "the language pool" in different ways and, even without positing a special language for poetry, may still draw from that reservoir selectively. Waldrop's alignment of "everyday language" with what slows change in mental habits may help readers distinguish her from those exploratory poets (Retallack is sometimes among them, as are Fulton and Wheeler) who deliberately open poetry to the language games prevalent in consumer and mass culture. The linguistic sediment Waldrop chooses to highlight and alter in her recent palimpsestic writing is language deployed with extreme care by intellectuals consciously pushing at conceptual and expressive frontiers. All three men work from a base in customary language games but extend them to enable fresh exploration and explanation of the universe we inhabit. Waldrop brings to their extraordinary (but gender-biased) interventions into everyday language and to the often not conventionally logical understandings they formulate the resources of her female body and (in part) not conventionally logical "feminine" mind. Section 23 of *Lawn of Excluded Middle* hauntingly describes this use of the body in relation to a "clutter" that surely includes the noise of everyday language: "It's true, the brain is desperate for an available emptiness to house its clutter, as a tone can only grow from a space of silence, lifted by inaudible echoes as birds are by the air inside their bones. So we reach down, although it cannot save us, to the hollows inside the body, to extend them into so many journeys into the world, so many words shelling the echo of absence onto the dry land" (60). Simultaneously reaching back into the ordering structures of exemplary yet provocative male-authored texts and reaching down (and beyond order) into the nothingness of silence and space inside her female body, Waldrop hopes to tap the vigor latent in everyday language for use in a gender-balanced language that is "uncommon" now but need not always be so. The ambiguities of *shelling*—suggesting at once a military bombardment and the release of seed—crucially demonstrate the unsettling combination of destruction and creation necessary to this transformative process.

Violation and destruction of received orders are readily visible in the collage by Joan Retallack that appears on the cover of her 1995 collection *AFTERRIMAGES*, just as they are foregrounded within its pages. The small black-and-white image of the entire collage (a portion of which is enlarged in dusty-rose monochrome on the rest of the cover) presents antique illustrations that have been not only cut into fragments but also eaten away by vigorous hole-punching (fig. 1). Consequently, the entire collage might be read as a shelled landscape of representations in which Newtonian science (figured by a boy covering one eye and looking with the other through a telescope—the activity that caused Newton to "[suffer] . . . from an after-image of the sun" [*AFTERRIMAGES*, unpaginated front matter]), traditional notions of masculine heroism ("La Liberté ou la Mort"), Eastern cultures (bits of Chinese and Arabic script), and Western gender roles (the stiff figure of the dairy maid, the more relaxed and empowered figure of the young astronomer whose hand rests on an armillary sphere modeling the solar system) are either being riddled with holes or exploding and bursting into flames.

Yet in neither the cover collage nor the poems themselves does Retallack's vision of a past in pieces emphasize despair or nostalgia, since, as with Waldrop, destruction is closely entwined with creation and apparent disorder with meaningful order. Here again, earlier texts, readily broken apart and manipulated, are a generative presence. Certainly, however, Retallack's work carries the somber weight of a postwar consciousness; *AFTERRIMAGES* is clearly situated near the end of a century of cataclysmic wars and after the

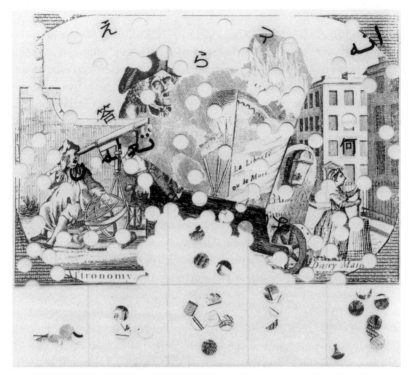

1. Joan Retallack. Cut paper and pencil collage, 1995. Photo by Neil Greentree. Cover design for Joan Retallack, *AFTERRIMAGES*, 1995. Courtesy Wesleyan University Press.

development of atomic weapons with power to destroy all life, all civilization. Read as *AFTER RIM AGES*, the title superimposed on the collage may position the writing as following after some decisive temporal boundary or shift. The postatomic context for *AFTERRIMAGES* is more directly signaled with the epigraph from Manhattan Project physicist Victor Weisskopff, who recalls that because of overlapping radio frequencies between the PA system at the Alamogordo blast and a local radio station, the first explosion of an atomic bomb was accompanied by a Tchaikovsky waltz. In addition to presenting an eerily ironic juxtaposition of different uses of human creative powers, this bizarre "accompaniment" of waltz and nuclear explosion positions the two within the same trajectory of human achievement, so that scientists' attainment of a sustained nuclear reaction is a historical afterrimage of elegant ballroom choreography.[19] Perhaps at the same time, this epigraph positions twentieth-century mass culture (the radio broadcast) as itself a grotesque afterrimage, a projection of Romantic traditions onto a world in which such anachronistic aesthetics are ludicrously and terrifyingly inappropriate. In contrast to the waltz with its regular rhythm, the bomb exists at the limits of human regulation: scientists tap the power of the atom, but once activated, the physical laws governing nuclear fission take over completely.

In her title sequence Retallack uses chance procedures to adapt the order of earlier texts to the world of the 1990s, tossing thirteen paper clips onto each page of collage palimtext she had composed and then transcribing on the lower half of the page only those letters that appeared wholly within the boundaries of the clips. This compositional practice makes visible the possibility of nuclear annihilation; the lower parts of the pages on which the sparse alphabetic afterrimages are scattered might well suggest the little that would remain after a nuclear holocaust. But neat dichotomies of wholeness vs. fragmentation, plenitude vs. emptiness, or fertility vs. sterility are not sustained here any more than they are on Waldrop's "lawn" of the empty middle or in the work of John Cage, whose central contribution to Western music—what Retallack terms a "paradigm shift"—is a release from binary divisions, particularly those between noise and music or sound and silence. Hence, the fragments of a multilingual literary tradition that palimtextually compose so much of "AFTERRIMAGES" are not a string of tortured ironies. They are precious and intriguing bits of language, elements of possibility whose meanings or potential for meaning are only enhanced by their fragmentariness and mutability.

Retallack's use of Chaucer can demonstrate.[20] In drawing upon Chaucer's texts—much like Waldrop's use of passages from Wittgenstein, Eddington, or Musil (and, one suspects, in deliberate contrast to T. S. Eliot's invocations of Chaucer in "The Waste Land")—Retallack enacts a freedom to change— to reinterpret and rewrite—that conveys delighting appreciation, polyvalent possibility, and feminist critique. On the first page of "AFTERRIMAGES," where the idea of balance is prominent, she places two lines from *Troilus and Criseyde* that might describe virtuous balance in a woman: "*So reulith hire hir hertes gost withinne, / That though she bende, yeet she stant on roote*" (5). In Chaucer's text, however, this characterization reflects a series of perhaps groundless male projections: Pandarus, addressing Troilus, expresses what he imagines Troilus to be imagining about Criseyde's state in a meeting between them that Pandarus claims will shortly take place. A modern prose translation of the passage runs: "Perhaps you're thinking: 'Although it may be so that Nature would cause her to begin to have a kind of pity on my unhappiness: Disdain says, "No, you'll never overcome me!" The spirit in her heart so rules her inwardly that, although she may bend, she still stands firmly rooted. What use is this to help me?'" (49). Pandarus goes on to assure Troilus that these supposed imaginings are false and that in fact Criseyde is primed to give in to his wooing. Inserted into Retallack's text, the passage is at once a compelling bit of found aural and visual texture, a trace from a foundational text of English literary tradition that offers an unusually complex early portrait of a female character, a demonstration of how thoroughly mediated by ideology and patriarchal projection literary representations of women tend to be, and a showcase for some stereotypical expectations of womanly virtue. An exchange between Retallack and Waldrop in their published conversation sheds light on this last dimension. There, Retallack expresses her discomfort with the term *heart* (Waldrop, "Conversation" 357). Waldrop concurs, explaining: "It may be because we are women, and the literary 'domain' of women used to be the emotions, the heart, the sentimental story or poem. We don't want to be defined—limited—this way" (359). Retallack adds, "Yes, there is that. But also more generally, there can be a sense that if you just feel something intensely enough—and this goes back to the unease with sincerity—that somehow it, ipso facto, has value of some kind, including truth value" (359). In its first appearance, then, the selection from Chaucer signals the distance between Retallack's aesthetic and one based primarily on emotional responsiveness, sincerity, or constancy.[21]

Alternate forms of precision invoked on the same page of "AFTERRIMAGES," scientific models and dictionary definitions, are perhaps better guarantors of value than intense feeling. But change is a governing principle of palimtext, so that they too are subject to mutation (as in "specificcrystallineformoftaxonomiccategories"). Intriguingly, the chance operations Retallack performed on the text preserved *"e hir hert"*; the afterrimage of Chaucer's lines might speak to the near indelibility of the linkage of the female and feeling, or it might demonstrate that the experimentalist's transformation permits what is elementally valuable—here, the capability of loving or feeling—to be released from its less desirable associations.

Other fragments from Chaucer that appear in the poem—several from the Man of Law's Tale and one especially well-known quotation from the Wife of Bath's prologue—also call attention to the subjugation of women in traditional gender roles: the expectation of virginal purity, marital fidelity, filial piety, uncomplaining endurance of suffering, and so on. But Retallack's fragmentation, deformation, and recontextualization of these narratives demonstrates that we need no longer repeat these misogynist patterns. Simply appropriating and compressing a received line—"HEREENDETHTHETALE OFTHEMANOFLAWE"—yields a proclamation of the end of the tale of man of flaw, whose use of narrative for sadistic multiplication of a woman's sufferings need not be our law.

The cultural baggage Chaucer carries is only part of the story here. In her essay "The Experimental Feminine," Retallack explains that "artists are artists because they have loved the work of artists before them; they spend their lives in conversation with the dead as well as the living. . . . The present is what we, in the urgency of the unprecedented, with the pressures of rapid-fire transformations all around us, make of the past" (*Poethical Wager* 98). Retallack's collage in "AFTERRIMAGES" of found pieces in many languages—Old Irish, Old English, Middle English, Latin, standard modern English, demotic English ("YO MAMA"), transcribed sounds ("schwoop"), and punning torquings of all these—is a palimtextual display of resources. As such, it stresses the openness of linguistic evolution and the vitality of evolving vernaculars (of which Chaucer's Middle English was one) as well as the somatic pleasures of seeing and speaking words. Old languages don't die, though we may recognize their vitality most readily in preserved literary texts or in etymological roots (*she stant on roote*) like those Retallack provides for "thicket." Retallack's lovingly irreverent, often humorous play with palimpsestic remains from these texts, with formulaic phrases, with individual words (as in: "Lana: Please machine give piece of chow / *(thanatoast)*" [20]) demonstrates the always available possibility of change. Language is endlessly malleable and resilient. The past is as present here as it was for Eliot, but unlike Eliot, Retallack focuses on using its mongrelized multilingual remains to provoke something new.

The book's title itself inventively disrupts received arrangements of language, introjecting an extra *R* into the word *afterimages*. "What a shock!" Randolph Healy exclaims in an insightful review. "A displaced letter in the middle of an established order. Words become highly unstable, fee/free, a single mutation launching them into an entirely different semantic field. . . . The reader was free to enlarge the scope of the poem in almost any direction by following such leads in whatever way they wish. Freed by just one letter. Her own initial" ("Eighteenth Letter"). The doubling of the *r*, an afterimage of that letter, introduces the word *err* and the concept of erring not only as going wrong and astray but also as the exploratory motion of rambling or straying. The verso side of the title page, printed as if it were a reversed transparency, adds further linguistic mutations, which when unreversed would read: "ALTERRIMAGES / AFTEARTHOUGHTS / AFTER/ORS / AFTERMATH." (The triangular image of that text then appears in afterrimage on the next page, containing four epigraphs.) Such transformations generate semantic polyphony with implications at once exciting and sobering. This particular series of linguistic permutations brings to the fore change and alteration, alterity, use of ear and mind, intellectually substantial art or theories of art, alternative prospects, and ores for prospecting, but it also suggests opportunities missed or things considered too late and the unpleasant consequences of what came before.

The top portions of the pages of "AFTERRIMAGES," which are palimtextual arrangements of fragments that have meaning for Retallack, acknowledge both the pleasures and the burdens of her position of afterness, especially of literary and linguistic belatedness and of postatomic insecurity. In not using the fragments to shore up old ruins, but instead subjecting her collage text to further decimation/transformation by chance procedures, she deliberately generates a further layer of afterrimage. Doing so involves a complex interaction of design and disorder. As N. Katherine Hayles has observed, the Cagean notion of chance procedures itself involves an oxymoronic combination of randomness and intention, of something that exceeds or escapes our designs on the one hand and a process by which we put our designs into effect on the other. What Cage referred to as "purposeful purposelessness" constitutes, Hayles notes, a "subversive intentionality" (231). These phrases capture the dynamics of Retallack's compositional procedure involving paper clips, a procedure that is subtractive, like the optical process of afterimaging described at the beginning of the text in "Color Plate 25." But paradoxically, it is with the addition of a chance-generated afterrimage that each page gains a kind of symmetrical order, though one in which text is mirrored more by its absence than by its repetition.

The breakdown of words into component letters that results from this "purposeful purposelessness" sometimes makes visible alphabetic patterns one would overlook when processing letter clumps as words. Such exposure of patterning has an ethical (what Retallack calls "poethical") dimension: as the predominant blank spaces call attention to the framing silence or space within which alphabetic sounds or letters acquire meaning, individual letters or letter combinations become freshly visible and audible. Looking to see where the afterrrimages came from in the text, we attend anew to the top section of each page, and in Retallack's view, "What brings art to life, what makes life—even the most difficult life—worth living, is a quality of sustained attention" (*Poethical Wager* 90).[22]

Even if the afterrimage portions of these pages suggest the deeply frightening, almost unimaginable aftermath of an atomic blast, at the same time these portions of the text carry an extremely positive valence, as prompts to attention and (a closely related phenomenon) as examples of "radical explorations into silence—the currently unintelligible—in which our future may make sense" (":RE:THINKING:" 358).[23] Sometimes no letters are preserved and only silence is produced—a silence that we have to attend to since it reverberates with the elimination of particular sounds. At other times, recognizable phrases acquire surprising resonance through chance selection, as already noted with the surprising preservation of *e hir hert* in the first poem. My favorite of these astonishing patterns occurs when a passage containing two parenthetic references to philosophical tradition—

(see a pre-Socratic on fire in the mind)
   nice being out here in the sun
      (or St. Augustine on time)
(7)

—yields an invitation to appreciate a pleasing pattern of letters accessible to anyone, not just those familiar with Heraclitus and Augustine:

(see   i   in   e
       in   e   in
             o
(7)

The pattern, moreover, seems an affirmation of connectedness, an instruction to appreciate apparently different elements as in fact existing "in" each other.

Another afterrimage where the unintelligible yields the surprising but polyphonically legible is one in which the only marks on the blank space read "s[   ]ent" (21). This brings to mind a Sapphic fragment, something already alluded to and all but named in the top portion of the preceding page:

Saph [.....................................]gment
UU -- -- --   -- --UU--?
(now she shines among Lyd...wom........)?

(6)

The pseudo-Sapphic remnant generated by Retallack's chance procedures reminds her readers that the processes, both social and natural, that limited the preservation of Sappho's work still operate and are likely to shape the literary record we transmit into the future. "S[   ]ent," moreover, suggests "sent" and "silent" (among other possibilities), both of which speak to the dynamics of chance operations here: text becomes silence and silence is rendered audible, while chance sometimes produces selections so readily meaningful that they appear "sent" by some higher power. Through the application of chance procedures, in Retallack's palimtext, regulation and disorder, determinacy and indeterminacy emerge as virtually indistinguishable.

"Icarus FFFFFalling," the second sequence in Retallack's *AFTERRIMAGES*, continues the bifurcated page format of "AFTERRIMAGES," but in this text the symmetry does not result from repeating on the bottom half of the page a chance-generated version of the palimtext that appears above. With thematic impact, Retallack shapes this late twentieth-century afterrimage of Icarus's fall to form a picture of progressive diminishment—a falling away in perspectival space—generated simply by a progressive reduction in the number of lines. After an eccentric first page, each of the subsequent nineteen pages has either the same number of lines as or fewer lines than the page before, and on each page the same number of lines appear above and, in afterrimage, below the bifurcating line of dots.[24] Above the horizontal midline, the text is single spaced, and below the line it is double spaced. (Perhaps this signals the several realms within which Icarus's tale takes place—air and land, or air and sea—and/or perhaps it registers the transformative character of any afterrimage.) In both halves the right and left margins are justified to generate a rectangular block of text, and since the line and page breaks seem arbitrary, the text invites reading as continuous—indeed, propulsively driven or gravitationally propelled—prose.

The earlier texts recognizable as palimpsestic sources in this poem are versions of the tale of Icarus, most notably Ovid's telling of that tale in *Metamorphoses*, though versions by W. H. Auden, W. C. Williams, and Muriel Rukeyser also contribute. But the "source texts" here are only a point of departure, as is suggested by Retallack's introductory acknowledgment of assistance from those who moved outward into the public realm to flesh out their understanding of a work of literature: "Thanks to the students in my August 1987 Language & Thinking workshop at Bard College, who when asked to go out and photograph Icarus falling found him everywhere" (36). Provoked by her students' discoveries, Retallack turns her attention (and her readers') to the omnipresence of young men's reenactment of the Icarus story, and to the cultural forces determining that reenactment.

"Icarus FFFFFalling," then, is in one sense grounded in the ordering form of a well-known narrative, one portraying a father who pushes his son to take risks even while warning him to be careful, and a son who discovers the exhilaration of risk taking, goes too high, and consequently plummets into the sea and drowns. It provides no coherent recounting of that story, but fragments of Ovid's telling, both in Latin and in English, are interspersed throughout Retallack's palimtext, and the opening page would seem to acknowledge Ovid's story as in some way foundational. That page presents a facing-page translation of the beginning of Ovid's narrative, where the English printed on the right is a kind of afterrimage of the Latin on the left, providing what Retallack in "AFTERRIMAGES" calls a "delicious asymmetry of sight and sound." Overlaid on—or falling through—the center of the facing-page translation, and partly covering it, is a slightly curved column of disjunctive text whose short lines incorporate Latin, pig Latin, French, and English. Many of these fragments, besides highlighting linguistic translation and metamorphosis, invoke some kind of up or down motion that we might associate with Icarus's flight and fall—for example, "dark islands up light / appetizers cheese dip" (37). However, as the surprise of that last punning phrase indicates, Ovid's narrative is a pattern from which to spin off—not the text's center, but a complex of relations and interactions launching its numerous divagations.

Perhaps the best figure for describing the complex organization of this palimtext, its way of re-forming old orders for the present, is fractal form. Fractals are "complex symmetrical forms that repeat themselves across every available scale but always with variations that never resolve at any scale into simpler forms" (Hayles 233), and Retallack sometimes refers to them or to a "fractal poetics" in advocating art whose complexity is consonant with the contemporary world's (*Poethical Wager* 15). In literature, it may not be possible to repeat anything at *every* possible scale, but certainly "Icarus FFFFFalling" has a quality of self-similarity in providing innumerable reenactments of the Icarus pattern at various scales, whether these be social (individual, familial, regional, national, international) or textual (letter, phoneme, word, phrase, clause, sentence, paragraph, page or succession of pages, and story).

From multiple perspectives and on constantly shifting scales, "Icarus FFFFFalling" exposes the ways in which Western society, in its glorification of male athleticism, forces young men to undertake terrible risks, manipulates them into being "ready to die for theher thefamily thetribe therace thenation thelaw the onthemoney big idea" (51). The father's desire to have his son perform his own understanding of masculine freedom has been so thoroughly normalized by social codes that both parties are blinded to the dangers involved: "father instructs son on rules of flight sky Walker Matt Jack George Ethan Gabe Josh the the fixes strange wings on boys shoulders *laeva parte Samos* not goodbye forever or a suicide note just what's to be expected on every wall on every scrap of paper on every matchbox" (38). Denaturalizing such expectations, Retallack underscores the price paid for our aspirations: the brilliant flash of light made by the first atomic bomb is rendered an afterrimage—that is, a fractal self-similarity on another scale—not just of other military displays ("Mussolini said a bomb exploding in the desert is like a rose bursting into bloom" [47]) but also of the flash made by Icarus falling ("you see a flash of light you hear a splash" [40]). The father's quest rehearses various socially approved ways adult males attempt to assert control and dominance: "*caelum certe* defacto anon unknown über-object always to prepare them for WARS BLASTS VECTORS VALENCES PROCLIVITIES TROPISMS developing tastes for horror shut in by land'nsea UNDER SOCIAL CONSTRUCTION" (38). "Icarus FFFFFalling" presents Daedalus's compulsion to return to his homeland as an individualized manifestation of ideologies of nationalism that encourage war and colonial expansion. Thus, while at one point he is called "Dead-o-Lust" (overdosed on testosterone, perhaps), the father's eroticism appears to have no object beyond the expansion of his own powers. This suggestion of onanistic egotism is reinforced by the verbal similarity of *penis* and *pennes*, Latin for the feathers with which the famous inventor constructs the wings that extend his reach. The absence of the mother from Icarus's tale ("where is I's mother not that she or any other . . . could save him now" [43]) and her submission to or complicity in the patriarchal order propelling its events comprise another thematic formation recurring in multiple scales in Retallack's poem. Woman's collusion with the system might be read in the lists of middle-American foods provided for a family reunion, as in the "furtiva lacrimosa mother" who, it seems, doesn't dare even to weep openly for the loss of her son.

Even the initial letter of Icarus's name itself propels the poem toward other enactments of the same structuring dynamics. It provides a link to stories of others whose names begin with *I*, including Isaac (another horrifying example of patriarchy's readiness to sacrifice its sons) and Iphis (whose father ordered her put to death at birth because she was not a boy, but who grew up passing as a boy, and in Ovid's story is ever-so-fortunately transformed into one). The letter *I* as first-person pronoun also highlights cultural obsessions with personal identity: a focus on *I*, that "clever one-eyed mechanical monster," makes one particularly susceptible to consumer hype—fostering the need for accoutrements of acceptable gender identity—itself another level of enactment for the fractal pattern of this palimtext.

Because of the fractal structure in which it is manipulated, Ovid's narrative does not function as a containing form; what is most striking in the experience of reading "Icarus FFFFFalling" is the simultaneity of its multiple concerns/reenactments, the startling complexity of its polyphony. Pulsing with verbal energy, tumbling pell-mell without punctuation or transition from the Beatles to the Sex Pistols to Mozart to "Palistrami" (a fast-food version of Palestrina), from Reebok sports equipment to pop art to Mendelian genetics, from Socrates to Freud to an immigrant fresh off the boat entering the land of "Anglo-Terror," from Malcolm X to the X chromosome to Alamogordo, the kaleidoscopic text actively discourages an untangling of its elements. Instead, it propels readers into the densest possible din of contemporary culture, which includes past culture as well, where Icarus is perpetually falling. Here is a sample:

> perfect palmer his sweet penisship de scribed on de texticular nite you did not withhold your son from me bless you Abe babe or Malcolm ex-ladies man nights they serve baked beans 'n fries modesta peduncle punch errasty Hells Proverbs live from hell EXTERIOR WASH WAX WAYNE ENTER

RIGHT EXIT LEFT THANK YOU HAVE A NICE stamp out fires with
Morris dances bird he soar too high he soar on his own wingding laws dis
courage to think of other order exorcise the male the sport of archery as

. . . .

Zeno's arrows fly in no time
(46)

Rhythmic and highly charged, the "buzzing noise" of this richly varied
palimtext doesn't add up to one chorus or settle in to one tune—but it has
nonetheless the elegant design of an infinitely complex fractal geometry.

Whatever its infinite potentialities might be in disclosing more and more
Icarus material, the poem moves toward silence, since Retallack has chosen
to replicate in the poem's visual form something like Daedalus's view of Icarus's fall: a progressive disappearance into nothingness. The text dwindles as
Icarus would appear to diminish as he fell away. On the last page, there are
no words above the dots and only two below: "fall over." These follow from
the text on the preceding page, but characteristically the syntax moves in
several directions at once, precluding any single understanding even of their
syntactic function. Thus even the visual closing off of the text functions as
open-ended and ongoing. Backing up, one reads, "just trying on the sadness
of the verb to be we hope is not too fffffallen to [page turn and line of dots] /
fall over" (55–56). In one reading, the concluding line announces the end of
the young man's fall: it's over. It also suggests he will fall and is falling over
again. Additionally, "fall over" might suggest tripping over obstacles, whether
the "sadness of the verb to be" or the glorification of aggressive athleticism.
From another perspective, the two words reenact the down and up combination of the first page, since the preposition *over* suggests movement above
something, while *fall* denotes descent. Read that way—as at once a downward
and upward motion—*falling over* becomes an encompassing figure for the
seemingly endless levels on which gender is constantly being constructed and
the scales on which its impact is manifest, so effectively conveyed in the intertextual language of this fractal poem.

For Retallack, as for Waldrop, the challenging quest for alternatives to
the disastrous "logics of a purely masculine power" requires what Retallack
calls the "experimental feminine" (*Poethical Wager* 93). It is because "feminine" approaches to experimental form refuse to exclude the (traditionally
feminine) unintelligible, incoherent, illogical, and inconsistent that they are
potentially adequate to the necessarily confusing dimensions of the truly
contemporary. Yet even as Retallack identifies the destabilizing feminine
with experiment—with "violations of masculine orthodoxy" (98) and with

"all that is not business as usual" (90)—the "experimental feminine" depends upon masculine and feminine as "dynamically interrelated principles" (99); similarly, "experiment and tradition, should, in an ideal world, form the dialogic energy that creates vital cultures" (91). From her compelling perspective, conventional binaries such as tradition and experiment or masculine and feminine are best regarded as complexly permeable parts of dynamic systems. (Waldrop's *Reluctant Gravities*, the sequel to *Lawn of Excluded Middle*, in which male and female perspectives alternate and interweave suggests her similar understanding.) Thus, experiment involves an "interrogative conversation between the insistent intelligible and the silent unintelligible, intention and chance, structure and process"; to maintain the productive tension within that transformative conversation, unintelligibility needs some modicum of structure, design, regulation (97–98). This is one motivation behind Waldrop's and Retallack's shared interest in imposing patterns and in using earlier texts as one means to do so. Via skillful and skillfully varied exploratory uses of palimpsestic layerings from previous texts, Waldrop and Retallack achieve exemplary success in generating "fields of pattern-bounded unpredictability" through which we may, without overwhelming disorientation, orient ourselves anew to the complex moment in which we live.

five

POEMS LIVING WITH PAINTINGS

Cole Swensen's Ekphrastic Try

The painter is standing a little back from his canvas. He is glancing at his model; perhaps he is considering whether to add some finishing touch, though it is also possible that the first stroke has not yet been made. The arm holding the brush is bent to the left, towards the palette; it is motionless, for an instant, between canvas and paints. The skilled hand is suspended in mid-air, arrested in rapt attention on the painter's gaze; and the gaze, in return, waits upon the arrested gesture. Between the fine point of the brush and the steely gaze, the scene is about to yield up its volume. (3)

This suspenseful description opens part 1 of *The Order of Things: An Archeology of the Human Sciences*, Michel Foucault's famous tracing of the gaze and the "cycle of representation" (in which representation comes into being, reaches completion, and is dissolved once more into the light) enacted in Velázquez's masterpiece *Las Meninas*. Foucault uses this painting, which dates from 1656, to demonstrate the shift from the Renaissance to the classical episteme, a reordering of signs as well as a breaking off of knowledge from *divinitas* that took place as one system of thought replaced another. While marking the culmination and the dissolution of the Renaissance order, Velázquez's painting is seen also as suggesting, via what is crucially invisible, the key change that will initiate the modern episteme, the invention of *man*.

Foucault's way of thinking about and representing the painting provides a foil useful for setting off Cole Swensen's 1999 volume of ekphrastic poems, *Try*, since her approach to paintings in some ways accords with but also contrasts significantly with his. Her poetic engagements with paintings suggest a fundamental concurrence with Foucault that works of visual art allow profound insight into historical epistemes. In part her project is, like his, an intellectually ambitious archeological one, in *Try*'s case aimed at illuminating some of the key differences between Western ways of knowing or systems of understanding at the close of the twentieth century and those of earlier times, particularly the late medieval and early Renaissance eras. However, just as Swensen avoids inventing narratives like Foucault's that firmly position the painter "back from" the canvas, she eschews Foucault's own pose of "stand[ing] . . . back" from the painting to provide a confidently objective analysis of its dynamics. His distanced stance is the same one taken not only by most art historians when they interpret paintings but by most ekphrastic poets as well, and it is a positioning Swensen deliberately rejects.[1]

Foucault accomplishes his epistemic analysis by tracing the gaze—whether the gazes of the represented figures, Velázquez's artful complication of perspectival sight lines, or the spiraling movement of the viewer's gaze. He explores especially the ceaseless oscillation of the viewer's gaze with the painter's (because the painter's gaze is directed at someone positioned where the viewer stands, the spectator is also the spectacle and that spectacle is constantly changing) as well as the "metathesis of visibility" (8) proposed by the mirror at the back of the room in which appears the image of the royal couple, who are gazed upon by most of those in the painting but positioned outside it: "In the realm of the anecdote, this centre is symbolically sovereign, since it is occupied by King Philip IV and his wife. But it is so above all because of the triple function it fulfils in relation to the picture. For in it there occurs an exact superimposition of the model's gaze as it is being painted, of the spectator's as he contemplates the painting, and of the painter's as he is composing his picture (not the one represented, but the one in front of us which we are discussing). These three 'observing' functions come together in a point exterior to the picture: that is, an ideal point in relation to what is represented, but a perfectly real one too, since it is also the starting-point that makes the representation possible. Within that reality itself, it cannot not be invisible" (14–15).[2] As my discussion of the prologue to Swensen's volume will demonstrate, she, too, is concerned with the gaze, with paintings' arrested moments, and with the invisible subjects pointed to by painters' images, but in her ekphrasis the gaze takes considerably more unsettled and unsettling forms than Foucault's tidy circling and "exact superimposition." For although Foucault emphasizes the reflexivity of *Las Meninas* as a painting "in which representation is represented at every point," the positions of the various gazers remain fixed, the trajectories of their vision clear, and their identities decipherable (though subsequent analyses suggest some of Foucault's attributions were erroneous[3]) (307). In themselves, the paintings Swensen writes about generally exhibit considerably less self-consciousness about representation, yet she interprets the gazes and the subjectivities of the gazers as far less stable. Indeed, she cultivates their mutability and intersubjectivity.

Ekphrasis, usefully defined by James Heffernan as "the verbal representation of visual representation" (3), goes back in Western literary tradition to Homer's description of the shield that Hephaestus makes for Achilles in the eighteenth book of the *Iliad*, but not until the Romantic period does ekphrastic work in English take the form of self-sufficient, freestanding poems, as in Keats's "Ode on a Grecian Urn." Critical discussions of this subgenre generally assume some form of competition or at least envy between the visual and verbal arts. The single most influential piece of scholarship on this genre has been Murray Krieger's essay from 1967, "The Ekphrastic Principle and the Still Movement of Poetry; or Laokoön Revisited," in which Krieger uses ekphrasis to demonstrate "the generic spatiality of literary form" (105). For a poem to be successfully poetic, he claims, it must convert its "chronological progression into simultaneity, its temporally unrepeatable flow into eternal recurrence" (105). Countering Lessing's desire in the *Laokoön* to keep the mutually delimiting sister arts distinct, Krieger sees all poetry aspiring to the "still" condition of the visual art object. Ekphrastic poems dramatize this general aspiration, since they are, he claims, poems that "in imitating a plastic object in language and time, make that object in its spatial simultaneity a true emblem of itself" (108). Partly following Krieger's lead but without endorsing his emphasis on ekphrasis freezing time in space, more recent scholarship like that of Heffernan and W. J. T. Mitchell has considered ekphrasis as staging the paragonal relation between literature and the visual arts, that is, as a struggle for dominance between image and word.

Swensen is aware of this perspective but would like to move beyond what she perceives as its limitations. Such a view is limiting, she observes in her essay "To Writewithize" (2000), precisely because "it accentuates the separation between the writer and the object of art": "The writer not only remains mentally outside the visual piece, but often physically in opposition to it, i.e. standing across from it, in a kind of face-off, in a gallery or museum. And often the physical stance echoes the mental: despite the apparent homage, there's frequently an element of opposition, a tinge of rivalry and/or challenge inherent in this mirroring."[4] She goes on to identify three alternate modes of ekphrasis discernable in current poetic practice, each of which in its own way minimizes the separation between writer and art object. The first mode of stretching traditional ekphrasis "holds closest" to the received sense of the term (as writing that registers the writer's contemplation of an artwork) "and yet," she hazards, "is perhaps the most radically different of the three." These works "don't look at art so much as live with it. The principal difference here is not in the verb, but in the preposition [that is, not in *living* versus *looking*, but in *with* rather than *at*]. There's a side-by-side, a walking-along-with, at their basis." In such works, "the operative relationship is not so much between a writer and a work of art as it is between verbal and visual modes of experience, both of which the writer lives." The second mode of interaction between contemporary poetry and visual art identified by Swensen incorporates the visual in literal ways through a heightened attention to page space, using the page as a visual field: "writing as art." The third mode, more often undertaken by artists than writers, truly literalizes "writing on art" and "takes visual art as a writing surface," using letters and words as principal visual elements.[5]

Swensen's *Try*—the 1998 winner of the Iowa Poetry Prize—I see as exemplifying the first mode, what she proposes in "To Writewithize" as a radically different "liv[ing] with art."[6] The poems of *Try* generate a significantly different experience of paintings than those offered by, say, Auden's "Musée des Beaux Arts," Williams's *Pictures from Brueghel*, or even Ashbery's "Self-Portrait in a Convex Mirror," and I hope the nature of those differences will emerge in the examination of her poetry and poetics that follows.[7] However, attempting to determine exactly how radical her own or other postmodern poets' break with ekphrastic convention may or may not be is not my aim. My hope, rather, is to illuminate what Swensen achieves through the nonparagonal instabilities of her ekphrastic writing, especially the range and the coherence of the ideas brought into play as she weaves in and out of a referential approach usual in ekphrasis. I will proceed by pursuing the imprecise but generative notion of poetry living with art in an extended examination of the poetic prologue, and then through more selective examination of subsequent poems in *Try*.

Like W. J. T. Mitchell, who asserts that culture has taken a "pictorial turn" so that the problem of pictorial representation "presses inescapably now, and with unprecedented force, on every level of culture, from the most refined philosophical speculations to the most vulgar productions of the mass media" (*Picture Theory* 16), Cole Swensen assumes that a cultural "shift from aural to visual apprehension" has taken place ("To Writewithize"). She even goes so far as to claim, "For most people in the western world today, poetry is primarily a visual experience." Less contentiously, she says this shift necessitates changes in the ways we talk about verbal/visual relationships. Some key terms in which Swensen thinks about verbal/visual relationships appear parenthetically—in the guise of offhand examples—beneath the title of the essay in which she makes these claims, "To Writewithize": "(as in 'to hybridize,' 'to harmonize,' 'to ionize,' etc)." Probably alluding to the three terms "(projectile (percussive (prospective " appearing beneath the title of Charles Olson's "Projective Verse"—a manifesto that had a profound impact on poets' use of page space—these terms illuminate Swensen's strategies in *Try*. In attending to the verbal and visual as realms united within the experience of the writer (both "lived by" the writer), she ostentatiously keeps the aural, the textual, and the visual constantly in play, while often entwining the haptic sense with sight and hearing; her work, then, emphasizes and extends the ways in which poetry inevitably mixes or hybridizes the information of several senses or "modes of experience." Like Mitchell, she would have readers understand (to adopt one of Mitchell's polemical claims in *Picture Theory*) that "the interaction of pictures and texts is constitutive of representation as such: all media are mixed media, and all representations are heterogeneous; there are no 'purely' visual or verbal arts" (5). The second term, *harmonize*, is useful for describing the way in which her ekphrastic poetry "breaks down the division between art and daily living" ("To Writewithize") as well as the conventional opposition between the "sister arts." Although her poems are composed of often dizzyingly disjunctive collage, the juxtapositions are not between visual and verbal, between image and word; rather, these realms are combined to allow participation in and movement through the revelations and disturbances in each.[8] Swensen's third term, *ionize*, denotes giving atoms an electric charge and thereby making them chemically active and electrically mobile (generating conductivity, for instance). Ionization, then, is a process of generating change, motion, and interactivity. As I hope to demonstrate, her poetry is filled with motion in ways that seem directed at generating vitalizing change as well as undermining notions of ekphrasis (or indeed artistic representation generally) as a stilling of movement. Because ionization affects the repulsion or attraction between atoms, the term has particular resonance for this collection, which is especially concerned with touch and with forces enabling or preventing contact.

A cursory perusal of *Try* suggests that Swensen's poetic mode of "living with" art does indeed "hold close[ly]" to traditional ekphrasis. The cover illustration, van Eyck's stately painting *La Vierge du chancelier Rolin*, prepares readers for the volume's reflections on a number of specific art works, most of them late medieval and early Renaissance paintings depicting scenes in the life of Christ, along with some later paintings or sculptures—and one recent video—on secular as well as religious themes. Individual artists' dated works—for instance, "*Auguste Rodin*, CHRIST AND THE MAGDALENE, *1894*"—often appear as titles or subtitles of poems; some poems are identified as being "after the work of" a specified artist; and particular paintings are identified within poems in distinctive font as the immediate subjects of subsequent lines.

As "To Writewithize" would lead us to expect, however, Swensen does not maintain a distance—or any consistent relation—between the writer and the painting: shifting among subjectivities and perspectives, her poetry moves rapidly in and out of the painting and among its subjects or pictorial planes. The reader, following the writer, never sees from one perspective for long. Another distinction from conventional ekphrasis is suggested by the title, *Try*, which, while signaling an interest in experiment and process, points also to procedural constraints on the book's form by marking the *tri*adic structure that infuses the volume on a great many levels. The book—whose cover image, composed in three neatly delineated planes, includes a conspicuous triple arch—contains nine poems (three times three) framed by a prologue and an epilogue; each poem has three parts and a one-word title containing the prefix *tri* (as in *triune, triptych, trilogy, triage*). Paintings are discussed in terms of three planes—foreground, middle ground, and background—and Swensen plays with the consequences of perspective's creating the illusion of three dimensions.[9] Words, phrases, and lines sometimes repeat three times, Swensen occasionally presents three variations, and so on. Such triadic patterning of Swensen's poems "on," "after," or "with" paintings highlights the constructed and conventionalized nature of any poet's representation of an already constructed representation. In so doing, it denaturalizes the familiar conventions of traditional ekphrasis and resists naturalizing its own.[10]

The prologue to *Try* also seems initially to offer something close to a conventional ekphrastic portrait—or, rather, a series of portraits of five specified Italian paintings produced between 1310 and about 1500—but while each depiction begins from the distanced observational stance fundamental to traditional ekphrasis, none remains there. The received conventions of ekphrasis, as well as the conventions of Christian iconography, are certainly on Swensen's mind as she opens the section designated "Prologue," consisting of a poem titled "Whatever Happened to Their Eyes":

Throughout the history of painting
Risen until caught in rising. Arrested.
Even stunned and so for a moment
stilled and toward
(3)

Emphasis on the motion of narrative "stilled" recalls Krieger's ekphrastic theory of poetry and Foucault's scholarly representation of *Las Meninas*, while the lines allude to Keats's celebrated ekphrastic ode on that "still unravished bride of quietness" in which the several meanings of *still* function in tantalizing balance. Quickly, however, we become aware of additional, complicating semantic possibilities. The language of being "caught" and "arrested" suggests that rising is a crime or transgression and—if we assume the rising takes place within the scene in the paintings—positions the artist as a kind of police officer, even one wielding a stun gun. If so, the traditional Keatsian ambivalence about art's at once preserving and preventing experience acquires a peculiar edge here, as if the artist's act of representation risks enacting a violent repression. Indeed, "risen until caught in rising" might suggest that throughout the history of painting, humans have imagined Christ as risen only *until* they have seen him depicted in that process—as if the artist's fixing representation impedes transcendence or viewers' ability to believe in it. These lines, then, seem to present painters—or, perhaps more accurately, painters as we have been taught to read their works by art historians and ekphrastic poets—as having acted in effect as a kind of anti-ionizing law enforcement, impeding transformative motion.

In contrast to the initial emphasis on representation as arrest of motion, the first description of a specific painting that immediately follows suggests that the actors shown in paintings are far less settled than has been assumed throughout the history of painting—or the history of commentary upon it. The figure in "My angel of Giotto, MADONNA / OGNISSANTI," has a split gaze: "the right eye / traveling, planned, fled and / the left fixing forward" (3). Neither of these phrasings registers achieved stillness, since even the left eye is not fixed but in the process of a directional fixing. Moreover, we cannot attach that eye to any single body. In the actual painting, the figure with the obviously dual gaze is the Madonna, but in the poem, the next line's mention of "he who watches" might point to Christ, an angel, or a saint instead. Slippage of identities becomes more pronounced as the viewer (who might even be "[h]e who watches" and/or might be addressed as "you") loses location reliably outside the painting:

He who watches him who wings
world without end and where
were you when she spun around and stared
and my God what on earth
has happened to their eyes?
(3)

By this point, *description* has obviously become an inadequate term for what Swensen is doing as she shifts from the familiar ekphrastic projects of mimesis or of converting a fixed scene into narrative to provide a strikingly polyvocal version of what Heffernan calls "the prosopopeial envoicing of the silent image" (136).[11] The speaker no longer poses as art historian, objective recorder of right and left eye positions. Now the speaker sounds shocked, and the immediate drama of the speaker's vernacular ("my God what on earth"—the last phrase also a joke, since what has happened is supernatural and not at all earthly) positions him or her as much within as outside viewing the scene.

That is, the speaker's highly emotional query could suggest that she or he has in some way entered the painting and is living the scene it portrays. Similarly, "she" who spun around might be a viewer in an art museum or Mary either in the painted biblical narrative or at the actual Annunciation, while the "they" of "their" might exist prior to the painting (as actors in Christian history), inside the painting, or outside viewing it.

Such multiplication of unstilled positionalities emerges as a defining trait of this form of ekphrasis, reflecting a nonparagonal relation between word and image, a fluidity of boundaries between writer and work of visual art. This open-ended and mobile intersubjectivity is explicitly announced in the first set of poems, in which Mary Magdalene is dubbed "Mary Mary quite so many" (revising the nursery rhyme's "quite contrary"):

> I, who can never be
> single, splayed through a chiseled bevel
> into the blues and greens and she's
> wearing red, which is why she
> gets the breadth, thus does not end.
> (9)

The intersubjectivity has a gendered resonance here and throughout *Try*: just as aspects of the prismatically multiple self of "I" appear in the often-painted and variously colored Marys, possibly Madonna as well as Magdalene, the many facets of female subjectivity in particular are readily captured in the shifting surfaces of Swensen's ekphrastic writing.[12] Given the emphasis on a prismatic spectrum of identities, it's not surprising that Mary Magdalene's gesture in the *Noli Me Tangere* scene of "reaching and always / toward that receding / land and body" also recurs in a rainbow of versions so that *Try* is an unstable palimpsest of myriad, often indistinguishable, reaching hands (9).

The prologue's speaker—whom I will from now on designate with the feminine pronoun—retains some degree of singular consciousness; for instance, the appellation "my angel of Giotto" suggests both personal investment and individualized idiosyncratic perception. Yet her avoidance of conventional linguistic orders, or perhaps their inaccessibility to her, leads to her occupying a range of spatial and temporal positions. The same indeterminacies of language push the reader to test various positionalities and entertain multiple interpretive possibilities. The twists of Swensen's syntax render even the question/exclamation "what on earth has happened . . . ?" ambiguous or multiple: the query may concern artistic representation (what have the painters done to their subjects' eyes?) and perhaps historical developments in such representation (how have painters' representations of eyes changed?); it could involve degradation of paintings over time (what has happened to the paint that was applied to represent the eyes?); or, entering into the world represented, the lines may ask what happens to either the organs of sight or the perceptions of those who have witnessed the divine or experienced a divine miracle. Readers are invited to consider a spectrum of options, not necessarily to choose among them.

The next description of a painting (the Strozzi Altarpiece) demonstrates several destabilizing techniques that prove typical of Swensen's ekphrasis. There is a characteristic motion among temporal locations—far from being stilled, time loops vertiginously between the present tense, the ongoing temporality of gerunds or the past perfect, and the completed past—and an equally characteristic swerve from one syntactic construction to another. The passage begins not with "the plague has passed but has left" but instead with "The plague has passed but leaving," while the grammatical subject shifts unexpectedly from being "the plague" to "the eye": "The plague / has passed but leaving any eye at the center of a painting drilling, stopped in / shock from all moving but forward to where a body barely now is standing" (3). If we refer to Orcagna's painting, the eye at the center would be Christ's, but again Swensen's verbal indeterminacies push us to envision alternatives. After all, it was Orcagna rather than Christ who survived an epidemic of plague, and "any eye" drilling at the center of a painting might be the eye of any plague survivor or of any viewer over subsequent centuries, just as the body (barely body, or barely standing?) might be that of Christ or of any viewer who faces the painting and meets the forward gaze of the represented Christ. Poetry conventionally opens more interpretive possibilities than most other forms of discourse, but when syntax so insistently points in several directions at once and when interpretive options are so foregrounded, instability becomes the most notable aspect of the reader's experience of the painting.

We might hypothesize that these proliferating perspectives reflect the process of "living with" art, a phrase that implies ongoing familiarity, whether valued intimacy (as one might live with one's close friend or lover) or resignation to a less pleasant condition of existence (as one might live with a chronic illness or lots of street noise). Just as one's thinking about the conditions of one's daily life constantly shifts, so quotidian familiarity with a work of art, whether loved or not, would generate varying reconfigurations of the painting in one's thoughts. Some working notes on *Try* that Swensen published in the electronic journal *HOW2* provide a way of understanding the poems' perspectival ambiguities that does not rely on but can supplement such speculations. There she presents representational painting itself—especially representation of events in stories with human actors—as fundamentally and deliberately ambiguous in its positioning of the viewing subject:

"One of [*Try*'s] recurrent themes is the position of the viewing-subject in rela-tion to the depicted subject—who is the subject of the narrative implied in so many of these [paintings]. It's clearly a matter of intending (con)fusion, . . . thereby reinforcing the stories themselves and initiating the viewer into the culture as a participant" ("Working").[13] The freedom of mind that I suggested would likely accompany "living with art," then, simply gives readier access to a mobile fusion/confusion of identities inherent in viewing representational art, perhaps allowing heightened consciousness of the ideological indoctrina-tion any representational painting performs.

The next passage in "Whatever Happened to Their Eyes" points to some-thing else at stake in the intertwining of viewing subject and depicted sub-ject besides cultural initiation or reflection upon such initiation: the survival of art itself. The lines—loosely interwoven with internal rhymes on "ace"—speak most apparently for the painting or those painted there, but perhaps for the painter or the poet as well; they offer a stuttering prayer for a binding of viewer and viewed so that the artwork may continue into the future:

> viewer hold me to you, lace this fracture to a future
> lace this
> lace which
> is mostly empty space seems to hold the very air in place.
> (3)

The ancient tradition of art offering a kind of immortality for those repre-sented (for instance, the sonneteer preserving the ephemeral beauty of his beloved, or the painter the vitality of his patron) is here reversed; the emphasis is on art's depending for its living on (inter)actions of the live viewer. The art-ist and/or the artwork pleads for a kind of touch—thematically, an important gesture in this volume, as will be evident shortly—and for an artful threading that will attach this broken language or this shard of visual representation to a future.[14]

Crucially, if somewhat paradoxically, the ties the viewer is asked to gener-ate, in figures of the archetypically female art of lace making, are "mostly empty space." Indeed, the syntactic ambiguity in that last line invites us to read here an assertion that "empty space" itself is what keeps the world together (whether our world or that of the painting). This suggests a nota-bly secular perspective, pointing to a vast epistemic gap between what Orca-gna's painting would have "said" to viewers in the fourteenth century, when "space" was the heavens that were anything but empty, and what the painting "says" now. This gap helps explain why a radical open-endedness may seem necessary specifically to the contemporary ekphrastic poet, whose cultural perspective is largely secular. A formal acknowledgment of empty space may be particularly necessary to poetry when, as Wallace Stevens put it, it has to take the place of empty heaven and its hymns. Swensen's writing, though only sometimes arranged to leave generous space or visible fractures on the material page, is always full of empty linguistic spaces—of missing referents, absent explanatory or connecting phrases, unfinished clauses, vacated subject positions, and the like. These important lines suggest that the poet's act of leaving out, of leaving spaces for readers to play at filling and emptying and refilling, is what currently sustains life through and in art.[15] No wonder the writer's interaction with an art work in this "living with" mode of ekphrasis serves as much to loosen as to secure the bonds holding what the visual artist, or the writer of traditional ekphrasis, has "arrested." We might say, reversing T. S. Eliot, that she undo the police in different voices.

Among the rigid forms that Swensen challenges in what I would term her *lacework aesthetic* is that of single-point perspective. Having chosen, for this volume of poetry, to "live with" multiple paintings created shortly before or after the invention of perspective organized around the vanishing point, Swensen in her prologue critiques that sweeping and monofocal organization:

> What they saw. For to see

> is to see everything. Inverted sky. Inveterate spy. From late medieval times through the Renaissance, one loaded site drives down to a point, and one could say no it is the face surrounding but and though the mouth, but no you're lying:
> (4)

By rearranging letters and sounds to create quite different meanings (*inverted sky* becomes *inveterate spy*) and by proposing visual alternatives ("one could say no it is the face surrounding"), she emphasizes the arbitrariness of linear perspective's order (though from an ideological perspective, probably far from arbitrary), its coercive narrowing of possibilities.[16] In her changed mode of ekphrasis, Swensen aspires to release the act of seeing from the drive toward a single point (potentially, a form of hybridizing), and the image of lacing, of intertwining loops giving shape to empty spaces, formalizes the nonlinear, multifaceted perception she seeks.

Only at this point in the prologue, when a monofocal perspective has been rejected on many levels, does Swensen allow the first-person pronoun to enter the poem; what precedes has effectively cautioned her reader against relying on one I/eye for unlying vision. Nonetheless, personal apprehension—inevitably, fundamental to perception—and personal testimony apparently have their place. The speaker claims to have witnessed a significant change in the world represented in a painting, or in painting more generally: "I saw someone leaving / and I saw the world, which was meant only for background, come to life" (4). Characteristically indeterminate, the lines do not assert a causal relation between that departure and the perceived change any more than they specify who departs. However, if the departing figure is supernatural—Christ or the annunciating angel—the disappearance may represent the disappearance of God, whether in an individual loss of faith or a more general epistemic shift to a secular perspective. Such a departure changes the setting that had been only background for the Christian narrative into something of vital and inherent interest in itself.[17] That is, a turn from religious belief transforms into landscape the earthly realm that the medieval or Renaissance painters meant to be only background.

The final painting considered in this prologue is by an artist known both for his emotionally compelling religious images and for his landscapes, in which he handled natural light with particular skill. Bellini's *Christ Blessing* (1460) directs the viewer's gaze toward spiritual salvation:

> (*Giovanni Bellini* your CHRIST BLESSING, climbing eye over eye some
> inside stair, a spiral that raises two fingers, one hand, heading toward heaven
> with a hole in it and a hole in the other one: twinned sun and absence see
> (4)

Yet the classical revival meant that Renaissance painters, unlike their medieval predecessors, were interested in accurately depicting the material body in space.[18] Thus, while Bellini's Christ points toward heaven, his mortal body gives the impression of solidity (in the painting, his nippled chest is exposed through a tear in his robe) and blood from the stigmata stains his hands. Swensen observes: "[T]he phrase 'the sight of blood' could mean something utterly else / and saw that it was / and made the body clay made the body, from the eyes down, fall away in / sheets" (4). To Bellini, the sight of Christ's blood—reminder of his having suffered the human condition—presumably meant redemption and immortal life, yet Swensen suggests that in representing the body so that it falls away in such a tangible way, "in sheets," the painter conveys the strength of the sensory world. Even in Christian images intended to point toward paradise to come, that intent may be countered by the aesthetic achievements of those same images, which teach the sensual power of art itself and the richness of material life.

The I/eye-witness testimony loops back, slightly changed, to close Swensen's poem: "and I saw someone leave and I saw the world that thrives on light clench and / cleave" (4). The world that thrives on light would be the visible material world in which plants photosynthesize and humans abide and/or the represented world visible in the painting. "I" perceives it clenching, a gesture of resistance against loss and leaving (as in "viewer hold me to you"), but also cleaving, a double term that can designate splitting or separating as well as clinging. The repeated claim of "I" to have observed a change in painting that reflects a dramatic (perhaps epistemic) shift—the emergence of landscape and of the "body clay"—is one that Swensen will test and explore from a number of angles in the rest of *Try*. The modern world's contradictory resistance to and embrace of living without a transcendent faith, its movement toward living instead with a faith in the sensory world, is—as I shall now demonstrate—explored especially in the volume's examination of touch and its prohibition, of the several meanings of flight (fleeing and flying), and of hands that reach and point both inside and outside the simultaneously visual/verbal unstilled realm of Swensen's ekphrasis.

Most of the paintings of Christian subjects that figure in *Try* treat one of two scenes from Christ's life: either when Joseph "took the young child and his mother by night, and departed into Egypt" (Matt. 2:14, King James Version) or when Jesus, resurrected but not yet ascended (in the prologue's terms, "rising"), in transition between human male and god, appeared to Mary Magdalene but commanded that she not touch him. The latter scene derives from the book of John, where the weeping Mary looks into the holy sepulcher, discovers that Christ's body is gone, is addressed by two angels sitting in the tomb, then turns to leave and is addressed by the risen Christ, whom she does not recognize:

> Jesus saith unto her, Woman, why weepest thou? whom seekest thou? She, supposing him to be the gardener, saith unto him, Sir, if thou have borne him hence, tell me where thou hast laid him, and I will take him away.
> Jesus saith unto her, Mary. She turned herself, and saith unto him, Rabboni; which is to say, Master.
> Jesus saith unto her, Touch me not; for I am not yet ascended to my Father: but go to my brethren, and say unto them, I ascend unto my Father, and your Father, and to my God, and your God. (John 20:15–17)

This tale and the paintings representing it add a new context for the early line in the prologue "and where / were you when she spun around and stared" (3), rendering it a question about how "you" (who could include us, the readers) is to be positioned in relation to this narrative of desire and rejection, loss and transcendence, obedience and authority, female longing and male law, flawed vision and aborted touch. The flight into Egypt, because treated by many painters as an opportunity to render landscape, provides another context for

"I saw someone leaving [that is, taking flight] / and I saw the world, which was meant only for background, come to life." These echoing interactions of later poems with the prologue can perhaps begin to convey the intricate interlacing of scenes and subjects, phrases and gestures, that takes place across the volume. Swensen's rapid interweavings create a vacillation between keeping historically distant perspectives distinct and merging them in palimpsestic overlay. This vibration among different views serves to suggest both that epistemic difference exists and that it is difficult to discern reliably because of epistemic overlaps and because we at least intermittently project our own epistemic perspectives onto whatever we see.

The first of the nine trios of poems in *Try*, "Triad," "lives with" an early fourteenth-century representation of the *Noli Me Tangere* scene by an anonymous Spanish painter. What captures Swensen's initial interest is Christ's having been given an extra appendage—what she presents in part 1 as the eruption, in a moment when the painter's vigilance slipped, of excess flesh: "Should the painter be distracted, should some sharp noise alarm him or pass- / ing thought disarm. All the saints in their flaming skins. And at first glance / seem to have an extra finger" (7). It seems that, unintentionally and perhaps against his will, the medieval painter offered testimony to the attraction of embodiment.[19] Even in an era of faith "[w]hen the sky was still gold," the painter affirms not so much Christ's eternal life as Mary's, as in the already quoted lines from the third section, "and she's / wearing red, which is why she / gets the breadth, thus does not end" (9). (Lines from a later poem explain, *"blue for the world that never touches ground; red for the living who love living / and thus live on"* [37].) Mary is, traditionally, a figure of worldly pleasure redeemed by Christ, but rather than implying that she has been rescued for eternity from her earlier sinful love of this world, Swensen suggests here that it is precisely Mary's sensuality, her material substantiality, perhaps even her/woman's childbearing ability (manifest in her hips' breadth), that enables her to "live on." Insofar as the sensuality attributed to Mary is stereotypically associated with women, Swensen underscores the value and enduring vitality of the feminine.

Considering paintings of the *Noli Me Tangere* scene enables Swensen to interlace a thematized critique of the misogynist elements in Christianity, and more generally of Christianity's attitudes toward the material world (so often attitudes of ambivalence or wariness, if not active rejection), with her formally enacted critique of traditional ekphrasis that imposes distance and opposition between visual and verbal experience.[20] Jesus's response to Mary is, after all, another version of "standing back." This in turn suggests that the set of attitudes motivating conventional ekphrasis impedes contact not just with paintings but with the material world and the sensory riches it offers (including the resources of female sexuality), and that Swensen's approach to ekphrasis aspires to foster an alternative relation with the sensory world. Her mode of changed ekphrasis, then, not only formally illuminates stances toward paintings but also enacts and reinforces stances toward experience that her poems thematically endorse.

In the middle poem of "Triad" Swensen offers three stories that might be discerned "as you back away from / the depicted" (8), that is, from the more objective viewpoint associated with traditional ekphrasis. But even stories (responding still to the fourteenth-century representation of *Noli Me Tangere*) are as elliptical as the biblical narrative itself, offering multiple possible understandings of what Mary's touching Christ—or touch more generally—could mean. According to the first story, "If you touch / the sky will turn blue," which could suggest that nothing would change (the sunlit sky has always appeared blue), that a secular age would begin (in which sky will no longer be represented as gold), and/or that the material world would seem spiritualized. The second story stays closer to the biblical text but implies a modern psychoanalytic reading of Christ as ambivalent about female sexuality:

Story Two:

If you profane   this is not flesh   with your supple
seething soon to be saintly and I

with a lock on the body and the sunlight cutting straight through me and I

picked up a brush and what's breathing
is not necessarily living

not that I have left but leave my

in your moth-fingered hands, in your million-fingered hands, a third story:
(8)

We hear Christ proclaiming to Mary the special status of his embodiment: that although breathing, he is not living in the ordinary sense, so that what Mary would profane with her touch is not flesh. His image of her hands as "moth-fingered" and "million-fingered" suggests a cleaving doubleness: a sensual longing for the delicacy of her potential caress and a fear that he would be overwhelmed by the erotic power of her touch. ("[S]eething" occupies a position of syntactic ambiguity, perhaps referring to her "supple" body, perhaps to his "soon to be saintly" one, perhaps to both.) The alliterative music of the passage, not untypical of Swensen's writing, underscores the pleasure of physicality. Yet "what's breathing / is not necessarily living" asks us to take seriously the claims underlying Christian asceticism: eternal spiritual life is what counts. We may also hear there the voice of the painter admonishing the viewer that a representation accomplished with a brush is not flesh, and that even the most lifelike image is not living, or lives only in the viewers' hands.

The third story replaces the Christian narrative of prevented touch with contact. Thematically important to *Try*'s central ambitions, it warrants quoting at length:

> Now everything is sky and
> where the body joins the body
> a flickering solidity
> encounters the returning
> touch finding a different erring
> and recognizing the difference,
> which is how hands are formed and then lives:
> miles sewn back on each other and the seam
> some secret plenty.
> (8)

Here touch "sew[s]" two people together, via the recognition of individual separateness or difference within the context of shared flawed mortality ("finding a different erring"); according to this story, flesh is not alarming excess but a marvelous plenitude.

That third "story" of touch as a possible "seam[ing]" together of different individuals (also a lacing together, since a joining of "flickering solidit[ies]" suggests airy lacework) represents, I am arguing, a potential in human relationships analogous to what Swensen aims to achieve via a form of ekphrasis that does not divide verbal from visual apprehension, that allows for their difference and also their interpenetration. But what is the historical or epistemic status of this story? Swensen's practice throughout *Try* of dating the paintings she has in mind invites her readers to consider the historical implications of her lines, yet the instability of her ekphrastic positionings can make it difficult to specify a historical location for her observations. Has that story been available since the scene was painted in the early fourteenth century, or does it reflect recent developments in Western attitudes toward bodies touching introduced by the late twentieth-century poet? Does it come last of three stories to represent a chronological development that Swensen wishes to highlight, or is it a timelessly available stance she would like to endorse? These questions prove fruitful for approaching the poems that follow, since they focus the reader's attention on the ways in which Swensen's ekphrastic method, with its ionizing movement among multiple perspectives, as well as her deliberate arrangement of the poem trios, juxtaposes different eras to sustain an evolving comparison of modern perspectives on touch with those of earlier periods.

Thus, the first trio of poems on a fourteenth-century vision of *Noli Me Tangere* is followed by a trio that presents prohibited contact in the modern context of a museum.[21] In the spare, plain-spoken lines of "Trilogy," a female visitor—and perhaps a male museum guard as well—touches the surface of an art work, quite probably a representation of the *Noli Me Tangere* scene. (Its gold sky and the guard's counting of fingers suggest it is the very image considered in "Triad.") A notable difference between the events in this poem and the Christian narrative is that the modern subjects defy authority and touch the forbidden other. However, they do not consequently experience more satisfying contact than the fourteenth-century's Mary Magdalene. When the female museumgoer touches the painting, she is desperate for attention and response:

> She touched the painting
> as soon as the guard
>
> turned his back. Respond.
> I said turn around. I
>
> screamed, I drowned, I
> thought you were home.
>
> I touched the surface of the canvas.
> It was I, the sound of salt. And fell
> and is still falling through a silent earth.
> (14)

The woman (whose act of defiance timelessly echoes those of Eve and Lot's wife, and perhaps Orpheus) may be as eager for response from the guard or from someone in her own domestic life as from the figures represented on the canvas or from the representation itself. Consequently, the scene stages not so much the struggle for power between image and word registered in traditional ekphrasis, as the agonizing difficulty of making contact, regardless of whether the attempted means involve written or spoken words, inarticulate sounds, visual images, or touch.

While connection appears no easier now than it was centuries ago, something that has changed from the ancient representation to the contemporary one is the modern woman's relation to the gaze. The museumgoer, after all, is not just the object of the gaze (while Mary Magdalene, frequently represented

with her naked body covered only by her long hair or as a languorously peni-
tent prostitute, is in Christian iconography the female object par excellence);
she is also the one who gazes, both in the museum and outside it. Poem "Two,"
which seems to follow the same woman as she "quiets // Outside" after the
outburst depicted in "One," presents her at an outdoor café watching a man
as one might observe figures in a painted scene: "Look, he's speaking, lean-
ing over to his neighbor. // Look how the lines around his eyes and mouth"
(15). In the next section, however, the woman crosses the square in a bright
red coat, becoming the object of the gaze, and as much spectacle as painted,
red-robed Mary Magdalene: "Look how they look at her, look up // from their
talking" (15). For these twentieth-century observers, unlike Christ, "There is
no thought / here of leaving" (15). But this doesn't guarantee connection, as
these lines are followed by "There is no thought" (15). In "Triad" Mary was
the "one alone [who] must stay on earth" (9); in the contemporary setting of
"Trilogy," Swensen still emphasizes the woman's aloneness: while some people
cross the square in small groups, people are also "alone in great numbers," and
the woman in red is one of those (15).

The final section of "Two," however, recasts her aloneness as individual
distinction and self-determination. Swensen's referring here to "*Joseph Albers,
THE INTERACTION OF COLOR, 1975*" may suggest that this is a distinc-
tively recent perspective. "[N]o one is ever repeated," applies to women as
much as to colors; each woman defines for herself what is "her own" (16). She
may repeat earlier gestures—of longing, of transgression, whatever—but she
determines her own path. Thus "Trilogy" concludes:

> She had to cross the square in order to get home.
> She was one. And one by one, they looked up and watched.
>
> When the guard turned around, the gesture was gone.
> A woman stood back and said no.
>
> She stood back, looking at the painting and said isn't it fine
> that a woman wearing red could arrive at a gold sky. Remind.
> Or else in falling. And nothing broke. The rift
> shifts open the devout. A finger that exceeded number, a
> fingertip.
> (18)

In this instance, standing back seems a gesture of valuable self-definition or
self-preservation—a refusal on the part of the modern woman to enter the
abject pose of Mary reaching toward Christ. After her "no," her refusal of the

old narrative devaluing female desire, the museumgoer offers an entirely secular and aestheticized reading of the *Noli Me Tangere* painting that focuses on the pleasures of color: a woman in red arrives at a gold sky. From this secular perspective, the fall itself is nothing serious ("nothing broke")—a dramatic break in human history for the devout, not for the unbeliever. Arriving at a gold sky wearing red may even suggest the possibility of something like paradise achieved through sensory experience. What remains powerful for the modern woman is the image of extra fingers; while they may not point toward supernatural grace and eternal life, presumably they signal the potential resources of touch.

That the next trio of poems, "Triune," explores those resources via contemporary art suggests that, indeed, a full appreciation of touch may be most accessible in a post-Christian era. These poems are "after paintings" by Olivier Debré, a French abstract painter (1920–1999) whose work appears to accomplish that vision of the third story in "Triad," in which "everything is sky and / where the body joins the body" (8). "Triune" beautifully conveys art's ability to foster emotional connection to the material world; "walking along with" Debré's paintings allows Swensen to render a seamless linking of the sensual with the spiritual realm. Significantly, Debré's appreciation of sensual contact with the world accompanies an appreciative perspective on woman and female sexuality. Woman, as Swensen finds her in Debré's painting, is first of all a person ("Person, pale, female"); her desires are appropriate to ordinary existence ("Thirsty, she picked up / the empty cup and left the room"); and her fertility is a liberating gift:

The pale green makes the woman
seem freer than the rest of us.

Inside her is a blue egg.
She lives with it,
which is why she looks like that:

No one has wings.
No one lies.
(21)

Those last lines recall the representations of religious subjects depicted in *Try*'s prologue—"He who watches him who wings / world without end" and "you're lying" (3, 4). Debré's work is secular—no annunciations by winged angels and no virgin births, no ascension, no fabulous tales or untruths about, for instance, female sexuality or eternal life.

If no longer imagining angels and eternal heaven constitutes in some ways a loss, Swensen provides a lovely rendering of the compensatory gains, especially in the last poem of this set, where she articulates Debré's achievement in terms of contact with the world. (Perhaps she is responding to a painting that presents the deep blues or greens of river water; in Debré's work, the "sense of color drowns the eye" [22].)

Deep deepening of the Loire

You can keep on joining.
You can join for years.

The natural extension of the hand
is the world is
reflected in its
proper motion here
(23)

The natural extension of the hand could be the practiced painter's brush making contact with the canvas, and it could be whatever extends the trajectory of a person's extended fingertips—anything in the world one touches or reaches toward. Wondrously, this sensual joining with the world need not mean entrapment in the body. Each poem in the trio is titled "Liberty," and in that last one, art's reflection of the world's proper motion is like a magic pebble with which the viewer can recall and reenvision a carefree state of innocence that, via its shadow, approaches pure liberated mobility:

Three children stand on the bank of a stream
throwing stones, laughing, jostling.
Look, their shadows flick through the water like fish
free of their bodies.
(23)

This vision contrasts sharply with that of the medieval painter Hieronymus Bosch, "after" whose work the next set of poems, "Trio," is written, in agitated prose that aptly suggests the crowded frenzy of his works. Perhaps better than any other medieval or early Renaissance painter, Bosch captured in his grotesque protosurrealist vision the Christian terror of hell, to which the pleasures of the flesh could lead. Bosch's work enables Swensen to explore one significant vision of the pleasures of touch that did exist in ancient Christianity. Her line, "A million people died or will die of similar affections," by substituting *affections* for *afflictions*, conveys an extremism that tended to see all desire as lust, all touch as potentially profaning and warranting eternal punishment (27). The collective speakers in this trio—who may be located within one or several of Bosch's celebrated triptychs, such as *Haywain*, presenting existence in paradise, earth, and hell—offer no vision of touch that incorporates spirituality or allows for valued selfhood. In the single breathless sentence that makes up the second prose poem, "Here," after the whole sky burns with hellfire and that world has burned down, people living on earth gaze on the beauties of a paradisal ocean/garden and proclaim their intention to come back. Their strongest desire, however, is for this world and "the bodies that breathe." Swensen's lines suggest a more subtle critique of their orientation than the argument about sin usually perceived in Bosch's work. Her speakers want touch that begins lightly but leads to a self-annihilating encounter in which one body essentially absorbs another: "letting the other one drift around inside a bit where the cells open out and, in opening, renounce the gift of a single body, the graft of a private history, the tip of a foot that won't sink back into the painting" (28). Their joining, then, is an escape from singularity, an eradication of difference and individuality quite distinct from the touch Swensen renders elsewhere so compellingly— touch that enables recognition of otherness, as in "Triad's "returning / touch finding a different erring / and recognizing the difference" (8).

By this point in reading the volume, we can readily appreciate how the lacework aesthetic of Swensen's ekphrasis is operating on a large scale: just as she shifts among multiple perspectives and between visual and verbal realms within any passage or poem, while leaving plenty of interpretive space between them, she does the same in structuring her ekphrastic volume and arranging the poems within it. The poems are ordered to resonate against each other, but not, as in Foucault's *The Order of Things*, to lay out thoroughly systematized differences. Thus, the poems "living with" Bosch's works also expose another version of leaving, one that is not a generative transformation but an annihilation: "An absolute motion, [rather than the "proper motion" of "Liberty"?] now we are going. Look at us leaving and leaving nothing behind. A whole civilization once vanished from this very spot without a scratch. . . . I smile with a certain amnesia, an amnesia that knows itself certainly, certainly they all lived here once and they were beautiful then but only then" (29). The poem that follows this passage—the first in "Triptych," *Try*'s central trio— then explores a life-preserving version of the leaving motif: the flight of the holy family into Egypt to thwart Herod's efforts to kill the Christ child, as it has been variously represented in paintings spanning several centuries. Here Swensen at last develops the theme suggested in her prologue: the discovery of landscape and its representation in painting. The opening lines of the first poem, "The Flight into Egypt"—which may be read as Joseph's or Mary's prayer—suggest Swensen approaches her investigation of this historical shift not as a precharted voyage but as a flight of discovery for herself as well:

> Reach me to
> > new all other
> > land
> That flees
> Known.
> (33)

As "Prologue" indicated, painters' development of landscape gave center stage to what had been unimportant surroundings, the realm not of spiritual transformation but of ordinary existence. The story of the flight into Egypt— a narrative not about "rising" but about lateral movement within this world— provided the perfect subject to facilitate that shift since it allowed painters of religious subjects to depict a tiny group of people traveling through the world. This story presents "an / exile of flesh. And of what was left in the living world," not, as in *Noli Me Tangere*, a flight from flesh (36). Consequently, "looking closely at the background land- / scapes, [one sees] that the holy family enters not a heavenly but a very worldly world, a / world just like ours except that it's not and that it can't be reached" (34). Emphasizing the artists' involvement in the sensory world of ordinary lives, Swensen remarks upon details that convey a sense of the physical difficulty of the journey—"Someone is looking now at the painting, thinking Mary, that your back looks / just a little tired, the shoulder inclined to the right" (36)—and notes the bourgeois ordinariness of the holy family in several seventeenth-century representations: Elsheimer's night scene of 1603, "'carried them as near to the limits of / truth as such subjects can go without entirely' Dear, they could be camping; / darling, please pass me the salt," while Claude Lorrain (whose *Landscape with Rest in Flight to Egypt* dates from 1647) depicts "a simple picnic under trees" (37). She several times refers to "the miracle of the wheat," an apocryphal tale often represented in paintings of the flight, especially medieval ones; this story (in which the miracle is often attributed to the Virgin rather than Christ) links the holy family to nature's fertility and provides painters with a further opportunity to display the wonders of the sensory world.[22]

"There," the second poem of "Triptych," offers more abstract ruminations on the significance of these paintings and, as one might expect in the new ekphrasis, does so by setting multiple views in conversation. Thus the poem opens with two quite different assertions, perhaps quoted from art historians, "'an implicit assumption that the concrete world is inaccessible' / 'an implicit assumption that the concrete world is more loveable'"; it includes two versions of lines that I think speak for landscape paintings and faith directed toward this world, countering the stance *Try* has linked to Christ's *Noli Me Tangere*, "*Touch me and you touch the world*" and "*Love me and you love the world*";[23] and it offers three differing descriptions of the visual planes of a painting (foreground, middleground, background), for example,

> PLANE 1: People. often in action, often in contact: there a hand rests on an arm, there a foot steps on a robe or an eye touches your eye without blinking.
> PLANE 2: A city; at the very least, manmade structures. The middle distance. Like you could go away without leaving.
> PLANE 3: There is indeed the unspeakable, and it can't show itself; this is the real.
> (40)

No single view of the kind of contact with the world allowed by landscape painting or the set of attitudes underlying it can emerge from this kind of approach. Instead, Swensen underscores the sense of always extending possibility, of open-endedness that emerges from these representations. In contrast to an ascension "arrested" or an extended hand stopped, in the paintings now on Swensen's mind, rivers lead the viewer's eye farther, "reach can be content or at least resolved will continue to unfurl," and "one and / one and one what's done / is hardly done" (42).

At this point in *Try*, Swensen returns to *Noli Me Tangere*, considering in the third section of "Triptych" multiple representations of the scene, from the early illuminations through even a nineteenth-century image. As if contemplating representations of the worldly flight into Egypt has changed the way she sees representations of other subjects, her emphasis now is on Jesus as someone of this world—as gardener, as man made of flesh, as one who appreciated the pleasures and beauties of the sensual realm. (We might think here of the question posed in "Trilogy," "What would the touch / if it did not first // run up against / a man who is in the end a man" [13].) From the lacework of Swensen's ekphrasis, a complicated story is emerging of "the line between flesh / and everything flesh" (44). Its complexity is enhanced by her collaged recycling of phrases from preceding (and subsequent) poems. For instance, the following lyrical description of an image from 1375 recalls the swimming shadows of Debré's "Liberty": "Christ in grey / on silk he reaches down as if to touch as she reaches up but all their hands, / lost fans, fluttering like fins dying of fresh air" (and looks ahead to the discussion of the ginkgo's fan leaf in the book's final trio) (43–44). The following passage, in which Christ longs nostalgically for embodiment in the very moment he is losing it, gains much of its poignancy from the density of its echoes and allusions:

> Once wheat grew in a single day
> and I was running as now I'm running as something odd is falling but
> upward and you must have heard
> and now must run and tell my brothers "once
> he had ends to his fingers
> (45)

This poem revisiting the biblical story of prohibited touch and the role of Christ within it contains some of the most beautiful writing in the entire volume, combining the pleasures of striking image, modulating sound, and rhythmic echo in passages testifying to the loveliness of embodiment:

> Go and tell my mother
> it's the water of the flesh
> that rises unto heaven
> drop by drop there was nothing left to cancel
> it starts just below the skin
> and then can't stop beginning.
> Mary who remembers, who sees her face in rivers,
> raise your head a little higher;
> the vase on the window sill has fallen, and it was I who grew those flowers
> once when I was human I
> thought I saw something beautiful. What
> do you think you're doing
> with those arms
> (45)

Mary Magdalene's uplifted arms, reaching toward him, may well be the beautiful sight this Jesus once appreciated. In contrast to "Triad," Swensen's reconsideration of *Noli Me Tangere* in "Triptych" portrays a strong sense of physical connection between Mary and Christ: in Poussin's artwork, for instance, "[t]hey could have been dancing" (44); in Le Barouche's "it is Jesus, so hand- / some, who holds out his hand but still must say, 'Don't'" (48). And if there is more emphasis than before on Mary's pain, her tears, there is also an increased sense of Mary experiencing a perhaps fortunate fall. For we are first told, "And so her tears fell onto burning soil and her dress turned red and her body / fell down like a body," but a few lines later, "and fell into a garden; go / and tell the others that whatever grows does so forever" (48).

On the one hand, Mary's mistaking Jesus for a gardener reminds viewers of the paintings (in which he often holds a spade) that Jesus redeems the fall of another gardener, Adam. But Mary's being left in this garden east of Eden after Christ has had to fly from it reinforces again her association with fertility and the ongoing life of the natural world; she remains linked, without end, to whatever grows in nature. Moreover, in this key poem she is given the last word, challenging Christ's rejection of the flesh and of touch—especially of woman's flesh and touch—as essentially pathological:

and rose to ask
what disturbed
and deep mistrust
must run the flesh
of a woman with such
stunning face. You must
not touch.
(49)

Poems like this one complicate *Try*'s portrayal of the epistemic shift that seems to have occurred around the Renaissance affecting how touch was perceived, valued, and represented in Western culture. If Swensen's poems do seem to privilege the most recent art works, such as Debré's, as most seamlessly linking the spiritual and sensual realms in their love of this world, nonetheless her ekphrasis avoids simplifying visions of earlier artists being blind to the potential spiritual resonance in touch's power to join one person to another or a person to the surrounding world. Avoiding a fixed perspective helps Swensen acknowledge both historical change and transhistorical commonality. Lines like "*For Bellini so loved the world //* There's a world out there that isn't there" (42) remind us that even the most devout painters were, as their vocation indicates, drawn to the visible material world, and that figures like Christ and the Magdalene have enabled painters since at least the early Renaissance to explore the intersections of the material and spiritual worlds. While secular and Christian perspectives are certainly distinct from one another, they need not be opposed any more than visual and verbal experience should be; in exploring the shift from faith in the divine to faith in this world, and in implicitly arguing for sensuality as crucial to post-Christian faith, Swensen ultimately emphasizes the nonparagonal elements of the secular and the religious.

Swensen's method—because it involves considering multiple images of the same scene, revisiting the same image multiple times or from changed subject positions to acquire different perspectives, and reconsidering the same themes as manifest in different paintings—may be analogous to that of the fifteenth- and sixteenth-century painters treated in "Triarchy: Narrative in Pieces" who multiply the scenes on a canvas in order to present in one painting different events within the same story. She calls their approach "narrative by repetition" because one painting might present, say, the wounded body of Christ again and again in various stages of his death and deposition (54). The mobility—the ionization—achieved by her ekphrastic method perhaps relates to this visual methodology of bringing different times into a single painting. Both the Renaissance painters and the contemporary poet thereby invite an additive interpretation as well as a comparative one, an understanding of the present as "walking along with" the past. Thus, Swensen presents Rodin's sensual masterpiece from the end of the nineteenth-century, *The Kiss*, in terms that echo her description from the prologue of Bellini's *Christ Blessing*: "two bodies that break down to a / single point that lips. Which makes the bodies drape. Fall away / in sheets. Repeat" (74).

The final trio of poems in *Try*, in which those lines appear, offers further challenges to rigid narratives of epistemic shift or simplified notions of cultural progress toward fuller appreciation of sensual experience. The first considers the fanlike ginkgo leaf in the context of a late nineteenth-century landscape by Gauguin and of the mid-twentieth-century nuclear explosion that etched its image on walls in Nagasaki. If a historical narrative is implied here, it's of grim decline—the tree "borrowed / from an orient and drowned" (73). Yet the tree itself "dates from the world's second age. Nothing's changed." The leaf has retained its fan shape, like "the unphalanged hand"; pointing fingers (phalanges) would be an imaginative addition. The final piece is a short prose poem that opens with the (perhaps "lying") formulas of urban legend: "This happened to a friend of mine . . . and it really did happen this way" (75). In the brief tale, a woman says to the man with whom she has been "getting nearer and nearer to a physical intimacy," "there's something I think I should tell you; I have no left hand" (75). What are we to make of this unnerving tale? Does kissing now supersede touch with the fingers? Are people no longer using their hands to make contact? And are they also not using their eyes? Does this suggest that contemporary human contact is somehow missing the sensual world? Have we, even as we have weakened the prohibitions against touch, somehow reduced our access to its pleasures? Or can one hand touch so much in a post-Christian episteme that a second hand is superfluous? And how do we evaluate the difference between this modern woman who can speak about her own limited ability to touch and the Mary Magdalene who has been defined by her hands' silently reaching toward a man who refuses her touch? No single or simple message emerges from this contemporary anecdote about touch.

Offered as speculation beginning "What if," the epilogue to *Try* proposes ways in which the principles governing the new ekphrasis might enhance efforts to generate art consonant with contemporary experience and emerging perspectives. This is the only piece in *Try* that responds to work by a female artist—a 1993 documentary video of a journey across eastern Europe made by Chantal Akerman, an independent filmmaker born in Brussels in 1950 and often labeled a feminist. This is fitting, given that the stance toward embodiment *Try* helps advance is one that particularly appreciates woman's multiplicity, agency, sensuality, and sexuality. Akerman's film prompts Swensen to consider methods of "ionizing" an obviously hybrid art form that is inherently both visual and aural. What if instead of separating the cello music and the image of the cellist from the fifteen minutes of the camera's panning a line of faces, the video artist had "slowly over a ten-minute period brought the music up behind and faded the image of the single musician into and over the long line of human faces waiting for something" (79). That is, what if further steps were taken to ensure the arts were not set in opposition to each other: what if the single performer in a single medium was not a focus, and what if the aural and visual aspects of several scenes were interwoven? Swensen goes on to wonder, "What if all concerts were performed behind a huge screen onto which was projected a long line of faces all facing us and it had always been done this way" (79). What if all musical performances were given a visual dimension that blurs foreground and background, a procedure that would interfere with the privileging of one sense over another, of a single plane or focal point over another? The advantage of all this: "You can see hundreds, even thousands, of faces in fifteen minutes. It lets you lose track of the music" (79). Combining music with moving visual images—visual art now being understood as something decidedly unstill, historically permeable, and polysemous—in the way that Swensen imagines enables those in the audience to see much more, thereby investing themselves more fully in this world. It also allows freedom from systematic notions of regular temporal progression measured in musical beats, minutes, or neatly separable epistemes.

six

RESISTING THE
CULTURAL STEAMROLLER

Susan Wheeler's Source Codes

IN HER COLLAGE ESSAY "Poetry, Mattering?" (2000), Susan Wheeler explores the difficulties of maintaining poetry's significance in this media-saturated age. The essay asks how, at a moment when "political life itself has become Geraldo'd," poets can combat contemporary culture's pervasive flattening, its homogenization:[1] "What way out of this can be imagined that yet participates enough, in the culture at large, to have an *effect*?" (317). Having signaled the need for some degree of participation in mainstream culture, Wheeler acknowledges the risk—perhaps the inevitability—that the literary market will subsume even the most wary, those with what she calls "the best intentions": the slope between selective participation in "the culture at large" and undifferentiated merging with it, or between *alternative* and *central*, is a slippery one. As a case in point, she names Susan Howe, singular experimentalist who was elected in 1999 to the American Academy of Arts and Sciences and in 2000 to be a chancellor of the Academy of American Poets.

Wheeler might well have cited similar examples from earlier eras, since poets of many generations have struggled to find a balance between an ethically responsible connection to the culture from which they speak, on the one hand, and sufficient separation from that culture to critique its ideologies or escape its conventions, on the other. However, contemporary consumer culture's obsession with novelty has sped up the process by which any avant-garde is appropriated into the mainstream, while the recent globalized expansion of electronic media has accelerated that assimilation still further. The question of whether poetry can still matter, asked in a number of ways by recent poets, critics, and public intellectuals across the political spectrum, has acquired new urgency, especially for those who would link cultural significance with innovation.[2] Wheeler seems justified in her claim that the sincere desire for resistance has itself been assimilated, as she points to the fate of the Language writers, who, "affiliated by a complex understanding of, and resistance to, the commodification not only of personal identity but of utterance—even to the nuance of syntax, of verb form, of spacial distribution on the page—find themselves a market share now resisted by students with proximity to their endowed chairs" ("Poetry" 322). Demonstrating the dynamic she describes, the paratactic, fragmented structure of "Poetry, Mattering?" itself—which might be intended to resist generic conventions of the essay—renders it effectively a piece written in sound bites,[3] while the rapidity with which her reference to talk show host Geraldo Rivera has become dated points to additional challenges confronting those who wish to produce culturally significant art. Wheeler hypothesizes that "non-coopted" resistance to market-driven culture may be impossible unless the writing in question is "wholly unknown" (322).

What Wheeler's bleak view enables that a more programmatic, utopian stance would not is her unusual readiness to appreciate in a range of poetic practices, conventionally positioned as antithetical, a shared desire for unassimilability: "The poet who hopes he can, in some small way, alter the path of the steamroller by inserting the 'uselessness' of elegant form—the medicine perhaps sugar-coated with reassuring pronouncements—into the lives of the industry, political, [and] academic 'players' around him, is resisting the banal in no less strenuous a way than she who resists the reifying hegemony of conventional syntax in order to counteract the market's emphasis on *pleasure* (comfort, convenience, sexual stimulation) as value" (324–25). Her acknowledgment of diverse strategies of resistance accompanies an equally even-handed assessment of efficacy; Wheeler continues: "No less strenuous, yes, but—alas, perhaps no less ineffective at tourniqueting the homogenization of difference" (325).

The essay's penultimate section uses Wheeler's motif of steamrollered flattening against itself—a motif that evokes Fredric Jameson's critique of the "depthlessness" he attributes to postmodern art—to offer a more hopeful vision of what might be achieved through the combined resources of several aesthetics (Jameson 12). The section comes from a children's story published in 1950, titled "The Very Mischief," in which two siblings, Elinor and Lee, take apart the piano keyboard, the victrola, and the clock. Rather than scolding, their mother tells Elinor how much fun she'd have with a little girl who simply couldn't keep out of mischief and whose exploits would be truly "interesting." Wheeler's excerpt reads:

"Elinor dragged Rosa [the housekeeper] under the kitchen door to show her what Lee had done, and Rosa came out flat. She even sang flat, which wasn't like Rosa at all. We were very much distressed . . .

"'*Goodness!* What's that I smell? It's the peas burning!'

"We rushed out to the kitchen and found Rosa was so flat that she couldn't see anything as round as peas. She had forgotten all about them. So *she* cooked the steak which was flat, and *we* cooked the peas which were round." (326)

In this playful context, the very word "flat" turns out to be multidimensional, referring to musical pitch as well as a flattened body, while it figuratively suggests uniformity or monotony. Such linguistic shape-shifting itself calls into question the pervasive flattening Wheeler has described, along with the negativity of her characterization. Flat things may be nourishing, and there is more than flatness available. Representing an ordinary world or meal that is simultaneously flat and round suggests a faith that our familiar cultural context may offer significant creative potential; moreover, it suggests that currently developing creativity may best be nourished by combining the resources of different aesthetics. At the turn of the twenty-first century, Wheeler is one of a growing number of poets exploring such eclectic possibilities. Wheeler is unusual, however, in the extent to which she foregrounds an uneasy self-consciousness about the mischief—and fun—she is making with the stuff of multiple traditions. Her intellectually penetrating, often darkly comic poetry provides a keenly focused lens onto trends in current poetics because it so knowingly explores the risks as well as the resources of combining linguistically innovative poetics with elements from traditions not associated with the avant-garde.

"Poetry, Mattering?" puts in a broad social context Wheeler's impulse, articulated in other prose, to challenge conventional aesthetic divisions, particularly among contemporary poetic camps: "If we allow ourselves to codify our assumptions about what is inside and outside experimental work, we cannot expect our own work to remain radical" ("What Outside?" 194). In "What Outside?," a talk from 1996 on the insider/outsider binaries that, in Wheeler's view, dominate poetic fashion to the detriment of the art, she rejects the rigid oppositionality of iconoclasm in favor of a transformative molding or critique I will label *iconoplasm*: "Why not see the statue as mutable instead of breakable, borrowing from it, gouging it in order to build something that contains it or preserves it as irrelevant, as a blind spot on the plaza?" (192). An intriguing paradox emerges: it is through iconoplasmic borrowing—a version of assimilation—that Wheeler stages her own attempt at writing that she hopes will be, however briefly, unassimilable.

Wheeler's four collections of poetry to date reflect her iconoplasmic engagement with a range of predecessors from Stéphane Mallarmé to Lewis Carroll, Coleridge to Berryman, Frost to Ashbery, offering mutations rather than shatterings of her models and sources. As if she were simultaneously *both* the imagined poets in the paragraph from "Poetry, Mattering?" quoted above, Wheeler resists the banal through elegant inherited forms or through play with received rhyme patterns she calls "doggerel" and also by disrupting fundamental conventions of intelligibility.[4] Drawing on poststructuralist theories and the disjunctive and defamiliarizing strategies of Language poetry, while maintaining a strong interest in narrative, in clever formalism like Auden's, in non-sense verse, in lyrical musicality, and in pop cultural reproductions, Wheeler's poems enact affiliations with a greater range of traditions than those usually associated either with conventional lyric or with recognized experimentalist practice. Hers is, quite deliberately, a hybridized aesthetic.

Wheeler herself recognizes the problems associated with the hybridity in which she is invested. The questions she posed for a conference panel on "crossovers, or hybrid poetries" in 1997 acknowledge that such a position may opportunistically fill a market niche:[5] "Is it possible to remain unaligned with one camp or another—to move fluidly in the field, assimilating or raiding varied traditions? Or is this also a brand: hybrid poets are tagged with the marketing mythos of an independent: romanticized loner, idiosyncratic and skittish (generally female, think Dickinson/S. Howe) bookworm, expansive Marlboro-master, bitter crank, etc.—or minor colonialist, appropriating everything" ("A Tag without a Chit"). Wheeler is also well aware that poets who "raid" various aesthetics are likely to be seen by those invested in radically experimental writing as assimilating in a "wrong," superficial way the fundamental disruptions enacted by the avant-garde.[6] Confronting what might be termed an anxiety of assimilation in relation especially to Language writing, Wheeler's recent essay "Reading, Raiding, and Anodyne Eclecticism" considers the legitimacy of complaints against "mere aestheticism" that employs "'surface characteristics' (disrupted syntax or Oulipian generators, say) of (O Lordy, what will we call it?–a) more rigorous work, while it continues to, for example, foreground the drama of the individual self" (149).[7]

"Reading, Raiding, and Anodyne Eclecticism" challenges assumptions Wheeler detects underlying most such complaints: first, that assimilators are philosophically or politically naive, and second, that "'radicality,' both political and aesthetic," can be reliably distinguished. There is not yet, she asserts, "a convincing litmus test for a poem's engagement" (151, 155).[8] Unwilling to give up entirely on the possibility of a "successful assimilation . . . if 'successful' were to mean both ethical in its writing and ethically enlarged in its reading" (148), Wheeler advocates risking even an "anodyne eclecticism" in hopes that challenging the borders of recognized groups and approved practices will "keep the possibility open for exits that we have not foreseen" (155).

Iconoplasm—the constant warping and mutation of genuinely varied source materials—is a key strategy in this quest. Wheeler's deliberate combination of elements from diverse source aesthetics and cultural fields effectively resists without attempting to destroy either the simplifications proffered by the mass media or the truisms to which high culture sometimes retreats.[9] In an era when the national culture is dangerously attracted to simplicity—to belief in simple ideas of good and evil empires, in simple solutions for even the most complicated social or environmental problems, or, within poetry's subcultures, to simplifying divisions between viable and unviable poetics—Wheeler counters with unsettling mixes that insist on the necessity of complex thinking both in artistic performance and in audience response. Although her assimilative methods of creating what Joan Retallack would call "a complex realism" differ markedly from Retallack's radical pursuit of "unintelligAbility" through an embrace of contingency and chaos theory, Wheeler's practice provides an alternative enactment of Retallack's belief that "[t]he more complex things are . . . the more room for the play of the mind, for inventing ourselves out of the mess" (*Poethical Wager* 23).

The inventiveness of Wheeler's work has not taken the extreme forms that would impede acceptance by the literary establishment. Wheeler has garnered prizes for three of her four volumes of poetry, the first two published by the University of Georgia Press and Four Way Books respectively, and the most recent (*Ledger*, 2005) by the University of Iowa Press. A selection drawn largely from those four and titled *Assorted Poems* has just been published by the distinguished New York press Farrar, Straus and Giroux (2009). She has taught creative writing at a number of universities, including New York University, Rutgers University, the New School for Social Research, and, currently, Princeton University. A winner of several national fellowships and awards including a Guggenheim, and a contributor seven times to the Scribner anthology *The Best American Poetry*, Wheeler is hardly a marginal figure, although her books aren't particularly well known. (That may change now with the publication of *Assorted Poems*.) Reviews typically note a distinctive verve, describing her poetry as "adventurous," "audacious," "volatile," "gutsy," and "cheeky" or as demonstrating "edgy frivolity," "assured craziness," and "abrasive displacements of the ordinary."[10] These same reviews disagree on whether her poetry is close to the reigning style or outside of current camps. To some extent their differing assessments mark the rapid changes poetic fashion has recently undergone as experimentalism has become fashionable and versions of "crossover" poetics have become more common. Albert Mobilio, writing for the *Village Voice* in 1994, presents her first volume, *Bag 'o' Diamonds* (1993 winner of the Poetry Society of America's Norma Farber First Book Award) as proving "that craft-conscious, uncompromising poetry can be written without the author swearing allegiance to any one fashion" (14). Four years later, however, Robert Hass, in his afterword to her second collection, *Smokes* (1998), which he selected for the Four Way Books Award, acknowledges that the postmodern idiom Wheeler handles so skillfully—"irony, pastiche, non-sequitur, dark wit, wild shifts in diction, a funhouse falling away of narrative continuity from image to image and line to line"—is "familiar enough," before praising the "witty ear" that enables her to "make new inventions" by drawing on the work of past masters (55). For Stephen Burt, *Smokes* typifies what he sees as an emerging school, "Ellipticism," whose members he claims are "post-avant-gardist or post-'postmodern': they have read . . . Stein's heirs, and the 'language writers,' and have chosen to do otherwise."[11] Wheeler's third collection, *Source Codes* (2001), on which I will focus here because it calls most attention to its own mutation and recycling of preexistent source materials, has not received much critical notice. It elicited some admiring reviews, however, including one that Brian Kim Stefans published in his online journal *Arras*. Having observed that Wheeler brings together disparate aesthetics and cultural registers— "Wheeler skirts along the troubled borders where virtual reality and Robert Lowell's Maine lobster town vie for our central geographical tropes"—Stefans goes on to proclaim *Source Codes* a "remarkably subversive book," "at once an homage and an evisceration of what one might call the main line of U.S. poetry. . . . *Source Codes* synthesizes, even exhausts, the range of techniques that the 20th century provided for American lyric verse" ("Little Reviews," Rev. of *Source Codes*).[12]

Seeing *Source Codes* as perhaps more modestly subversive, I would modify Stefans's claims: in using a foregrounded assimilationism to resist assimilation, Wheeler's work challenges the very notion of exhaustion. Much of the volume's interest lies in the self-awareness, ambivalence, and wit with which it employs various forms of eclecticism—of deliberately mixed sources, discourses, and informational codes—to encourage multiple and even contradictory readings. This challenging multiplicity generates ethical pressures like those demanded by Charles Altieri when he asserts in "Avant-Garde or Arrière-Garde in Recent American Poetry" that if (avant-garde) art is to play a significant role in culture by cultivating readerly participation and freedom, "its undecidability cannot be primarily semantic. The basic undecidability is ethical—not a matter of what things mean, but of who we become in our dealings with those meanings or efforts to mean. We need enough meaning on enough registers to feel the pressures of demand and possibility, which, in turn, test how we will engage what we encounter. Then we have the kind of undecidability where selves are tested and responses prove inseparable from responsibility" (641). Some of *Source Code*'s more subversive manipulations of undecidability involve the three appendixes, especially one containing

HTML (hypertext markup language) code. At a moment when some poetic innovators (including Stefans) are turning to the resources of computers for "new media poetics," Wheeler uses computer language not so much to generate new forms of poetry as to focus readers' awareness on how one may manipulate received languages and codes, whether developed for communication between people or with computers, to impede and/or complicate assimilable ways of reading, knowing, and thinking.

Source Codes is a multigeneric hybrid preoccupied with the literary, cultural, and economic sources behind contemporary artistic production and with the problematics of information coding and communication in the postmodern world. The collection is introduced by a "Contents" list in which partial listings of sources for the works to follow occupy the spaces usually filled by titles. Those works are identified only by spelled-out numbers, and nearly half of them turn out to be photo collages instead of poems. Appendixes containing poem drafts and HTML code constitute the final third of the volume. The collection presents at least four kinds of informational codes: publically derived visual images created from mass media; verbal texts that subjectivize to varying degrees the materials of public discourse and shared cultural reference; autobiography, intermittently discernable in the "content" of poems or through material traces in the poem drafts; and computer code that is at once more and less individuated than the others. Through their interactions, which highlight processes of cultural hybridity, eclecticism, and assimilation, Wheeler emphasizes the epistemological and ethical resources especially of the visual realm and the perceiving eye to enrich human experience in the seemingly homogenized context of contemporary mass culture. Making mischief and cultivating error also emerge as acts with significant ethical, political, and creative potential. That these two activities may reflect incompatible worldviews—*error* suggesting a discernable order or truth not associated with the ludic (more postmodern) concept of *mischief*—is, I suspect, deliberate. By setting up irresolvable contradictions through her eclectic iconoplasm, in essence short-circuiting the usual interpretive systems, Wheeler produces work that, even as it assimilates, resists assimilation.

Mischief, error, and a visible version of hybridity—collage—are all introduced with the first photo collage, on the book's cover (see fig. 2). The image invokes the late 1950s or early '60s, when the space race fueled the development of elaborate ways of coding information for electronic transmission across huge distances. Large, finned two-door cars—patriotically red, white, and blue—are parked on a broad, sunlit urban street, where a few shade trees are dwarfed by a cluster of high-rise buildings. These are typical midcentury constructions, evidence of late-modernist attempts to impose rational order

2. Susan Wheeler. Postcard and magazine collage. Cover design for Susan Wheeler, *Source Codes*, 2001. Courtesy Salt Publishing.

on the urban scene. A couple of pedestrians are visible as tiny figures on the far side of the street, but the figure who dominates the foreground is an astronaut suited in white, with red and blue embellishments, who appears to be suspended from a rope. Actually an architectural feature—a narrow face of the building seen as a line because of the way sunlight falls on it—that seeming (miscoded or erroneous) "rope" appears to be secured to the top of one of the multistoried buildings in the background, and the astronaut, whose feet are below the frame of the image, floats or stands next to a massive fluted column.

This rationally preposterous image provides a thematically rich introduction to the volume. Most obviously, it points to sources of Wheeler's art in the cultural climate, including the visual data, of the era that shaped her youthful consciousness (she was born in 1955). It treats with irreverence midcentury U.S. aspirations for domination not just of the globe but of the solar system. Wheeler brings into one frame the faith in technology and the desire to conquer nature that NASA embodied, the vast unembellished geometries of the period's urban renewal, and the era's nationalistic emphasis on an anticommunist, flag-waving patriotism. The visual combination may point to the common ideology of capitalist industrial colonization these phenomena share. Wheeler challenges that ideology through her humorous iconoplasmic positioning of the astronaut in an incongruous setting and particularly through the "rope" that ties him to the high-rise in the background. The iconic figure of patriarchal technological triumph (one small step for man, one giant leap for mankind), looking like a yo-yo about to bounce back to the roof from which it was projected or like a cocooned Superman secured by the aerial equivalent of training wheels, is whimsically disempowered. At the same time, the suited figure defamiliarizes the American urban landscape, eerily rendering the nation an alien place, perhaps one where the air is not breathable or gravity not operating.

Like the cover image that situates a space-suited astronaut in the city, many of the photo collages in *Source Codes* contain displaced figures from other regions and cultures, distant historical periods, or different stages of economic development. In each, a single postcard image provides the setting, and the inserted incongruous figures tend to be reasonably close in scale; this might generate a piquant surrealism if the crudeness of Wheeler's cut-and-paste technique didn't create an effect of "wrongness." No attempt is made to integrate these "misplaced" figures seamlessly into the scene, while the deliberately grainy surface of the collages further highlights their artifice. Generated from preexisting images produced for mass consumption in films, souvenir postcards, or journalism, the collages avoid being in any obvious way personal documents; they deflect a tendency remarked upon in "Poetry, Mattering?" for the contemporary reader to approach poems in terms of personages. Rarely beautiful, the composite images also seem far removed from "mere aestheticism." These images convey a dual impression of being at once belated and distinctive, not particularly original yet notably unusual within the context of poetry collections. Through them, Wheeler positions her work in an iconoplasmic relation to collage modernism and the substantial tradition of visual/poetic combination that has followed from it.

Wheeler wittily signals her general interest in transforming rather than smashing icons by selecting a number of settings that in Western culture are literally iconic places: a large outdoor statue of Christ; three interiors of ornate cathedrals; a woodland shrine containing a statue of the Virgin; a grave site with a large cross on the gravestone. In several collages—for instance "Forty-nine," in which a bas relief wall niche in the Hague strongly resembles an altar (see fig. 3)—settings of touristic pilgrimage are nearly indistinguishable from sites of religious devotion. The disruption of these places of religious or cultural worship by Wheeler's mischievous insertion of inappropriate human figures perhaps foregrounds how the iconic settings are themselves implicated in particular economic dispensations and/or nationalist agendas. But it is difficult to determine the extent to which these images convey serious social analysis. Readers can observe, for instance, that the imported figures, who are frequently children or adolescents, tend not to be demonstrating the respectful formality that would once have been expected in such settings; they may, for instance, be dancing or passionately kissing. Now that these monuments of ancient culture and religion have been commercialized, turned into museums or even hotels, their changed function allows for a much wider range of behaviors. Contemporary culture's hybridization and increasing social flexibility are playfully on display. While the collages resist flat judgments whereby readers would simply celebrate or deplore this freedom, their exposure of interpretive possibilities challenges readers to untie this cultural knot for themselves.

One could read a number of the photo collages, especially those that place dark-skinned figures in or near Anglo-European monuments, as political polemics.[13] The deliberate incongruity of Wheeler's assemblages could be seen as contesting—or marking as contestable—the forms of territorial control that conventionally operate between nations, classes, races, cultures, generations, genders, individual bodies—and aesthetic camps as well. But other readings are equally plausible. What is the reader to make, for instance, of the nearly naked, grinning soccer fan, his body painted to display his nationalistic loyalty to the Nigerian team, standing in a cathedral in "Seventeen" (see fig. 4)? What significance emerges from the parallels between bodily decoration and the elaborate ornamentation of the cathedral walls? Is the reader invited to think of soccer as a contemporary religion, or as garnering for underdeveloped countries the kind of attention and status that artistic monuments gain for European nations? Is the reader encouraged to contemplate colonialism and the role played in it by Christianity? Or is the reader simply to relish the irreverence of this fiction in which display of flesh and celebration of physicality occur in an iconic setting long associated with denial of the senses? The

3. Susan Wheeler. "Forty-nine." Postcard and magazine collage, in Susan Wheeler, *Source Codes*, 2001. Courtesy Salt Publishing.

collaged images, calling forth a number of different interpretive codes, continually thwart the simpleminded formulas and easy political positions typical of America's "Geraldo'd" culture. To adopt Altieri's language, registering the "pressures of demand and possibility" encourages Wheeler's readers to confront their own assumptions and define their own commitments.

4. Susan Wheeler. "Seventeen." Postcard and magazine collage, in Susan Wheeler, *Source Codes*, 2001. Courtesy Salt Publishing.

The "round" semantic and ethical complexity of these images is further enhanced when one reads the photo collages as elements in the larger collage of the volume itself, constellated with proximate poems or pictures. Wheeler—playing at once with the constraints of procedural poetics and with the formalist traditions of concatenation—has signaled interrelations by linking the endings of many entries to the beginnings of the next. For example, the last word of the poem "One" ("up") appears as the opening word of the poem "Two"; the peace sign (also possibly a V sign) made by the defiant-looking girl in the collage "Eight" echoes the word "peace" that ends the poem "Seven"; "dead" at the end of "Nineteen" leads to "the grave" that opens "Twenty." Pairs or groups of poems and photo collages work together as fields—a term appropriately associated both with the poetic "composition by field" propounded by Charles Olson and Robert Duncan and with the visual art of Agnes Martin and Bridget Riley, mentioned in "Twenty-six." For instance, the photo collage "Nine," in which a man and a woman passionately embrace by the altar of the Capilla del Rosaria, acquires greater cultural resonance in the context of the succeeding poem, which is constructed from a passage in *Anatomy of Melancholy* (1621) where Burton spews forth vilifying depictions of women's bodies to prove that male lovers are blind to their mistresses' imperfections.[14] The setting of "Nine" may contextualize Burton's misogyny ("Ten") within institutionalized Christianity or emphasize misogyny's long standing within Anglo-European culture. Wheeler's poem, which could have been made by twice tearing a strip down the page of Burton's translated text and transcribing what appeared on it, may display the limits of iconoplasm's transformative power in that even literally tearing his canonical text to pieces leaves her still reinscribing it. Yet Wheeler's mischievous act of repeated de- and re-creation effectively spotlights this textual "statue" as "a blind spot on the plaza"; the "errors and imperfections" displayed here are not those of women but those encoded in Burton's text.

As this example suggests, Wheeler's iconoplasmic repetition of precedent texts sometimes overlaps with the "aesthetic of infidelity" that Lisa Lowe points to in Theresa Hak Kyung Cha's *Dictée*, which "problematizes the premise of translation as fidelity" because the enterprise of translation is part of the apparatus of cultural dominion (42). Like Cha's, Wheeler's refusal of faithful reproduction defies cultural norms, including gender bias. (One might note the gendered implications of "The Very Mischief," in which the mother surprisingly encourages her daughter, rather than her son, to dare misconduct.) Yet if a feminist awareness of misogyny's varied manifestations frequently emerges in *Source Codes*, Wheeler's play with sources and with concatenation tends to unsettle a single-issue focus and undercut polemics. "Twenty-three," for instance, presents a thin little girl holding a thermometer in her mouth with a blood pressure cuff around her arm seated next to a huge grandfather clock. The leg missing from her chair might speak to the precarious position of females in patriarchal society. Yet the source information in "Contents" identifying "Paper House" reveals that the imposing clock is actually made of paper, suggesting the fragility of patriarchy (grandfathers). The girl's three-legged chair is recalled in "Thirty-three," where a girl with one leg, seeming to hop with the support of a post, is passing before rows of kegs which the "Contents" pages locate on a "Sugar & molasses landing, front of Sugar Exchange, New Orleans, La." Perhaps readers are to revise the reading of patriarchy—and now capitalism as well—as only paper tigers: women *are* casualties, as were the slaves who worked the sugar plantations. But Wheeler's giving the girl mobility, despite her handicap, in the most miscegenated of U.S. cities may shift emphasis from the often rehearsed evils of patriarchy and capitalism to the resources of creolization—and implicitly, of poetic eclecticism—a process that refuses to position particular groups inside and outside. That refusal is fundamental to the ethics as well as the aesthetics of Wheeler's iconoplasm.

The photo collages in *Source Codes* are only one means through which the information coding of this volume explores cultural hybridity and the multidimensional (non-"flat" and also nonbinary) variety it may generate. The equalizing gesture of listing poems and photo collages indistinguishably in the "Contents" pages and naming one or several sources for each signals that verbal texts are constructed as much from disparate preexisting and public materials as are the visual collages. The variety in the source information—ranging from "Memory" to a list of eight movie titles, from citation of a scholarly article on obscure dialect structures in African American vernacular to "Unknown"—emphasizes the mixed origins of any art work in experiences, impulses, traditions, or specific models, only some of which are even identifiable. The source information in "Contents" also tends to highlight the distance between an art work and its specific, immediate sources by prompting awareness of how dramatically the meaning of the source material is transformed by its iconoplasmic resituation. Readers will recognize, for instance, that the body-painted "[s]ports fan, *BBC Focus on Africa*" would convey a very different message appearing in stadium bleachers instead of a cathedral (fig. 4). Just as the phrase *"Beyond genes"* in Wheeler's dedication of the volume to her stepchildren indicates that the sources shaping individuals and their bonds to each other go beyond the deterministic elements of biology, so the "Contents" pages of *Source Codes* remind readers that any work of the imagination goes "beyond" the sources from which it springs and to which it remains tied. That an art work originates in an apparently homogenized world and in its commercialized products does not necessarily mean it remains flat.[15]

The extensive possibilities for play upon—and beyond—literary sources in particular are apparent, for instance, in "One," for which the "Contents" pages offer: "Cf. Romanticism to the present re: 'self.'" This source information places the poem, and the volume it introduces, within ongoing debates about the viability of the post-Romantic forms of personal lyric. While recent linguistically innovative writing has tended to reject the kind of coherent self, consistent personal voice, and individual imagination conventional to the lyric since Coleridge and Wordsworth, Wheeler, predictably, employs a more iconoplasmic than iconoclastic form of resistance to lyric conventions, and a decidedly mischievous one.[16] Her poem, which follows Romantic models in locating a first-person speaker (not the indefinite pronoun suggested by the title) in a specific landscape, is packed with darkly funny, demoticized allusions to Romantic lyrics that challenge Romantic premises. "One" opens:

When the wind shifts, the dirt—uh, earth—kicks
up. It skirts the pages of the catalogues

that line the steel link, it scarifies the retina, it
scumbles up the new gas line in Mr. Rodriguez's

R.V. I see you levitate before you risk the
plunge. Swinging into the western blast, the screen

door sings although the brothers oiled it—gone
to flaxseed, gone to hay—afore the late moon dis-

appeared.
(1)

A corrosive "blast" replaces Shelley's Western wind or the breezes that play harp strings in Coleridge's "Eolian Harp" and "Dejection." In place of Wordsworth's Lucy "in her grave" or her spirit sealed in slumber, "Rolled round in earth's diurnal course, / With rocks, and stones, and trees," this poem features a buried dog, "Lester's // daft mutt Seagram" who died from being "spayed cockeyed" and whose shallow "grave the winds kicked / up" (1). Wheeler's "One" explicitly challenges the Wordsworthian focus on the continuously developing self (child as father to the man), substituting a characteristically postmodern "silt self." She posits as "self" an unconsolidated entity composed of innumerable particles, given temporary definition by the material body without intimations of spirit(s) beyond the whisky for which the mutt—a hybrid—was named. Whereas the breeze playing Coleridge's harp tells of "the one Life within us and abroad, / Which meets all motion and becomes its soul," in Wheeler's poem such possibilities are scorned "as if[s]." Using iconoplasm to generate a fresh presentation of views evident in a good deal of literature since modernism, the poem reveals not unified Life but embattled lack of control: "We reassert / the selves but the Seagrams of the earth [the buried corpses and the brand-name detritus] they // sift us with silt no mind our gear in a wind that takes / *going off* to heart" (1). "Dis[sing]" the assumption shaping contemporary personal lyric, part of the Romantic legacy, that the poet's special sensibility, eloquence, and insight are what give poetry value, Wheeler offers instead ethically charged stimulation via virtuosic play with a source tradition.

As the collection's first poem highlights resources in poetic tradition, its last poem manipulates source material derived from contemporary mass media and electronically transmitted information. "Forty-eight" uses old-fashioned formal patterns to combine references to political upheavals in Nigeria with allusions to Hollywood movies and television shows in a context emphasizing fraud, grief, and slaughter. Here are the first two of its three stanzas:

> The bog-man's stippled in celluloid, grist for the mill.
> The Mohican is Irish now on-screen, his father a shill.
> I've gone to the meadow,
> I've come back in loss.
> The wails of the widow,
> the brass of the boss.
>
> Quincy's props man packs the sham socks, he whistles this song.
> The airport in Lagos teems over, the reception's all wrong.
> We sing what we know of,
> we singe when we try.
> The poster head glowing
> against a dumb sky.
> (66)

One could read these stanzas as simply condemning the way in which television equalizes a fictional medical mystery (Dr. Quincy) and a nonfictional uprising (according to the "Contents" pages, the airport in Lagos "teems over" in July of 1998 because of rage and civil strife following the death of a prominent opposition leader) and the way contemporary mass media, including Hollywood movies, aestheticize violence, turning even horrific events to market advantage, "grist for the mill." When Wheeler indicates in her second stanza that the knowledge we are receiving via television news broadcasts, network series, or the "poster head" of billboard advertising (and/or the images through which we are receiving it) is "all wrong" and that we risk doing damage ("singe[ing]") when we work from such information, she could be adding her voice to those lamenting postmodern culture's reduction of dynamic geographic and social complexity to simulacra projected on media screens. However, her topical references seem to me to point to more specific concerns. As she evokes two contexts of contemporary postcolonial unrest, Nigeria and Ireland, Wheeler directs attention to difficulties faced by the politically conscious artist today, difficulties that perhaps necessitate an iconoplasmic response.

The poem prompts us to ask, What would constitute meaningful engagement for the poet? Clearly, the sentimentalized response critiqued via "sham socks"—evoking shamrocks, a thoroughly commercialized emblem that glosses over divisions within the nation—is irresponsible. But can one as easily dismiss the art of Daniel Day-Lewis, who in *The Last of the Mohicans* (1992) played Hawkeye, a cultural hybrid with strong allegiance to the last survivors from a tribe obliterated by Anglo-European colonialism, and the next year powerfully portrayed a young man from Belfast wrongly accused of an IRA bombing in *In the Name of the Father*? He is in fact—or in genetic code—the son of an Anglo-Irish poet whose English affiliations are more notable than his Irish ones. Do Daniel Day-Lewis's representations of characters identified with colonized victimization constitute corrupt appropriations, and/or might they contribute to valuable consciousness-raising? The mention of bog bodies (presumably as the subject of television documentaries) calls to mind the work of a "real" Northern Irish Catholic, Seamus Heaney, in his collection *North* (1975). Heaney was accused by some reviewers of using the ancient bodies to rationalize contemporary violence as inevitable, and of taking a voyeuristic position safely removed from the immediate conflicts. The controversies surrounding that volume's politics underscore the complicated interrelation of personal identity, artistic practice, cultural context, and political allegiance. Although Wheeler's poem has offered no fully satisfying model of politically engaged art, it is not clear that those concerned with art's mattering should simply dismiss the examples offered by either Day-Lewis or Heaney. For it seems unlikely that the artist can escape complicity with the appropriations of mass media, or with the brutalities of colonialism and nationalism. (Colonialism's persistent legacy is suggested, for instance, by the poem's later mention of the cummerbund, an article of Western formal dress adopted from colonized India.) A purist political stance that—like an iconoclastic stance in the arts—presumes a clear outside and inside, clear good guys and bad, simplifies irresponsibly and closes off possibility.

The poem goes on to trouble further any implied condemnation of mass media generally by suggesting that reception wasn't necessarily clear when we saw events and places in less obviously mediated ways. The final stanza opens with a question about epistemological clarity (albeit not an entirely clear question, given the mixture of present- and past-tense verbs):

How did we know what we see, when we saw through the mind?
What citizen without cummerbund could Columbo yet find?
What mourning is mete grief,
what picture is true?
The raveling of relief,
the singing eschewed.
(66)

"[Seeing] through the mind" could be understood as a permanent human condition, or as something people did in the distant past before the world was seen through film or TV, or as something people have been doing recently in acquiring information from the images produced by Hollywood and broadcast journalism. But whether or not "[seeing] through the mind" is distinct from seeing through the camera lens and the TV screen, ethical questions of appropriate feeling or action and of "true" representation remain. The poet could "eschew" song/poetry because of its inability to establish reception that's incontrovertibly right. But instead Wheeler *has* written a poem, one that does not ask how we might remove ourselves from the culture dominated by electronic media, but rather how we might responsibly see—and sing—it differently.

The third stanza, then, can be read as exploring this need for alternate modes of perceiving and communicating by posing questions that imply the possible existence of alternative ways of seeing or of responding emotionally that might be worth pursuing. The tentativeness of this hope may be suggested by the failure of the poem's juxtaposed lines, linked by meter but not by grammatical conjunctions, to define the relation between the questions (or the act of posing them) and either the "raveling of relief" or the avoidance of singing. Raveling itself may mean clarifying by separating the aspects of something, or it may mean becoming tangled, confused. Yet the stanza, with its sorrowful suggestion of singing abandoned, nonetheless conveys a desire for more adequate perception. If, in the contemporary context, we haven't seen well (ethically?) "through the mind," or if seeing through the mind was once a reliable mode of gaining information but is so no longer, are there, in a world saturated with media images, alternative ways of seeing that might yield a "true" picture?

Wheeler's procedures in *Source Codes* suggest an interest in the visual as a potential epistemological and ethical resource for poetry now. Given that, as Marjorie Perloff has noted, "[i]ncreasingly, so far as the media are concerned, the image is supposed to say it all," relying on sight might seem perversely inconsistent with any attempt at artistic unassimilability (*Radical Artifice* 87). Perloff has persuasively argued that in this era of riveting advertising images, of what she calls the *"videation"* of our culture (74), the modernists' poetic image and related notions of direct treatment of the thing have become suspect for poets; today's powerful advertising images "challenge poetic discourse to deconstruct rather than to duplicate them" (92). Yet, as Perloff also goes on to demonstrate via the work of Steve McCaffery, Johanna Drucker, and others, the visual techniques of advertising may be put to sophisticated use in highly visual poetics that serve a cultural critique. Wheeler's volumes suggest she shares Perloff's conviction that rather than maintaining a pretense of existing apart from commercialization, "art discourse must work, not just to reverse the 'commercial' stereotype, but to undo its own presuppositions about the stereotype in question" (133). In asking "what picture is true?" Wheeler is not endorsing notions of noncontingent perception or representation, or stable notions of truth. Rather, throughout *Source Codes* she uses readily visible twists of aesthetic convention, along with iconoplasmic references to the "videated" aspects of post–World War II U.S. culture, to display a multifaceted vision of, for instance, the Irishman pretending to be another Irishman and also pretending to be a frontiersman who lives like a Native American, that can function as currently "true." Wheeler uses highly visual forms of iconoplasm to display not just a world of simulacra but a potentially valuable hybridization characteristic of postmodern society and culture, and to mobilize the diversity beneath its seemingly flat surface. *Source Codes* explores how visual elements in, of, and in combination with poetic texts may further Wheeler's project of textual unassimilability, of finding arresting ways of artistic coding, and ultimately of maintaining poetry's power of proffering significant cultural critique and of posing ethical challenges for its readers.

"Twenty-six," which describes the changing appearance of the land during a transcontinental flight between San Francisco and New York, can be read as presenting through the visible, especially through visual metaphors invoking objects of material culture, the revitalizing resources of aesthetic eclecticism. The speaker's gaze focuses first on the western plains, usually considered flat but here registered in richly varied textures:

> The grid, west of Lincoln, Nebraska, could be
> Agnes Martin's: all purplish white,
> marked with hatching, Richart chocolates in
> a box—some squares ribbed, some chenille,
> checks close-cropped like a flat-top crew,
> some wavy orbs, some purled, some knit,
> some bisected by blue hypoteni,
> (35)

The gaze then pans gradually eastward to the worn curves of the Appalachians and beyond. One probable source is Gertrude Stein's depiction in *Picasso* of the American landscape seen from a plane as a cubist surface.[17] But where Stein sees in terms of a single contemporaneous development in the arts, Wheeler reads the landscape eclectically. Wheeler assembles metaphors reflecting the arts of different eras, indicating that the continental United States—like her "crossover" poetry—integrates into its presently visible surface many of its pasts. A stream's winding track registers as the "chunk coral's white spines of trilobites" (35); snow-covered mountains appear as a white quilt bunched up in the sun; and—in the passage quoted above—fields are plowed in patterns suggesting other domestic frontier arts, knitting or purling. At the same time, the landscape appears as contemporary consumer products, fine arts, and fashion design: in addition to Agnes Martin, the poem depicts landscape in terms of "a Reebok welt" (35), "Rayogram leaves in negative" (35), "Missonis in an earth / toned year" (36), "Bridget Rileys" (36), and more. The brand-name commodities that provide many of the poem's visual metaphors are associated not with flattened homogeneity but with distinct and distinctly beautiful locales. The temporally and socially eclectic terms of Wheeler's description give the nation's geographical diversity historical depth within the specific cultural and economic moment of the twentieth century's close.

Toward the poem's ending, more attention is directed to the process the traveler is involved in, a process of crossing and recrossing the continent that could figure the dynamics of contemporary "crossover" poetics:

> Now
> orbs, stripes, chutes are Missonis in an earth
> toned year or, beneath brown gauze, Twister,
> Bridget Rileys or make-up palette a giant
> lost —— what's lugged in getting there!—
> west, only to cross back again ——
> the clouds too clotted to release the grid or,
> summering, the grid a gaudy green.
> What is left behind—bagels, screen—what—well—
> Suffice—shores the variegated field of what is between.
> (36)

In alluding to some key poetic statements on modernist aesthetics—the opening of Stevens's "Of Modern Poetry" and the close of T. S. Eliot's "The Waste Land"[18]—the last two lines call attention to Wheeler's bridging of the divide modernist writers maintained between high and low culture.

Those modernist poems, confronting the ruin of traditional high culture, convey the burden of attempting to start from scratch (or rubble) in building an art adequate to the age. Like much postmodern art, this poem revels in the contemporary artist's vision being permeated by a jumble of existing art and advertising, though the speaker also admits that in distant overview "it's all a flat board" so that individual lives have to be conjured imaginatively (35). Wheeler asserts neither progress nor decline but takes as the contemporary artist's path an attentive crossing back and forth; her heavy luggage may figure the large number of traditions and precedents she requires on her journey. She refuses to lament what is left behind on either coast (Manhattan's bagels or Hollywood's movie screens?) or in any airplane cabin. Ending a moment of stuttering hesitation with resolve ("suffice"), she affirms that the past or its remains reinforce a valuably diverse "variegated" culture. Those variegated fields of betweenness, literally the terrain between the continental coastlines, also represent the capacious space of "crossover" art that draws on a range of traditions and existential perspectives.

Wheeler's particular form of crossing depends not only on a ranging visual attentiveness but also on an extreme flexibility of idiom. Along with formal and archaic language, her compressed syntax is packed with slang, slogans, jingles, and song lyrics associated with particular cultural moments—as in "Ballistic, he went ballistic," "Two mints in one," "gone to flaxseed, gone to hay" (16). These are often given a twist, as when the rich live "thumb to mouth" (7) or when Christ's "Not my will but yours" echoes chillingly in "*Fuck my will, fuck* yours" (3). The mix generated provides a comical form of renewal, very like that of the restaurant sign (*Buffle Chigkpen Wingf*) Wheeler imitates in "Thirty-nine." There the errors of "the flubbled words" that "agoline / her nights and then her days" render unpredictable the sketched tale of "Stenofto-see" (the name contains *to see*), whose likes and dislikes would otherwise be neatly controlled within the predictable regime of U.S. consumerism that occupies Wheeler's refrain: "*up and down this shopping strip*" (50).

Consumer culture is obsessed with the purchasable finished product. If poetry's power to resist is threatened by absorption into that culture, *Source Codes* counters by making visible a wide range of stages in a poem's production and thereby calling into question the appropriateness of considering any version of an art work as the finished and marketable one. This is one function of the appendixes, which highlight poetry's material metamorphoses. These visually arresting sections, which demand that readers think through their eyes, present codes and sources that do not have meaning and value in a mass market (though two of the three might have value in the niche market of library archives). Their inclusion insists that any poem is an extended multimedia production, evolving through many stages and in varied visual/

material forms. Collectively, the appendixes also highlight how readily language may be manipulated, whether to ease, complicate, or thwart communication. The multiplicity of compositional layers and forms of coding displayed requires of readers an intellectually complex mobilization of multiple interpretive strategies; these in turn may work in contradictory ways or may expose each other's limitations, making it easier to discard cultural and ideological baggage that might otherwise have remained invisible.

Like the presentation of figures from earlier economic dispensations in Wheeler's photo collages, the inclusion of handwritten text and scrawled emendations in the two appendixes of "Source drafts" emphasizes through visual information the interdependence and coexistence of disparate stages of development. Thus, readers familiar with Wheeler's work will recognize that lines from a draft titled "The Dog Track," though crossed out as if the poem were to be discarded, in fact survive in "Here Comes Sparky" (107). The drafts also show the production of art reflecting the artist's engagement in her social and cultural context. For example, the drafts of "Local Verb" (which became "Thirty-Eight") include not only lists of possible rhyme words and definitions of terms Wheeler toyed with, but also names of some contemporary poets (82). Similarly, a scrap of graph paper in "Appendix III," which has on the left handwritten bits that ended up in at least three poems from *Bag 'o' Diamonds*, also includes financial notes about distributing some percentage of the gross, while on the right torn edge "LANG" appears above "CEN," suggesting that Language Centered writing (as Language writing was sometimes called) was on Wheeler's mind at the time of that drafting (103).

The nonteleological, nonlinear notion of textuality emerging from these poem drafts is reinforced by "Appendix II," identified in "Contents" as "Source code." Made up entirely of HTML, it provides a visual reminder that the metamorphoses common in the development of any art work have only been accelerated and increased by the introduction of computer technologies.[19] Wheeler's hybridizing gesture of importing computer code into a volume of poetry also invokes a set of analogies and metaphors—involving machine-readable languages, coding languages, textual markup, and so forth—through which to consider anew what is meaningful, interpretable, or assimilable. Wheeler invites her readers to think about the sources for an art work—its precedent traditions, specific influences, prompting events—as acting like source code, which provides sets of high-level instructions from which one can create machine-level instructions and, from there, particular programs and specific documents. This conceit not only encourages an iconoplasmic sense that outmoded sources can be fruitfully modified for current use; it also provides ways of conceptualizing and better understanding the strategies Wheeler has used in the rest of *Source Codes* for impeding the progress of the steamroller. Poetry that presents the interpreter with irresolvable contradictions (for instance, a worldview that believes in error and one that acknowledges only mischief, or a speaker who seems at once individuated and constructed of received discourses) is analogous to programming that uses several source codes in one instruction to a computer: the result would be to jam the machine, to prevent its following its usual procedures. *Source Codes* keeps suggesting that the deliberate mixing of languages (machine languages with natural ones, or, more figuratively, visual and verbal media, varied levels of diction, dissonant cultural contexts, divergent traditions) usefully impedes processing as usual.

The section of code that makes up "Appendix II" is essentially a piece of found art and, as such, acquires most of its interest from being placed in a new context where it is perceived differently than in the original one. Placed in a volume of poetry, the computer code highlights issues and processes of literary interpretation. Its semantic resistance, particularly as experienced by those unable to read HTML, heightens consciousness about interpretive biases and procedures. Readers who encounter hypertext markup language as an unknown foreign language will discover several strategies with which they can respond to this section of text, with quite different results. The limitations of what each strategy can reveal suggest there are unassimilable aspects of virtually any text, though with more familiar textual—or cultural—forms readers and writers alike may tend to ignore rather than acknowledge and explore them.

One approach to "Appendix II" (already begun here) would be to consider its general identity as a unit of computer language and ponder the conceptual ramifications of Wheeler's incorporating into her volume of poetry a section of the code, usually hidden from sight, used to tell computers how to display texts. As Johanna Drucker has pointed out, computer programming languages reflect particular assumptions about the ways in which visual configurations factor into a text's meaning: "As a text is put into binary code storage or made into an element of a software program, should its typeface, style, and format be encoded as well? The question was answered in the negative by the original designers of HTML (hypertext markup language), the design software used to give graphical expression to texts, images, and websites. In effect, the decision that was made was that typography was *not information* in any *fundamental* sense. . . . Recent moves to rethink this decision . . . have begun to redress this oversight. But the advantage of the "oversight" was to call attention to the dramatic significance that attaches to the material information included in type and format decisions in a document" (Drucker 162). By including this appendix, then, Wheeler invites readers to contemplate the significance of visual "material information" to textuality and to textual interpretation. (If missed earlier, the pun on matter in the title "Poetry, Mattering?" becomes apparent.) In a related way, one might understand this section of the book as suggesting the endless possibilities for altering a text, a notion fundamental to iconoplasm. Its laborious coded instructions underscore the importance of spatial arrangement to both the production and the reception of text, as well as the complexity of the many choices that lie behind any arrangement of language on a page. The poet emerges as perhaps as much a space explorer as the astronaut who appears on the book's cover.

A second approach available to readers unable to read HTML would be to examine the text more closely, attempting to employ interpretive tools useful with more familiar genres. For instance, considering this appendix as a particular visual arrangement of text, one might observe how much this passage of HTML *looks like* formal verse in a variety of arrangements, many of which echo numbered poems in *Source Codes*. Thus, one page of the HTML code groups text in nearly identical three-line clusters that look like regular stanzas:

```
<AHREF="javascript:sizeLayer(\"+layPass+'\',\"+theFile+
    '\',2)"><IMG SRC="menubar/r2.gif" ALT="*"WIDTH="9"
    HEIGHT="9" HSPACE="1" VSPACE="0" BORDER="0"></A>

<A HREF="javascript:sizeLayer(\"+layPass+'\',\"+theFile+
    '\',3)"><IMG SRC="menubar/r3.gif" ALT="*"WIDTH="9"
    HEIGHT="9" HSPACE="1" VSPACE="0" BORDER="0"></A>

<AHREF="javascript:sizeLayer(\"+layPass+'\',\"+theFile+
    '\',4)"><IMG SRC="menubar/r4.gif" ALT="*"WIDTH="9"
    HEIGHT="9" HSPACE="1" VSPACE= "0" BORDER="0"></A>
```
(89)

These lines in a very new language might call to mind Wheeler's lines that play on the ancient *ubi sunt* trope:

Where is the suitcase packed and ready by a table?
Where do chandeliers swing over photographic equipment?
Where, where is the burglarized apartment?

Where is the lease they were ready to desert?
Where is the first love, departing with a Greek map?
Where, where do the many men march?

Where is the brother, late at the airport?
Where should the valise be expected, now?
Where, where does your mama call you from?
(45)

Elsewhere, a section of single-spaced lines all beginning "document .layers[x]" (91) recalls other anaphoric poems like "Forty-two," in which all the lines begin "Do not" (53). Similarly, the alternating capital and lower-case letters of the closing page of the appendix evoke Wheeler's method of registering the shifting voices in the section of "Forty-five" headed "July 20" (62). Simply observing how the very act of programming the display of a potentially marketable text produces visual shadow poems challenges simplified understandings of what defines a poetic text, and of the forces shaping it.

Another application of familiar interpretive tools would involve focusing on the letters and words, exploring ways in which the alphabetic text might be meaningful outside the context of computer programming. Awareness that literate people who see words are almost driven to try to make sense of them, and that such efforts can push minds in surprising directions, has been important for many Language writers; one can approach at least parts of the HTML code as one would approach linguistically opaque experimental writing.[20] In the context of a volume in which issues of identity (including those played out in the personal lyric), the usefulness of inherited artistic traditions, the resources of visual culture, and the layers or stages of artistic creation come to the fore, the following lines, for instance, are suggestive:

```
        VISIBILITY="inherit"></LAYER><LAYER
ID="content"TOP="32" LEFT="4" BGCOLOR="#FFFFFF"
        CLIP="0,0,192,164"
VISIBILITY="inherit"></LAYER><LAYER id="moveit" height="10"
(88)
```

Some lines invite more sustained readings; consider, for instance, the closing lines of this appendix:

```
window.captureEvents(Event.MOUSEDOWN | Event.MOUSEUP);
window.onmousedown = startmoving;
window.onmousemove = keepmoving;
window.onmouse = stopmoving;
// -->
```

```
</SCRIPT>
</BODY>
</HTML>
```
(97)

One might read this passage, too, as extending the volume's emphasis on sight and also its critiques of the Romantic inheritance, specifically the view of eyes as windows onto the world that allow the artist to "capture events" in mimetic representation. This traditional notion of capturing events—here, an action-packed mouse hunt (thinking of the mammal more than the computer accessory)—is accompanied by a linear narrative structure, in which motion begins, continues, and then stops. Suggestively juxtaposed against this are three words in capital letters whose relation to one another is open to multiple interpretations. One might understand them as apposites: HTML is the script for the text and, in a curious way, also its body, since the computerized text would have no formed body without it. Or one might see them in some dynamic interplay—for example, a script such as a poem gains material body through HTML. To my eye, the central placement of "BODY" suggests something like Charles Bernstein's reflection—leading us back into more conceptual reading strategies—that "the more disembodied our language environment becomes, the more we may learn to value the materiality of writing. The aura of the prior stages of linguistic production and reproduction increases as each is displaced" ("Response" 181). These prior stages might be associated with "SCRIPT" as the handwriting that appears on the xeroxed drafts of other appendixes. Incorporated into poetry, HTML and the electronic landscape it stands for may enhance, rather than disguise or displace, the materiality of the text.

Reading HTML code as one reads literature involves imposing a fundamentally different approach to language than that taken by programmers. As Drucker points out, programming languages are "more mathematical than linguistic"; they are "highly constrained and specific, basically aiming to eliminate ambiguity, nuance, or variable interpretation" (155). Poetic language goes to the opposite extreme, cultivating language's ability to suggest multiple meanings simultaneously. Treating HTML code "wrongly" as if it were poetic language deliberately introduces ambiguities where none were intended and fruitfully opens a range of interpretive possibilities.

A third interpretive strategy would involve asking someone who can read HTML for a translation of sorts.[21] Doing so, one learns that this particular text is not in fact functional. It is code that has been mischievously played with, much as Wheeler's photo collages are images that have been altered.

The section contains syntactic errors, while the content files it would apply to are missing; this renders the section analogous to the work of the experimental poet depicted in "Poetry, Mattering?" "who resists the reifying hegemony of conventional syntax in order to counteract the market's emphasis on *pleasure* (comfort, convenience, sexual stimulation) as value" (324–25). In this case, however, what is counteracted is not just the market emphasis on pleasure but the market itself, since this piece of HTML is too flawed to yield a marketable text (except, ironically and mischievously, within this book of poems).

The presence of text that a programmer would regard as full of errors raises questions about what constitutes error—not just textually, but epistemologically, socially, morally, aesthetically.[22] Dysfunctional computer code may still be functional as visual or visual/verbal art. Similarly, the visual "errors" of Wheeler's photo collages—that is, the seemingly inappropriate placement of human figures in alien environments—may figure cultural and social errors (of slavery, imperialism, uneven global development, or simply of decorum). But they also push readers to ask, From what position and with what knowledge can one appropriately judge something to be an error? Is creative mischief in fact distinguishable from error? What would enable one appropriately to judge aesthetic assimilation "wrong," or to distinguish true radicalism from an "erroneous" display of its traits? Dichotomies, including the opposition between mainstream and experimentalist, radical and assimilationist, become difficult to maintain, and that, for Wheeler, is one of the advantages of thinking in terms of source codes. Indeed, "Appendix II" itself might be read as an act of iconoplasmic resistance to/engagement with what some regard as the most innovative and most culturally engaged forms of poetry now as well as poetry's most vital future: "new media" texts. In itself a gesture of interest in digital poetics, "Appendix II" also flaunts nonassimilation, not even flirting with the kinds of dynamism and interactivity valued by e-poets. Wheeler's display of fixed and flawed code reminds us that virtually any poetic text, whether arranged on a page or morphing on the computer screen, has behind it an elaborate set of violable and usually invisible rules—whether instructions given a computer or conventions of syntax, punctuation, and lineation internalized by writers—and that interpreting *any* poem requires a highly interactive process.

Read as a challenge to the notion of "wrong" assimilation, "Appendix II" echoes Wheeler's achievements in those poems that most obviously rework found materials. "Seven," for instance, is similar to the appendix in being based on a selection of text in a "foreign" language with a limited readership—a statement in Latin erroneously cited in "Contents" as *Odium sine litter is mors est.* Presumably, the original would read *Otium sine litteris mors est*:

leisure without literature/poetry/reading is death. (*Litter* is a word in English but not in Latin, and *odium* means hate.) Wheeler's poem, nine twists on Cicero's epigram, does not seem a lament for the decline/death of literature, which many blame on the rise of computers. It does, however, in iconoplasmic fashion, offer wry mutations of Poe's (odious) assertion about the death of a beautiful woman as the proper lyric subject and of the Romantic definition of lyric as emotion recollected in tranquility: "The dead woman of leisure is without literature. / The death of literature is tranquility" (9). Once again, reshaping elements from "other" languages or aesthetic and cultural systems—even ones thought to be either dead (Latin) or deadly (Geraldo)—enables a multifaceted critique and perhaps a way out of their limitations. Even if inevitably composed from litter or detritus, this literature challenges us to think in complex ways about current realities.

In "What Outside?," observing how recent poetry anthologies attempt to sell their product by creating aesthetic identities defined against the competition's, Wheeler warns, "Now, consider the result of the action of this codification, this self-definition *against* an Other. Less to raid. Less to read. A snugger rug. New-found affinities. And a border to protect. An economy to support. A kind of nationalism complete with colonizing outposts in the classroom. Like the Other. More alarmingly, a codification of boundaries that turns what is 'outside' into what cannot be admitted 'inside.' . . . How else define a social or political conservatism?" (193). In her own poetic practice, as I have shown, Wheeler has cultivated forms of textual miscegenation that mix even incongruous media, levels of culture, registers of allusion, disparate languages, and poetic strategies; these she uses in *Source Codes* to critique and counter literary and extraliterary colonizing and policing of borders. At the same time that this mixing enacts some resistance to commodification, Wheeler knows she inevitably engages with commodifying forces and sources. The market itself is another Other, another outside, that the artist cannot afford to police as being inadmissible inside. In this context, Salt Publishing's procedure of presenting the bar code that sellers scan on the final page *inside* the volume assumes the cast of an ironic shrug: Wheeler appears to claim this commercial coding, conventionally relegated only to the outside, on the jacket or the back cover (where it also appears), as a piece of text in *Source Codes*. Refusing to glamorize artistic production as removed from other forms of capitalist output (cf. "Five," based on Frost's "Provide, Provide," in which rich consuming "beauty sluts" demand that the artist "[p]roduce, produce" [7]), she mischievously makes society's errors visibly her own. The appearance of her photo on the back cover, a common format, functions similarly. The photo brings to mind a question Wheeler poses in "Poetry, Mattering?" about "the *after-effect* of participation in the culture-at-large upon the poet": "At what cost was this packaging, this framing and branding, this construction of public personages?" (320, 321). Is Wheeler allowing herself to be made into a personage, the cost of which she identifies as a "(steam-rolled) flattening" (326)? I prefer to see this gesture as another act of iconoplasm in which a traditional procedure has been altered by its context and handling. Balancing the photo collage on the front, the photographic portrait on the back contributes to a self-conscious display of Wheeler's deliberately inclusive and necessarily "cobbled solutions" to the ongoing problem of making poetry matter (326).

seven

THE THING SEEN TOGETHER
WITH THE WHOLE SPACE

Myung Mi Kim's Visual Poetics of the Aggregate

THROUGH ITS TITLE, *Under Flag* (first published in 1991), Myung Mi Kim's first collection of poetry calls to mind words from the U.S. Pledge of Allegiance: "One nation, under God." Kim's revision of the phrase suggests her sense that nations exist not at God's will but as entirely human constructions, their unity maintained through systems of military force, social legislation, and ideological indoctrination for which a national flag is a visible emblem. As an immigrant to the United States displaced in childhood from her Korean homeland, Kim is particularly alert to the ways in which human lives and allegiances are controlled by conceptions of nationality and by the institutions and representations that sustain nations—including not only icons like flags, but legal, literary, and journalistic documents, and even the familiar formulas of ordinary speech. Around the globe, these received understandings and modes of representation help keep people "under" others' domination; moreover, they restrict conceptualization and the ability to generate alternative social systems.

This chapter might be understood as tracing Kim's exploration in later work of alternatives to what flags represent to her, for it will consider her interest in forms of assembly or even group identity that do not impose unity on diversity. The noncoercive groupings in which Kim finds value are mobile and adaptable, readily subject to permutation and recombination. This chapter is linked to the two preceding in also being concerned with Kim's interest in the varied ways things of this world may be seen (either in the sense of perceived or more literally observed) and in the role visual elements play in human understanding. If the flag as visual icon demonstrates the power of visible design to communicate and an attempt to do so in quite coercive ways, Kim is interested both in how defamiliarized attention to visual phenomena may support resistance to dominant ideologies and in how space and other visual information in the pages she produces may enhance her poetry's complex communication.

Like Paul Celan in "The Meridian," an essay she admires, Kim values an art very different from a flag or an anthem. That art is "a word against the grain, the word which cuts the 'string,' which does not bow to the 'bystanders and old warhorses of history.' It is an act of freedom. It is a step" (Celan 156).[1] This writing against the grain—in Rachel Blau DuPlessis's coinage, writing "otherhow"—is a consciously ethical practice. Joan Retallack's term "poethics," coined in the 1980s to "characterize [John Cage's] aesthetic of making art that models how we want to live" (*Poethical Wager* 44), is an apt term for Kim's aesthetic as well, since the often-noted difficulties of Kim's poetry reflect the challenges of seeking models of ethical living that are better suited to contemporary experience—or to the experiences of the imminent future—than those that are already recognized and can already be articulated. In Retallack's view, the poethical and the innovative are intertwined: "Every 'great' innovator was acutely aware of changing circumstances and forms of her or his own times and had to devise a distinctive writing procedure to accommodate them. It's in this sense that authentically innovative work is consciously poethical. It vitally engages with the forms of life that create its contemporary context—the sciences, the arts, the politics, the sounds and textures of everyday life, the urgent questions and disruptions of the times. It's these factors that make it different from earlier work and for a time unrecognizable—to all but a few—as significant extension or transgression of existing genres. For the work to become poethical it seems it must risk a period of invisibility, unintelligibility" (*Poethical Wager* 40). In Kim's work, noted for a difficulty not always distinguishable from unintelligibility, as in the works Retallack describes, the formal issues of poetics are inseparable from an inevitably politicized investment in change.

Explaining her politicized poethics, the several prose documents in which Kim presents the principles of her writing link linguistic disruption to the disruption of oppressive or limiting social systems. "Anacrusis" (1999) asserts, "Allowing for the floating materiality of matter that 'does not fit' or 'is not part of a metrical pattern' asks urgent questions about the terms under which ideas of the metrical pattern (that is, ideas of authority and maintenance of the superstructures that support these mechanisms) emerge and are validated." The mindset that wishes to uphold authority by following metrical conventions is, for Kim, the same mindset that unthinkingly supports political or social authority.[2] Kim's "Convolutions: the Precision, the Wild" (2007) sets the "[f]ierce unsystematic recombinatory potential of language" that her poetry taps and "[t]he task of aberration   disruption   the provisional" it undertakes against "[r]egularized language and knowledge. Standing for perceiving and thinking. Serving as arbiter of recognizability, and thus of affiliation. What is occluded in the sociohistorical index" (251). Here, too, what is regularized in poetry is not merely analogous to but essentially part of what is regularized in "the sociohistorical index." Again, in "Pollen Fossil Record," the section of prose notes that concludes her volume *Commons* (2002), Kim presents ethical imperatives in which the poet's experimentation with language constitutes an intervention in the language that constructs the public sphere.[3] Statements from the final section of *Commons* presenting the volume's aims include the following series:

> Counter the potential totalizing power of language that serves the prevailing systems and demands of coherence
>
> Contemplate the generative power of the designation 'illegible' coming to speech
>
> Enter language as it factors in, layers in, and crosses fields of meaning, elaborating and extending the possibilities for sense making
>
> Consider how the polyglot, porous, transcultural presence alerts and alters what is around it
> (110)

That last pronouncement, ambiguously an instruction to the reader and/or a description of the project of the writer, points toward the present chapter's focus on some of the strategies by which Kim attempts not only to observe the interaction between language and the larger world but also to alert and alter her readers' awareness. Kim exhibits an almost detached curiosity about how language performs to "[extend] the possibilities for sense making" (that last phrase suggesting at once the enhancement of sensation and the construction/perception of understanding), and she is also committed to tapping those resources in service of a politics that counters "prevailing systems." If what she and other like-minded writers do with language is to have an effect on the larger social world, it is not by fomenting political revolution or oppositional activism so much as by changing awareness and perception in individual readers, whose altered consciousness will, through what we might envision as a ripple effect, radiate outward to be shared by others whose lives exist "around" theirs.[4]

Her aim is in large part to foster through a highly visualized poetics what I designate an "ethics of seeing." This seeing has to do not just with what one's eyes apprehend, but with what one's mind constructs from this data— that is, with perception and comprehension. Kim's writing works to counter modes of seeing that aim for comprehensiveness, coherence, or totalization, since these she links to oppression, imperialism, and the suppression of difference. Both thematically and in their formal character, her poems, I will argue, encourage perception of diverse particulars in ways that do not impose artificial separations (as do the boundaries that divide nations) on the one hand but also avoid projecting visions of seamless or homogeneous wholes on the other. With a more ethical sight, singularities are recognized in their distinction and also as existing in or being able to form aggregates. The term "aggregate" I take from Kim's poetry; particularly in its zoological or geological definitions ("[c]onsisting of distinct animals united into one organism" or "[c]omposed of distinct minerals, combined into one rock" ["Aggregate"]), it perfectly conveys the balance Kim seeks between discerning and valuing difference on the one hand, and recognizing on the other hand the basis for community in the possibility of some fundamental human commonality.

Kim's careful arrangement of the visual elements of her texts and her deliberate—and increasingly unconventional—use of page space render her poems literal embodiments of this poetics of the aggregate, wherein discrete bits are disjunct yet function within patterns and relations. The activity of reading her poems, in part because it requires a careful attentiveness to their visual character, gives readers practice in the kind of attention to complexity and complex relationality that may push us beyond the received oppositional categories of thought, beyond received ways of knowing, toward more ethical modes of perception and representation and of human communion.[5]

The bulk of this chapter will examine *Commons* as a text that asks questions about how and through what framing ideologies people see. There Kim draws attention to the historical roots in the natural sciences of the fifteenth and sixteenth centuries of what Martin Jay has called the "objective optical order" that Kim in *Commons* links with imperialism and racial or gender-based oppression (Jay 6). Kim invites consideration of Western culture's interest in dissection and classification, wherein observation of difference provides the basis for hierarchy. She also introduces in *Commons* the concept of the aggregate, which encapsulates a mode of vision and of social organization alternative to the bounded separation of the kind of scientific perspective that emerges in the "age of discovery." A reading of *River Antes* (2006) in the concluding part of the chapter will demonstrate how the visual materiality of that text participates in and disrupts received modes of seeing. In *River Antes*, I will argue, the visual text embodies a (po)ethics of seeing that is largely absent from—and a crucial complement to—the verbal text.

The several meanings of the title word, *Commons*, point to the political and ethical concerns of this volume from 2002. It focuses on the experience of common people, those the OED speaks of as "the lower order, as dis[tinguished] from those of noble or knightly or gentle rank." It also explores issues of how an equitable community can be provided for or supported, in line with the definition of commons as "[p]rovisions provided for a community or company in common" ("Commons"). At times, the inadequacy of available rations or daily fare—another definition of *commons*—is also a concern; the text notes the conditions of want experienced by ordinary people across the globe who are subjected to war, displacement, or imperialist domination—for example, "Terms stringent for lack of food . . . // Weeks of slaughter and remonstrance / Fed the children and animals first" (23)—or as a consequence simply of human overpopulation, as in "The heat of the midday sun is obvious, but the pressure of populations on the inadequate areas of flat land has to be inferred" (18). Responding within these contexts to what humans have in common, the poem takes as its responsibility "[t]o mobilize the notion of our responsibility to one another in social space" (111). I am particularly interested here in how Kim connects social space with the space of the poetic page—in how her use of the visual possibilities of the poetic text in *Commons* contributes to the ethical and political mobilization she seeks. Consequently, the spatial meaning of *commons* as land owned or used jointly by residents of a community—as in a common room or Boston Common—is particularly relevant here.[6] I argue that the space of Kim's page itself becomes a commons, where combinations may form and reform without depending on exclusion and marginalization.

Commons is organized in three sections followed by the fragmentary prose notes on poetics, "Pollen Fossil Record," from which I have already quoted. The introductory section, "Exordium," has five pages, each containing three evenly spaced passages of two or three lines presented as prose. This section introduces the book's ambition to generate ways of knowing and of using knowledge that do not duplicate those practiced earlier, particularly those associated with the history of Western civilization. It opens: "In what way names were applied to things. Filtration. Not every word that has been applied, still exists. Through proliferation and differentiation. Airborn. Here, this speck and this speck you missed" (3). Kim is interested in the way things have been labeled and conceptualized in the past, largely so that she can discover the cracks in that edifice of linguistically codified knowledge. The word "filtration," associated with that past, suggests a process of exclusion that is discriminatory. The "speck[s]" that have been missed, that floated away (airborne)—or were generated (born)—unnoticed, offer potential as materials for building quite different structures.

The second group of lines makes the same point in relation to numbers rather than names: "Numbers in cell division. Spheres of debt. The paradigm's stitchery of unrelated points. What escapes like so much cotton batting. The building, rather, in flames. Does flight happen in an order" (3). The passage suggests that the biologist's or the economist's use of numbers allows for the imposition of false orders—paradigms that bind together points that are in fact unrelated. Again, Kim quickly shifts attention to what doesn't stay within that paradigm or taxonomy—to the batting that escapes the confines of the mattress cover, to the building that suddenly vanishes, or to the motion ("flight") that might be a bird's improvisation in air or the chaotic scramble of refugees on land.

In "Exordium," the ways of knowing demonstrated by the historian, the chronicler, the cartographer, the geologist, and other specialized experts are invoked and challenged. They do not adequately capture the experiential realities of upheaval in our unstable world where—like the flapping of butterfly wings that chaos theory says may affect the weather—small shifts may generate dramatic transformations: "Alterations through the loss or transposition of even a single syllable. The next day is astronomical distance and a gnarled hand pulling up wild onion" (4).

The artificial categories and boundaries traditional epistemologies impose do not hold, either in nature or in language. Kim notes, "Cutworms in tomato beds. Roots of a tree close to the property line have gone out under the neighbor's cornfield. Whatever kin of word is. Partnership of words is one of many members" (6). Words are like social communities or natural ecosystems in that they have relationships and interdependencies that make them stray from their assigned places, and this vagrancy from regulated orders, this crossing of borders, is something that Kim wants to foster. Congruently, she seeks to render language something other than the vehicle of taxonomy, division, and hierarchy. Thus, the last passage of "Exordium"—which may echo Yeats's romantic dream of Innisfree while also evoking a traditional Korean house construction—announces the work of the rest of the volume as pursuing an intelligence closely aligned with a mindful caring and a language in service of the commons: "Standing in proximity—*think* and *love*. See, meet, face. Incidence of generation. Walls of wattles, straw, and mud. A laundering stone and stones for the floor. Gently, gently level the ground. This is the leveling of the ground" (7). Here, relations between words—in this case, verbs of invisible actions—are presented as physical relations; words are "standing in proximity" as people in a room do, or as walls stand to form a building. Such respect for the materiality of words and their relations, it seems, enables a shift away from hierarchy toward equality at the ground level of the commons.

As Kim moves into the announced leveling process in the second section of the volume, titled "Lamenta," she begins to open up her text spatially, visually. Undertaking what the opening lines call "[t]he transition from the stability and absoluteness of the world's contents / to their dissolution into motions and relations," Kim abandons the neat, proportionally spaced three-part arrangement of "Exordium" and allows the pages varied forms, inviting her readers to think about how the visible arrangement of the text may be meaningful (13). Many of the pages present widely spaced short lines without end punctuation, but no two look alike. Text sometimes appears in solid blocks; elsewhere, spacing within and between lines varies considerably. Sometimes lines are composed of a few letters ("*s-s-s*" [18]) or a single pair of words at once linked and separated by a centered dot ("say . siphon" [13]); sometimes they are complete discursive sentences ("If the woodness lasts three days without sleep, there is no hope of recovery" [16, this one taken without acknowledgment from the *Book of Mediaeval Lore from Bartholomew Anglicus*]). While there are no dramatic manipulations of typography, Korean words sometimes appear in italicized roman text; at one point English words and Korean characters—a phoneme and its roman transliteration—are arranged to look like mathematical fractions:

$$\frac{\text{bellrag}}{\text{bellslip}} \qquad \frac{\text{ㅈ}}{jw}$$

(20)

That particular example is a good one to demonstrate how resonant small visual devices become in *Commons*. Neither "bellrag" nor "bellslip" is a readily recognized word, though "bellrags" appears in the OED as a name of a water plant. Because they are not familiar, they become examples of verbal compounds in which one might find reference to modes of dress that invoke poverty or degradation—rags—and femininity—the no longer common item of women's underclothing, the slip. The visual arrangement may invite readers to consider these items relationally: bellrag is to bellslip as the character ㅈ is to its transliteration *jw*. The presentation as ratiolike analogy brings "rag" and "slip" conceptually closer than they might usually seem, indicating the feminization of poverty at the same time that it highlights the gap between a Hangul character and its transliteration, suggesting that their different cultural contexts render them as different as separate words. The horizontal lines also signal the mathematical operation of division, a term that might in the context bring to mind the division of the Korean nation or other forms of social and (inter)national schism. Issues of difference and similarity, separation and unity, emerge in quite complex formation from the simple technique of a fractionlike visual display.

Quotation marks are another small visual device that Kim uses with significant fresh effect here. In a number of places in "Lamenta," phrases that sound as if they come from journalistic sources are visibly set apart as quoted text, as in "'war-torn' / 'turbulent homeland'" (16), "'peacekeeping troops' / 'tanks beneath the windows'" (43), "'helicopters hover' / 'embassy compound'" (38), and "'left their homes after two solid days of attacks' / . . . 'religion and capitalism intersect in the muddy village twenty miles north of'" (39). By setting phrases apart—allowing them to "stand in proximity" without syntactic glue—the quotation marks invite readers to contemplate these bits of language more thoughtfully than one might if they were not visibly recontextualized within this literary text. They also signal a documentary impulse. However, in contrast to the 1930s documentation of particular places and crises—as in Muriel Rukeyser's use of congressional testimony to expose the Gauley Bridge mining disaster in "The Book of the Dead"—many of the documentary elements in *Commons* serve primarily to document the common discourses that have had little impact on the all too familiar situations of violence with which they are associated. That unspecified muddy village torn by competing economic and religious interests could be located in any number of countries on any continent, and the quotation could come from any of hundreds of pieces of journalism.[7] The quotations are like artifacts from a kitchen midden, linguistic shards from familiar modes of thought Kim seeks to critique and replace.

An interest in common patterns of language and thought seems reflected also in the quoted documents for which a specific source is cited. These include a series of four scattered pages, each titled "Vocalise," which are distinguished from the rest of the text and linked to one another by their arrangement as prose in which each line is introduced by a quotation mark. Three of the "Vocalise" pages quote Renaissance scientists exploring anatomy through human dissection and/or animal vivisection, while the last records the condition of an adolescent girl dying in Hiroshima on August 6, 1945. These are chilling passages, demonstrating a desire for knowledge apparently divorced from human feeling and propelled by a sense of privilege, of knowledge acquired "[i]n the bowels and studies of inferiors" (36). Kim explained in an interview published a few years before *Commons* that she had been thinking "about the way anatomy emerges as a science around the time of voyages to the 'New World.' The idea of looking at the body— more, looking inside it— . . . to inculcate a culture of dissection (discovering / owning / naming)" (Kim, "Myung Mi Kim" 99). Although the link between imperial expansion and dissection is not explicit in the "Vocalise" passages, it is implied there and also by the surrounding text. Scholars, too, have recently been exploring this connection, which is importantly linked to a valorization of vision as impersonal observation. Robyn Wiegman, for instance, when tracing the role of natural history and its mode of rationalized observation in establishing a visually based understanding of race, acknowledges that "natural history was not alone in securing the process of vision to a highly ordered and regularized material realm. Indeed, its systematical understanding of vision and form was remarkably similar to what Martin Jay in 'Scopic Regimes of Modernity' calls Cartesian perspectivalism (6). Jay demonstrates a relationship between the English Renaissance's aesthetic understanding of vision and the scientific perspective founded on the researcher's dispassionate eye" (Wiegman 26).[8]

The distortion of seeing involved in the anatomist's figurative voyage of discovery is evident in one of the "Vocalise" pages from 1543 where Vesalius in *De Fabrica Humani Corporis* describes his vivisection of a dog for the benefit of some friends who wanted to see the nerves:

"When I finished this demonstration of the nerves, it seemed
"good to watch the movements of the diaphragm in the same dog, at the same operation.
"While I was attempting this, and for that purpose had opened the abdomen and was
"pulling down with my hand the intestines and stomach gathered together into a mass,
"I suddenly beheld a great number of cords as it were, exceedingly thin and beautifully
"white, scattered over the whole of the mesentery and the intestine, and starting from
"almost innumerable beginnings.
(31)

Quotations like this one—which concludes with the author's being "struck by the novelty of the thing"—suggest a critique not only of the process by which the West conducted its quest for new, objective knowledge, but also of the attached sense of ethics and aesthetics—of what is "good" or "beautiful." Obviously, perception of "good" here does not take into account the perspective of the creature being experimented upon, while perception of the beautiful is also severed from its contexts and costs. Three of the "Vocalise" passages recount scientific observation of (sometimes pregnant) women or female animals, suggesting how readily women's bodies have been appropriated for scientific experiment and for display, and how readily women have been regarded merely as reproductive animals.[9]

The "Vocalise" page from da Vinci's notebooks summarizes the orientation of those who have undertaken this kind of scientific quest. The thoroughness with which he examined the human body as he "destroy[ed] all the various members" and studied their constituent parts rendered the process so slow that he had to dissect more than ten bodies: "'it was necessary to proceed by stages with so many bodies as would render my / 'knowledge complete" (41). For da Vinci, and for Western science generally, the end, which is comprehensive knowledge, justifies dehumanizing means. And while his ultimate aim may be to enhance human powers and human health, his immediate focus is self-serving: *his* complete knowledge.

Leonardo da Vinci and other men of science are known for their acute observational powers, but there are crucial blindnesses involved in their deployment of their visual faculties. That such distorted vision is evident as much in the recent past as it was four centuries ago is documented especially in the "Vocalise" page from Hiroshima just after the atomic blast. The scientific and/or military observer quoted seems to have had no anticipation and no understanding of the human damage inflicted by this kind of explosion. He is baffled by its invisible workings: "'. . . I didn't understand why she died. I can only surmise that her insides had imploded. / 'Acute internal injuries and not one mark on her body. No one ever knew who she was" (50). Western science, it seems, has difficulty perceiving the collateral and not immediately visible consequences of its manipulations of matter. (Perhaps one could say that there is a failure of peripheral vision, which Kim counters by expanding her attention to include the marginal—i.e., collateral—spaces.) In addition, the speaker demonstrates blind self-centeredness: rather than lamenting the girl's death, he puzzles over his own lack of understanding, and in regretting the general lack of knowledge about her, he takes no account of the family and friends who presumably knew this girl well. Other parts of "Lamenta" that sound like quotations similarly record without feeling or judgment the horrifying consequences for nonhuman life forms of the scientific advance of nuclear fission: "Abnormalities included growth retardation, fasciation, malformation, and variegation, / with the latter being most prominent"; "New buds did not sprout from the damaged side of trees within 700 meters of the / hypocenter. Among the herbs that regenerated rapidly, there were sweet potato, taro, / dwarf lily turf and big blue lily turf" (53). Jay's characterization of Cartesian perspectivalism as being in league with a scientific worldview in which natural objects "could only be observed from without by the dispassionate eye of the neutral researcher" again seems apt (9). Although ethical questions may have a place in scientific observation, in such a scopic regime they are readily pushed aside: here destruction and regeneration command the same dispassionate interest.

In their content, the "Vocalise" pages effectively foreground the issue key to this poethical text of how people see—the issue of what people notice, of what process enables their attention, and of what they do with the information or insight gained from observation. (Kim's substituting an *s* for the *z* in *vocalize* calls attention to the syllable that is a homonym for *eyes*.) If, as the poem asserts, "The fundamental tenet of all military geography is that every feature of the visible world / possesses actual or potential military significance," other approaches to the natural and social spaces of the visible world may yield other forms of significance that Kim suggests would be less destructive to life on this planet (32). Thus, in this poem that repeatedly refers to the hunger and suffering of refugees fleeing from war, lines like the following point to the importance of bringing one's emotional intelligence to bear by imagining how what is reported feels to those undergoing it:

One among fled many
　　　　felt
(20)

On the same page the assertion "It burns" cannot be seen simply as documenting "[f]urther carbonization of matter"; readers are invited to hear the declaration as also recording an agonizing sensation.[10]

In addition to endorsing emotionally engaged, nonobjectifying sight, this visually and syntactically disjunctive poem repeatedly enacts a noncomprehensive immediate knowledge, a knowledge in glimpses and fragments that contrasts with the "central organizing myth of comprehensive knowledge" that captivated da Vinci and many others since (44). Thus, the page that begins with the just-quoted phrase ends with a line of observed ephemeral detail, "Color of robin's egg against spring grass."

Color is a recurrent motif in this poem so concerned with ways of seeing. Seeing color is distinguished from the "Vocalise"/scientific/imperialist mode of perception in several ways. For one thing, color is presented as existing relationally, as being produced partly by its context; the pale greenish blue of the robin's egg is defined by the bright green of spring grass. In addition, color is culturally relative, prompting recognition of cultural difference. Kim thus presents in Korean a color that does not have a name in English: "*cho-gah-jiib* : a color—straw and wintered grass" (19). Further, perception of color is privileged in "Lamenta" because, in contrast to the fixed systemization of knowledge valorized by Western science, color is processive, modulating according to the quality of light, which shifts with the hour, season, and location. And it is often difficult to pin down: "This is some color but what color is it," Kim notes (39). Color, then, exemplifies the thesis at one point straightforwardly announced: "All that we see could also be otherwise / All that we can describe could also be otherwise / The thing seen is the thing seen together with the whole space" (16). That last line points toward the notion of aggregation; it claims one sees truly when one sees not just the individual component but that component as part of and in relation to a much larger (and changing) assemblage. Attending to color is a good way to make the "transition" Kim desires from received ways of seeing to alternative ones, "from the stability and absoluteness of the world's contents / to their dissolution into motions and relations" (13).

Kim's poem doesn't just discuss unethical and ethical seeing and provide textual examples; it also enacts them on the space of the material page. The arrangement of the "Vocalise" texts as blocks of prose suggests a connection between conventionalized observation in service of an ethically dubious epistemology on the one hand and conventional linguistic and formal organization on the other—the kind of linkage we saw directly asserted in Kim's statements of poetics. We might say these practices occupy the same social space. In the documentary "Vocalise" pages, Kim deviates from ordinary prose only in repeating opening quotation marks at the beginning of each line and in providing no closing quotes. Through its visible arrangement, then, this highly regularized discourse is emphatically distinguished from the poet's, while the unclosed quotes suggest such language use is ongoing.

When contrasted with the other pages of "Lamenta," the look of the "Vocalise" pages also signals materially how little space there is within such received discourse for intervention or invention. For the biggest difference between these pages and the others is that the others have much more space, and that space surrounds smaller units of text. This difference encourages different kinds of visual attention, analogous to the alternative modes of observation that the thematics of the poem clearly call for. These modes of seeing are holistic without being comprehensive—that is, bits of text appear in an arrangement readily apprehended as a visual pattern in which parts relate to each other, but those parts also retain an integrity that is reinforced by the surrounding space. Single words or word pairs, and sometimes longer lines, spatially separated on the page, demand from the reader distinct acts of focused attention. Often, the words' relations to one another are unclear; even individual lines or phrases are syntactically ambiguous, and such ambiguity is frequently reinforced by Kim's use of words that can function as either noun or verb and sometimes adjective as well.

Consider, as an example, the page headed "317," which reads:

—to settle refugees—to remove land mines
And their task leaked

cho-gah-jiib: a color—straw and wintered grass

The question is labor
Skin loosening from bone is age

Ages longer than drought or rain

Grafted

ee   .   은
(19)

The spacing asks us to pause over each line or pair of lines, an action that generates awareness of how tenuous and yet how various the semantic links among these lines are. Resettled refugees are, we might posit, like grafted plants, asked to grow on roots and soil not native to them. One might also think of skin grafts, needed by those whose skin was loosened from their bones not by age but by land mine explosions. The Korean word as well as the Korean grammatical markers that appear at the bottom of the page, one in romanized form and one in Hangul, might suggest a specifically Korean diaspora. The shift between languages and between different ways of representing Korean suggests perhaps another "labor" of the refugee—the learning of a new language, perhaps a grafting of one's thought onto another linguistic scaffolding. The movement from the bodily aging of a human being to another kind of "age," a more geological temporality bound to shifts in climate, is easy to observe, but its significance is ambiguous. How does the human sense of time fit with the "[a]ges longer than drought or rain"? Is the urgency of the manmade crisis involving land mines contrasted to, or linked to, equally life-threatening crises like drought or flood? Are humans responsible for both, or is one human engineered and the other purely "natural"? And does the dry grass color serve to suggest a graft that didn't take, a dead plant? What does it mean to say the task (was that the removal of land mines?) "leaked"—that it spread and grew larger? That it was not effectively conducted? Or does the text suggest a wartime "leakage"—a dangerous crossing of boundaries—of supposedly secret information?

The spacing helps the reader notice those "[a]lterations through the loss or transposition of even a single syllable" that can be so consequential (4). One observes not only the difference an *s* makes when added to "age" (particularly when read as a noun) but also the different character of the verb "is" in the two lines placed together at the center of the page: skin loosening from bone is a sign, a condition, or a consequence of age, while the question is not a sign, condition, or consequence of labor. Is that distinction related to the difference between *ee* and 은, which, I have been told by a native speaker of Korean, are used interchangeably but are not the same, one being usually a subject marker and one a topic marker?[11] The movements, positionings, and graftings of letters, words, languages, and peoples jostle one another in this poem; the shifting inconclusiveness of their relations leads to potentially fruitful lines of inquiry about such things as different forms of temporality and the impact of human behavior on "natural" disasters. Here, as throughout "Lamenta," the lines' spatial isolation establishes their distance from conventional hypotactic ordering, from totalizing systems, and from closure. But it does not preclude the lines' relation to each other. In terms already quoted from Kim's prose notes, the aim of this deployment of page space is to "[e]nter language as it factors in, layers in, and crosses fields of meaning, elaborating and extending the possibilities for sense making" (110).

As already indicated, the word that I believe best characterizes this kind of page poem is one that opens the volume's final section, "Works": "Aggregate." For Kim, "aggregate" (whether noun, verb, or adjective) clearly pertains to that social space within which she seeks a sense of people's responsibility to each other: "Levels of aggregation," she announces later in "Works," "may be extended in principle and without limit, / multiple nested units between household and world" (85). She speaks of units, not unity; a unity is likely to require the kind of filtration and exclusion one lives with "under flag," while an aggregate is an inclusive combination that allows for recombinant energies. Its "nested units" may themselves, like the household, be nestlike spaces of security and nurture. Admittedly, some of the aggregates depicted are horrifying testaments to human brutality—"[t]he heap by which we know burnt children" or "[s]omeone had sorted the femurs" (97). Yet others speak to the human drive toward mutually protective collectivity: "And the houses, provisional houses sprung up together, around each other, haphazard, / in a formation—in a form seeking shield from the wind" (97) or "Rudimentary sinew connecting library, school, and public land" (92). The pages of *Commons*, where often unlikely aggregates of words hunker in the white space, enact this kind of provisional, haphazard, but socially responsible development, semantically, aurally, and visually. At the same time, they remind us often of the common failures of community evident in public life: "the schools had been burned down / the teachers had been starved to death / the road had fallen into decay / the bridges were gone" (89).

Since *Commons* suggests that "our responsibility to one another in social space" is significantly motivated through and in language, it is not surprising that one form of linguistic aggregation Kim focuses on in "Works" involves the coming together of different languages via translation, transliteration, or simply interpolation (111).[12] This cross-cultural aggregation models—and tests—transnational forms of social responsibility in a global age. Unlike Theresa Hak Kyung Cha, whose *Dictée* provides an influential model of using interplay among multiple languages (Korean, Chinese, French, Latin, and English) to explore the struggles of colonized and diasporic Koreans, Kim works with only two languages, Korean and English, but Kim's Korean appears in three forms: as Hangul characters, as standard roman transliteration, and in Kim's own transliteration of Korean as she hears or speaks it (as in *"nuph-juk-pahn / nubh-jjuk-paan"* [18]).[13] This calls attention to the way in which languages are themselves aggregates, formed through the hybridizing interactions of cultures via trade, war, and imperialism. For instance, the distinctive page titled "Siege Document," in which five lines of Korean are written all three ways, highlights the international history embodied in written Korean (76). Hangul—a phonemic alphabet of fourteen consonants and ten vowels—was invented in the 1440s partly to establish distance from China at a time when the existing writing system of Hanja used Chinese characters. Initially associated with people of low status (the commons), Hangul later became associated with nationalist pride, particularly since it was banned during the Japanese occupation early in the twentieth century. The romanized form of Korean, meanwhile, would not have existed without the global domination of Anglo-European nations since the "age of discovery"; its arbitrariness and its distance from Korean speech is highlighted by Kim's insertion of her own alternative phonetic transcriptions. This presentation, moreover, allows readers to see languages as aggregates of the various codes in which they are transcribed.[14]

Sometimes Kim translates the Korean she presents; often she does not. In one largely untranslated page that opens, "Sometimes they dug holes and ordered us to get into them," she records in her own hand—the Hangul of someone whose writing proficiency in Korean never developed beyond the middle school level—what seems to be the testimony of a Korean elder exiled to Siberia (83). What carries meaning for readers who cannot decipher Hangul is the effort of even flawed transcription, the slightly uneven script's attempt at communicating another's particularized experience of colonial deracination and oppression.[15] This is evidently an act of responsibility for another in social space—and page space. Elsewhere, too, the reader who does not know Korean may have a very different experience than the Korean-speaking one. The former cannot necessarily distinguish a Hangul phoneme from mere play with sounds and letters. Consider, for instance, *"aba . apa,"* which one might take as an exercise in consonant substitution, one example of the poem's frequent play with the sounds of words that deviate from one another only by a letter or two (69). For the Korean-speaking reader, however, the italicized letters are words meaning *father/daddy* and *hurt* or *it hurts [me]*. With this information, the line, which is immediately preceded by "A bereft," may register the pain of a refugee torn from family, the suffering generated by patriarchal authority more generally, and/or Kim's own pain at her father's sudden death when she was fourteen. Kim's decision not to provide a translation may suggest that some meanings do not move well from one language to another, or that some parts of experience belong in a particular language. Nonetheless, the poem's visible aggregation of English and Korean suggests there is something potentially valuable—or socially responsible—simply in having the two languages interact on the page. The procedure itself promotes cross-cultural interaction—even if only in the literal sense of encouraging a non-Korean reader to consult a Korean one—while it fosters awareness that we are constantly gleaning information of varied kinds from multiple languages in our environment. That point is reinforced, for instance, by the following lines from the first page of "Lamenta":

Sign scarcity, the greeting—*have you eaten today?*

Signal of peonies   singing given to bullfrogs
(13)

The greetings in a community implicitly communicate its particular living conditions, just as the blooming of peonies—a seasonal language—tells those in tune with the natural world to listen for the mating season of frogs. Like the italicized letters that may or may not be meaningful in a language the reader does not know, the blank spaces on the page can similarly encourage readers to listen and watch for sounds and correspondences that have not been previously intelligible.

These speaking silences, lacks, and hungers are poignantly evident on the page from "Lamenta" on which appear only two widely spaced lines, each in brackets: "[when my father died and left me nothing] / [this is how I speak]" (37). Too rarely, *Commons* suggests, do we hear the voices of those who have nothing or whose social value is deemed by the powerful to be close to nothing; moreover, as the brackets and open spaces suggest, their expression will not fit the preexistent norms. This is why Kim's poethical desire "[t]o change the position of enunciation and the relations within it" takes her beyond recounting or documenting the experiences of refugees and of oppressed women; it takes her beyond writing that is conventionally legible or intelligible into literal and figurative spaces where language, freed from its usual arrangements, might convey alternative perspectives and ideologies (99).

In some passages, the unconventionally deployed punctuation or non-alphabetic marks available on the computer keyboard help her speak "otherhow." For instance, the page facing the one in her own Korean hand contains entire lines and sections of lines made by repeatedly touching the equal sign on the keyboard so as to generate closely spaced parallel horizontal lines. In context, these marks seem to signal an eradication or erasure of traditional cultivation rights by an invading power, a process that leaves the common people unable to produce or afford sufficient food. Rather than describe the destruction, which has been repeated in many places and continues to be reenacted, Kim chooses to perform a kind of systematic but generalized visible obliteration on her page. She thereby underscores a widespread pattern of eradication evident in varied specific situations. Remaining at the center is the phrase "being atomized," which denotes the imposed opposite of becoming aggregated:

Cultivation rights

============= =

=====================

================= =

too bad

The lower level of the social hierarchy ===== made up of ===== who tilled and ========= the food

========= being atomized=========occurs
=================price lists =================
==================

As they enter, they cut down grains, tear down the inner and outer walls, and fill up the ditches and ponds; they exterminate the aged and the weak

In the calendars available, shortages are documented as a result of human actions: civil wars, piracy, failure to transport food where needed
(82)

It appears to be Kim's hope that this kind of movement into a visually uncommon language opens readers to additional transformations in perception involving other senses besides sight—"The snapdragon's crimson / Understood as a potential sound" (103). In the spatially exploratory pages of *Commons*, multiple languages aggregate, as do multiple ways of seeing. These, Kim hopes, will mobilize new forms of conversation, of learning, of responsible or ethical interaction with languages and people different from oneself.

Kim's 2006 publication *River Antes* significantly extends the spatially exploratory quality evident in *Commons*. In order to understand the challenges the poem's pages pose for readers, it is useful to consider a distinction Alan Golding makes in his essay "Visual Materiality in Bruce Andrews" between poetry in which the visual components of typography, layout, drawings, and the like serve an expressivist function, bearing a direct relation to thematic content (as in the work of Susan Howe), and work like Andrews's, in which visual elements are among the "tools of a materialist poetics" serving the poet's "overall project to counter politically suspect modes of representation." *Commons* and the volumes preceding it, all of which demonstrate careful deployment of page space, fit predominantly into Golding's second category—though devices like the lines of equal signs acting as an obliterating force on the page of *Commons* certainly point toward expressivist possibilities. That is, the generous space of Kim's typographic arrangements materially extends her text's asyntactic freedom, with the aim of helping release it from the constraints of conventional orders of thought and language. As we have seen, both in her prose statements and in the poetry of *Commons*, these conventional forms of representation are linked to varied forms of social injustice and inequity, including imperialism and gender-based oppression. Kim's elegant chapbook *River Antes* presents a more complex practice of visual poetics in which a materialist "counter[ing of] politically suspect modes of representation" combines with an expressivist enactment of an important but largely unverbalized thematics.[16] *River Antes* presents, then, greater challenges if we are to respond to the work as an aggregate—as a whole, in which the visual and verbal texts need to be seen in relation to one another. For, as I will argue, the visual character of *River Antes* in its expressivist dimension is largely at odds with the prominent thematics of the verbal text. Kim has spoken of poetic form as a means of "presencing contestitory [*sic*] forces," and here the formal elements that enable such contestation are primarily the visual ones ("Generosity as Method"). The visual (counter)text speaks its own thematic language that is essential to the poem's meaning. Indeed, the reader who does not bother to read the visual text—that is, who fails to appreciate Kim's poetics of the aggregate—would be mired in the violence and grief of history while missing the more hopeful potential that the visible material encodes. This chapbook, Kim's most richly and complicatedly visual publication to date, offers her fullest demonstration of an ethics of seeing.

Although "River Antes" will be included in Kim's next volume, *Penury*, the small edition of the chapbook, the work of Michael Cross's Atticus/Finch press in Buffalo, New York, quickly sold out and is not readily available. Consequently, a description of this extraordinary work of art is in order.[17] The 6" x 9" book has a black inner cover with a sewn binding, around which wraps an outer cover of slightly textured tannish-gray cottony stock. The outer cover is folded in over the inner one both in the front, where it is attached with glue, and in the back so that the black inner cover is almost completely hidden. The outer cover's design of embossed, swirling calligraphy in darker gray extends seamlessly from the front cover around to the front overleaf, and from there to the back overleaf and the back cover. This flow of the decorative detail from the front to the back of the book might in expressivist fashion suggest the work's coherence or a riverlike flow of its parts into one another.

As a particularly distinctive feature of the book's material construction, five of the ten (unnumbered) pages in the second half of the book are twice the expected length and are folded in half to fit within the cover. When unfolded, those pages make triptychs (see fig. 5). They can be refolded in several ways, breaking the work into various units and blocking different pages from view. One can even open the book so that four pages are visible at one time. The folds, then, demonstrate the recombinatory possibilities of the aggregate, usually less dramatically staged via disjunctive lines that invite varied grouping; the folds offer physical dividers that readers can use to temporarily define units to approach as aggregates.

Extending a tendency in Kim's earlier work, the text appears minimalist, with lines and groups of lines surrounded by lots of space—as we observed with *Commons*, a key material for opening alternative ways of ordering experience. No page in the first half has more than twelve lines of text; a few have only one line or three, and those lines may be widely separated. In the second half of the book, where the folds appear, blank space predominates even more: all five folds have nothing printed on the sheet that precedes the long folded page. Each double-length page has on its back side only a simple graphic image made of a single virgule about five-eighths of an inch tall centered over a line that contains a virgule of the same size followed by a period, some space, and then a pair of virgules (see fig. 6). When folded, one page appears blank and the other is empty except for the pattern of marks in the lower right-hand corner.

In addition to the recurring folds, each repeating the same graphic image, repetition occurs in the several patterns of textual arrangement that recur unsystematically—while allowing for considerable variation—on some pages

5. Three fold-out pages in Myung Mi Kim, *River Antes*, 2006. Courtesy Atticus/Finch Chapbooks, designed by Michael Cross.

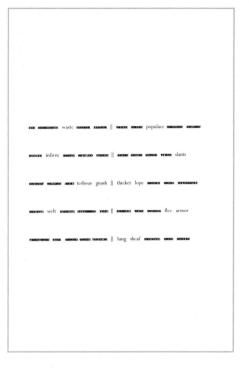

of the triptychs. For instance, one visual pattern presents irregularly spaced centered lines of varying length, like this:

Calling of name sound, turned

Tumescent

Pick at   root out

An elder (old tailor)   needle ear threading   keeping eyes on us

Light of the full poor cell

Another pattern involves longer lines of words, eight or ten per line, in asyn-tactic lists divided in the middle by pairs of vertical lines. On two of those

Bent at the waist nose nearly touching ground

Trolling sense

Toppling expert shores before home hunt

Continue hunt Lightning help hunt

Pursuant time and place vital prohibit

Operations rush first wave shield

Marred apart swarming hand-held

Green color on the face Tiger Fury

Wear down tamp unit time and place

Knotted heavy holy swear free flash

transcript 904

pages, a divided line lacks a half line; in one, the blank space appears on the right, while in the example below the left side is empty:

wicked rounding swept cliff || burial mound numb dispense

guard ravine hoarse hail || pilfer citizen signal extract

|| mendacity one head four faces

On the third such page, individual words on each of the five lines (doubling the length of the other two) appear to have been typed over so many times that those words are illegible, leaving only thirteen discernable words on the page (see fig. 5).

In addition to the page where the words are overwritten to the point of illegibility, two other pages are particularly unusual in their visual character. The final section contains a page on which no alphabetic text appears, only a kind of visual rhythm created by many short lines of virgules or double virgules with an occasional period. A page in the penultimate section or fold looks as if it might once have contained three columns of text, but these appear

6. Page in Myung Mi Kim, *River Antes*, 2006. Courtesy Atticus/Finch Chapbooks, designed by Michael Cross.

to have been cut up or shattered so that only three words have no letters or parts of letters missing. Not arranged in straight lines, the broken columns or shattered words, when viewed as a single page design, give the impression of a delicate word cloud, floating in the space of the page (see fig. 7).

While there is no entirely regular system to the visual arrangement or construction of *River Antes*, the general effect is of careful order created in and with generous, quiet space. What I call the visual text—the visual elements that may be used by readers to discern expressivist meaning—creates a sense of harmony, even serenity. The sheer beauty of the book, with its heavy, cream-colored paper, lovely muted shades, and clean typeface, is likely to generate a kind of reverence in handling that prompts a deeply pleasurable savoring of the tangible and visible object. This sense of almost ceremonial harmony is reinforced particularly in the second half of the book through the slow pace of reading determined by the reader's having to take the time to unfold and refold pages, while making choices about what to read first and what to re-cover. The reading of the folds generates an awareness of options that may always be available to readers but are obscured by convention. The options are neither overwhelming in number nor irreversible, so they further add to the pleasure of reading. Here, it's clear that one could as legitimately

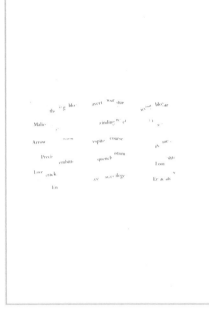

7. Page in Myung Mi Kim, *River Antes*, 2006. Courtesy Atticus/Finch Chapbooks, designed by Michael Cross.

read the opened folds from right to left as from left to right. And one is invited to try reading selectively, since a triptych can be partially folded so that only one of its pages with words, or one page with words and one with graphic marks, is visible. The reader experiences a gentle freedom in the material text's invitation to choose, to rearrange, to try different combinations, to reread in different arrangements.

Admittedly, there are some aspects of the visual text that suggest violence or disorder, repression or erasure. The exploded cloudlike page (fig. 7) might be one example; the words overwritten with other letters (fig. 5), or even the black paper of the inner cover and the prominent tie of the black string, might be others. The visual ambiguity of such elements precludes perception of a simple opposition between the visual and material aspects of the book on the one hand and the semantic character of its words on the other. Yet, overall, the careful harmonies and repetitions of the book's space-filled design, the necessarily slow speed with which one can read, and the almost serene order of the chapbook's cohesive visual patterns seem to me at odds with the verbal text, which is a disjunctive construction in which the language of war and aggression, social division, cultural fragmentation, and environmental degradation predominates.

The verbal text of *River Antes* is highly elliptical, and few pages convey a coherent narrative or unified thematics. Perhaps the broadest unity of the work is suggested by *antes* in the title: the poem as verbal text seems preoccupied with looking back to what has come before, both in individual and in more collective public history. Thus, the first half of the chapbook opens with the words "*household radix*," which, positioned unobtrusively in small italicized font at the bottom right-hand corner of the page, seem to function as a section title for pages that focus on historically prevalent social inequities, and particularly on women's constraint in domestic roles. The page following "*household radix*" begins:

[conjugate]

she, the weeping work
parade of earnings

I take the instruction to conjugate as an indication that we are to regard this scene as repeating over time—she performed the weeping work, she is performing the weeping work, she will perform the weeping work, and so on. Part of this work is child rearing:

: Why don't you take mommy swimming? It'll be fun—

He is not making rent.
She is tired of being alone with the child

The societies for which this particular conjugation is relevant privilege males: "within a few years it learns to read—if it is a boy—and in this place / the catalogue of books may be inserted[.]" The option to insert whatever catalog of books is appropriate again suggests that this general situation is widespread. Even when pages refer to a historically particular social system of hierarchy— as on the page that cites a tablet from 692 BC depicting prisoners working at a quarry (and approaching a river), a chariot pulled by servants, and war trophies that seem to include severed heads—the effect is of a historic scene that could with slight variation have been found in many cultures, time periods, and geographical locations. In biology, *radix* refers to a root or point of origin, and such scenes may be included here as sources for current realities. This may be part of what's suggested by the line "plethora of roots || mowed lawns" if we read the second phrase as pointing toward contemporary middle America. (The lines may also suggest a complexity covered over by the establishment's love of neat containment.) Presumably, one point of the attention in *River Antes* to "root" knowledge of what has gone before is that it enables a clearer view of the social structures and structures of knowledge we have seen Kim critique in *Commons*.

Within these generalized historical sketches, an "I" is glimpsed twice. The first time, this "I"—presumably female like the poet—depicts herself putting her own needs and interests second to those of others: "I am in the house / I clear the books, the many books, so others can eat // The children will play // corn | corncob[.]" The transformation of corn to bare cob shorn of its nourishing kernels suggests how this role can similarly consume the speaker's energy and resources. The other representation of the "I" in this first half of the collection is introduced by a page on which appears, in small font on the lower right (as with "*household radix*"), the word "*fell.*" Perhaps it signals a fall from an Edenic childhood innocence, for on the next page the first-person speaker is isolated and grieving, perhaps mourning the death of her father: "I go to my father's house / I wear a grief hat / I am told to put on coarse hemp and to proceed on my own[.]" (My impulse to read these lines in terms of the death of the father is no doubt influenced by my knowing that Kim's father was killed in a car accident only a few years after her family had immigrated to the United States.) If it seems plausible that this first-person speaker goes to her father's house to mark his death, this depiction of personal loss complicates the critique of patriarchy suggested elsewhere. Her roots or radices lie in her father's household, and proceeding on her own is part of her mourning, a form of suffering, not liberation. If one finds no suggestion that the grief hat signals the death of the father—if, for instance, one sees the father sending her off on her own, banishing her to adulthood as Adam and Eve were banished with their fall—it is still clear that the situation is one of mourning and of a consequent isolation and exile.

Those words about the grief hat, the coarse hemp, and proceeding "on my own" are the last words before the folds begin. If we regard the book as a metaphorical river that flows generally in one direction, then the section of folds that follows might track the speaker's solitary journey, her attempt to confront and understand not only her personal losses but also the social dynamics of the cultures from which she comes and from which she feels alienated. By constructing the visual and material text as something that has data literally hidden inside folds, which may then be refolded, perhaps so as to change what was originally encountered, Kim (with Michael Cross) has created a text in which the reader has to imitate the poet's search for her own understanding, her own path for proceeding. The folds, then, which clearly defamiliarize the reading process, encouraging unusual ways of processing text and heightening awareness of both the materiality of the text and ("politically suspect") conventions of literary composition or comprehension, may also have a mimetic function. One begins to appreciate the expressivist significance of the book's cover design: the reader initially encounters a light gray cover and has to look to find the stark black one within. Similarly, the folds may suggest a process of intellectual or psychological quest, wherein one has to take action to get beyond what is initially evident, or where one perhaps has to don one's "grief hat" and confront painful losses or forms of destruction.

Let us take such action and seek out the meanings to be found in the verbal text within the folds. Meaning is not easy to locate here, since asyntactic arrays of words predominate. These arrays seem to suggest multiple narratives, which is to say that the words function as shifting aggregates, related together but not in any fixed or clearly bounded way. These shadow narratives convey to me a sense of varied, often violent actions. Consider, for instance, this page from the first fold:

spar wanton drear dear forbid || hold facing simple adore one

regard ally press fray reason || rest cleft hold avarice swift

rights tie wallow heaving cause ||

While many of these words could be verbs, they certainly do not convey any single story. In attempting to find meaning, we can note that a number of the words—such as *spar, press, ally*, and *fray*—might suggest conflict and struggle, perhaps in a situation of war. This verbal array might lead a reader to imagine situations of desperate action involving swift flight or pursuit, though it's equally possible to discern (in terms like *drear, hold, tie*) a situation of dismal imprisonment as well as glimmers of love and caring (*hold, adore, rest*). For me, the disjunctive realms evoked by the words convey a sense of disparate situations, emotions, and actions coexisting in a kind of chaos. That is to say, the tenor of the verbal text differs dramatically from that of the generally stately and harmonious visual matter.

The words on the next page to the right are less chaotic, but again one encounters varied actions, now in a vertical list of ten past-tense verbs that appear beneath a bracketed line—"[_____ years and ____ months]"—a space in which to designate some duration for phenomena or experiences that presumably could last varied periods of time. More clearly than the words on the preceding page, the verbs here suggest actions likely to involve collectivities such as tribes or nations. These are verbs one might find in reportage on American military actions in Iraq, for instance, though they designate widespread processes of social change such as diaspora, immigration, conquest, colonization: "Restored / Crossed / Led / Captured / Implemented /

Confronted / Launched / Removed / Spread / Stabilized[.]" These larger social developments provide a context within which we briefly glimpse the first-person speaker once more—in the left-hand side of the triptych—perhaps as a child under an adult's watch: "An elder (old tailor) needle ear threading keeping eyes on us[.]"

This particular triptych is typical of the folds in suggesting a consideration of the forces behind both social change and stability, particularly in a context of military violence. In some of the other folds, the preoccupation with military conflict and invasion is more explicit, as in lines such as "Operations rush first wave shield," "bunker buster bomb," "you are now leaving the American sector," or "Fighting house by house / You saw it and you heard it?" Sometimes—as was the case also in *Commons*—environmental devastation is alluded to, as in "Cobalt Incident" or "when the fish are killed at once / and appear on the banks all at once." Overall, the tenor of the words is far from tranquil.

Up to this point, I have proposed a reading of *River Antes* as a confrontation with painful aspects of the past—which may include the very recent past leading to the present—a past both private and public, individual and collective. I have suggested that the folds, a key part of the innovative visual text, might in part figure elements in individual or collective experience that can be approached in varied ways but require some effort to discern or are painful to confront. I have also suggested that the ample blank space associated especially with the folds, combined with the repeating visual patterns of orderly textual arrangement, creates a counter tone of serenity.

What are we to make of this tension? I would contend that a crucial function of the visual text in *River Antes* is to model ethical modes of individual behavior and social interaction alternative to those that are evident in history, or in the recent news. The very form of the text suggests a need for calm, for patient and careful attention, and for an openness to alternative arrangements as one attempts to "proceed on [one's] own"—that is, to proceed without imitating the problematic behaviors of one's antecedents or one's contemporaries that have led to war, dislocation, unnecessary suffering, and environmental disaster. The open spaces of the textual arrangement of *River Antes*, then, are expressivist models of a mindful exploration and creative openness, as well as material erasures of politically suspect conventions. The visible spaces of *River Antes* become an expressivist image for the space of art itself, especially of experimental art: a potentially ethical space in which to contemplate, to come to terms, to reassemble, to find new paths, to create new modes of representation. Appreciating both this hopeful view and the challenges it must encounter requires expanding Kim's poetics of the aggregate to encompass the entire text as a composite verbal/visual entity, allowing its visual and verbal elements their separate substance while also reading them as bound to one another.

The final lines of the penultimate fold suggest a comparable negotiation as they reinforce an optimistic view of the future while also conveying a somber warning. They read, "Grass grew from the sternum / Roots took over the mandible[.]" That grass grows in the spaces where the body once was, in the spaces between the bones, suggests the potential fruitfulness of a quest willing to face the grievous costs of past modes of behavior and to substitute other forms of life. Space—emotional, intellectual, and material—is crucial to this generation of new life, new ways. At the same time, the image of roots taking over the jawbone has a double valence: if the innocent life form of grass is taking over a part of the skeleton associated with rapaciousness and aggression, that is surely a hopeful vision; but the jaw is also necessary to speech, and it has been silenced. Moreover, the word *roots*, associated with *radix* and with the past, is also a reminder of how much what precedes us mitigates against such rebirth and just how difficult it will be to escape from what the text calls "River's fray." Such complications are, of course, part of the value of this art that avoids simple polarities or easy claims to superior sight. Without proffering simplistic solutions to the complex problems of contemporary social space, Kim has made visible space legible in *River Antes* in such a way that the open spaces and the differing verbal and semantic combinations they allow provide her reader with ethical alternatives to the modes of action and perception responsible for the devastations that dominate recent history.

eight*eight*

CODA

Thinking On

PERHAPS THE OBAMA AND POST-OBAMA YEARS in the United States will offer a more receptive cultural climate for complex thinking than what has been experienced by intellectuals, writers, artists, and scholars in the recent past. Whether that will be so remains to be seen, but in any case forward-looking poets in the decades to come are likely to feel a continuing, no less urgent need to push toward fresh ways of engaging in complex thinking in and through the forms of their art. Digging out from the many messes in which we find ourselves in the post-Bush era will require escape from the habits of language and thought that have kept us asking versions of the same questions and offering essentially the same answers. That is one reason for the continued relevance of exploratory poetry as a cultural and intellectual enterprise. In her 2007 essay "What Is Experimental Poetry & Why Do We Need It?" Joan Retallack explains, "A poetics that can operate in the interrogative, with epistemological curiosity and ethical concern, is not so much language as instrument to peer through as instrument of investigative engagement. As such it takes part in the recomposing of contemporary consciousness, contemporary sensibilities."

Although it is beyond my powers to imagine what new questions might emerge from such explorations, the work of the poets examined in the preceding chapters—both what I have discussed and what they have published more recently—suggests some of the issues likely to remain in focus. Poets are sure to continue grappling, for instance, with the implications of print and digital production in an increasingly digital world, just as they will be testing further the visual resources of the printed page to find where those two-dimensional resources falter. The Web is already opening possibilities for integration of visual images and sound elements with print text, in addition to increasingly sophisticated forms of mobile and interactive textuality. Whether digital media will dramatically expand the readership for poetry or discourage the kind of attention poetry requires will depend on many factors, but poets' approaches to this technology will surely figure among them.

Issues of gender and its relevance to cultural production are likely to remain subjects of keen debate in this purportedly postfeminist era, just as race will remain a fraught category for poets both to mine and to challenge in what some regard as a postracial time. Identity politics surrounding ethnicity, race, and gender contributed to the ascendency of personal lyric in the 1970s and thereafter. Consequently, issues of social identity are likely to inflect continuing debates concerning the viability of lyric, particularly its ability to respond to the changed understandings of subjectivity and language derived from poststructuralism as well as to changed understandings of the human emerging from science and from posthumanist discourse. The current revival of lyric studies suggests that some of the renewed interest in lyric will be retrospective in its focus. Nevertheless, work such as Fulton's exploring throughout *Felt* (2001) the dissolution of "the intergown of difference / severing self from = = nonself" (17) or Wheeler's edgy overlapping of financial and religious language in *Ledger*'s lyrics points in more prospective directions. At the same time, the markedly varied ways in which poets such as Waldrop (as in *Blindsight*, 2003) or Swensen (as in *The Glass Age*, 2007) continue to manipulate the prose poem, as well as continued uses of proceduralism by Waldrop, Retallack, and others, suggest that the drive to generate alternatives to lyric, and even to collage-based poetic construction, is far from exhausted.

As is evident from C.D. Wright's recent ventures into a collaged form of social documentary in *One Big Self: Prisoners of Louisiana* (2003) and into an agonized version of political reportage concerning the war in Iraq and other disasters of capitalist imperialism in *Rising, Falling, Hovering* (2008), poets will continue to employ poetry as a means to raise political consciousness. And they will do so while arguing among themselves about the relative efficacy of various artistic approaches to public politics. (In Wright's recent volumes, the powers of poetry emerge as tremendously important, since "the first task is to recover the true words for being" [*Rising* 28], which poetry can do, and also starkly limited: "Poetry / Doesn't / Protect / You / Anymore" [59]). Multilinguistic texts—an area into which Kim was beginning to venture in *Commons* and that might also come to mind in relation to Waldrop's and Swensen's extensive work as translators—may provide one forum for invention that keeps abreast of our globalizing situation.

Taking complex ethical issues as the terrain of poetry, poets in the coming years will be grappling with the implications of scientific advances in such fields as genomic research and biotechnology. They are likely to play a particularly visible role in environmental debates in this era of global environmental crisis; poetry's long association with nature and nature's sublimity has paved the way for this engagement. Retallack, for instance, perhaps responding to environmentalists' calls for less anthropocentric discourse, has begun to advocate a "poetics of reciprocal alterity"—that is, a poetics in which the imagination does not simply inhabit the supposedly empty spaces of otherness, but in which alterity has opportunities to "speak back." In her view, proceduralism remains a resource here, because it can assist the poet in following John Cage's principle of attempting to imitate not nature's appearance but rather nature's processes or manner of operation. Jonathan Skinner's journal *ecopoetics* is one place where one can already see some radical reinventions of nature poetry that resist the traditional dichotomizing of urban/rural, wild/civilized, and animal/human as they, in Retallack's words, "reinvestigat[e] our species' relation to other inhabitants of the fragile and finite territory our species named, claimed, exploited, sentimentalized, and aggrandized as 'our world'" (Retallack, "What Is Experimental Poetry?"). Given that renaming, in a broad sense, will be fundamental to such reinvestigation, the exploratory poet has a key role to play.

The challenges faced by those currently aspiring to produce thinking poetry are immense. How can they effectively resist the always powerful forces of conformity and complacency, and manage to "surprise the mind's dumb regularity" (Fraser, *Translating* 10)? Will they be able to reinvent not only their own idioms but the languages of globalized communities? Will they succeed in pointing, in a time of scarce resources, to social arrangements that will direct humankind beyond war, beyond unsustainable consumerism, beyond violent tribalism and nationalism? And can they do so while still attending carefully to the local and particular, long counted among poetry's special strengths? Will they be able to expose the layers of incoherence and inconsistency, the rigidities of received thinking, while enabling us to remember and learn from the past?

The poets examined in the preceding chapters have resisted narrow definitions of poetic camps, courageously pursuing their own alternative ways of thinking with the poetic page. Their examples, and the history they represent, suggest that our best hope of approaching these meaningful goals—however partially, provisionally, or fleetingly—lies not just in an expansion of poetic strategies and forms but also in a diversification of poetic groups. Complementing such diversity, we need a critical discourse that resists the temptation to plug in old historical or stylistic categories routinely or to invent new pigeonholes for critical convenience. To recognize fully the accomplishments of thinking poetry in the future, we who read poetry will have to do our best to embrace it with our own equally complex thinking.

NOTES

1. Thinking Poetry

1. Early anthologies such as *The L=A=N=G=U=A=G=E Book*, edited by Bruce Andrews and Charles Bernstein, *"Language" Poetries*, edited by Douglas Messerli, and *In the American Tree*, edited by Ron Silliman, provide excellent introductions to Language writing. A number of Language poets, including Bruce Andrews, Rae Armantrout, Charles Bernstein, Lyn Hejinian, Steve McCaffery, Ron Silliman, and Barrett Watten, have by now published collections of essays elaborating their poetics. For books of criticism on Language poetry, see George Hartley, *Textual Politics and the Language Poets*; Bob Perelman, *The Marginalization of Poetry: Language Poetry and Literary History*; Megan Simpson, *Poetic Epistemologies: Gender and Knowing in Women's Language-Oriented Writing*; and Ann Vickery, *Leaving Lines of Gender: A Feminist Genealogy of Language Writing*. Marjorie Perloff, the first critic to bring Language writing to the attention of the academic world, has continued to write insightfully on the subject. In *Differentials* she presents as the "animating principle of the movement: poetic language is not a window, to be seen through, a transparent glass pointing to something outside it, but a system of signs with its own semiological 'interconnectedness.' To put it another way, 'Language is material and primary and what's experienced is the tension and relationship of letters and lettristic clusters, simultaneously struggling towards, yet refusing to become, significations' (Supplement 2)" (158).

2. In an interview published electronically in 2002, after acknowledging that "the borders were never clear" and "a number of poets who would never have wanted the label—Michael Palmer, Leslie Scalapino, Susan Howe for instance—have now been called Language Writers," Bob Perelman provides a useful listing of the key figures: "There were two major groupings with friendships and correspondence in between. . . . The Bay Area scene included [Ron] Silliman, [Barrett] Watten, Lyn Hejinian, Carla Harryman, Steven Benson, Rae Armantrout, Kit Robinson, Tom Mandel, Alan Bernheimer, [Robert] Grenier and myself. Silliman and Watten met in the 1960s, but

most of us met in the 1970s. Grenier and Watten started the magazine *This* in 1971. A while later, the New York scene coalesced around Bruce Andrews, Charles Bernstein, Ray DiPalma, Alan Davies, and Steve McCaffery" ("Ten to Ten"). That list includes thirteen men and three women. In a 1982 essay, "Partial Local Coherence," Kathleen Fraser provides a longer list of names often seen in "Language Writing journals," dividing them into categories of West Coast, East Coast (twenty-seven, with seven of them women), and affiliates "tangential to and preceding" Language writing (fourteen, of whom four are women) (*Translating* 74).

3. The introductory chapter of Linda A. Kinnahan's *Lyric Interventions: Feminism, Experimental Poetry, and Contemporary Discourse* is particularly useful in this context, as are Kathleen Fraser's essay "The Tradition of Marginality" (*Translating* 25–38) and Rachel Blau DuPlessis's "For the Etruscans" (*Pink Guitar* 1–19). Other valuable work on recent experimental writing by women that does not center on Language poetry per se includes DuPlessis, *The Pink Guitar: Writing as Feminist Practice* and *Blue Studios: Poetry and Its Cultural Work*; Steve Evans, ed., *After Patriarchal Poetry: Feminism and the Contemporary Avant-Garde* (a special issue of *differences*); Elisabeth Frost, *The Feminist Avant-Garde in American Poetry*; Elisabeth Frost and Cynthia Hogue, eds., *Innovative Women Poets: An Anthology of Contemporary Poems and Interviews*; Laura Hinton and Cynthia Hogue, eds., *We Who Love to Be Astonished: Experimental Women's Writing and Performative Poetics*; and Deborah Mix, *A Vocabulary of Thinking: Gertrude Stein and Contemporary North American Women's Innovative Writing*.

4. The version of this essay published in *Translating the Unspeakable* revises these sentences as follows: "While the structural preoccupations of language-centered theory and practice are stimulating and concretely useful, the aesthetic distaste for *any* self-referentiality introduces (yet again) the concept of prohibition. For a writer whose awareness has been tuned by the growing need to claim her own history and present tense, Language Writing's directives are often encountered—if not intended—as the newest covenant" (76).

5. Similarly, Oren Izenberg, in an essay published in 2003, speaks of the "ever-widening appeal of a Language-informed poetics and the energy with which it has charged the scene of contemporary poetry" ("Language Poetry" 132). The Language-influenced work discussed in this book, however, does not produce the "peculiar anaesthetic boredom" that Izenberg finds characteristic of Language writing, which in his analysis is "uninteresting . . . on principle" (157, 158).

6. The first of the original Language poets to serve as chancellor for the Academy of American Poets is Lyn Hejinian, whose term began in 2006. However, noted experimentalists began to serve in 1999 when Michael Palmer became chancellor, followed in 2000 by Susan Howe and in 2001 by Nathaniel Mackey.

7. See, for example, Steve Evans's impassioned piece, "The Resistible Rise of Fence Enterprises," published in his blog *Third Factory*. Evans deplores what he terms the journal's "ideology of merge and market" and the "vacuity" of its editorial stance, identifying the four historical conditions fostering its emergence ca. 1997 as follows: "first, the deepening erosion of intellectual and practical resistance to incursions of

market logic into social relations where they have no place (i.e. reification); second, the aging, routinizing, and reductive stereotyping (from within and from without) of language-centered writing, and with it—by virtue of an illegitimate but effective conflation—the avant-garde project as a whole; third, a generational crisis within the dominant poetic establishment that, notwithstanding its continued monopoly of institutional power, can no longer command the respect, allegiance, or even attention of much of their captive audience of MFA candidates; and, fourth, the glaring absence of any regularly appearing journal capable of rearticulating radical poetic values within the much altered circumstance of post-1989 global capitalism." Evans's controversial essay and the lively responses it generated are collected in Evans, *Third Factory*.

8. My scare quotes around *mainstream*, necessary because it is hard to say with certainty what the dominant conventions are now, mark another area where critical awareness and terminology fail to keep up with rapid developments in poetry. "Scenic mode" is Charles Altieri's term, central to his argument about poetry of the 1970s in *Self and Sensibility in Contemporary American Poetry*.

9. Kinnahan's book traces the history of that wrestling—that struggle to find viable positions somewhere between the I-focused personal lyric and the banishment of the subject—and offers more open models of reading female poets' reconceptualizations of subjectivity.

10. The anthology with that subtitle, coedited by one of the conference organizers, Claudia Rankine, had its beginnings in that conference at Barnard College.

11. Among the poets treated here, Swensen and Waldrop are represented in *Lyric Postmodernisms*, while Fulton, Kim, Waldrop, Wheeler, and Wright appear in *American Hybrid*. Only Retallack is not included in either one.

12. A further distortion sometimes evident in such anthologies and stemming from the desire to collapse received binaries involves appropriating into the "new" category ("hybrid" or "lyric postmodernist") work that on formal or historical grounds doesn't really belong there. For instance—something Alan Golding called to my attention—early poems by Rae Armantrout, one of the ten writers producing the collective autobiography of the Language writing scene between 1975 and 1980, *The Grand Piano*, are included in *American Hybrid*. While Armantrout's usually short poems have garnered a broader audience than the work of most Language writers, attempting to shift them from being Language writing to being "hybrid" works speaks to changes in the institutions surrounding poetry but says little that's meaningful about the texts.

13. Perhaps their lack of interest in group identification and their failure to fit into a dramatically polarized critical narrative help account for how little commentary there has been on their work compared to, say, that of Adrienne Rich, Audre Lorde, or more recently Sharon Olds on the one hand, and Lyn Hejinian or Susan Howe on the other. An online search of the MLA International Bibliography on January 2, 2009, using the "author as subject" option gives a sense of the academic attention these poets have enjoyed: Rich, 344 entries; Lorde, 175; Olds, 31; Hejinian, 57; Howe, 88. In contrast, search results for the poets in this book, from greatest number to

least, are as follows: Waldrop, 23 entries; Wright, 12; Kim, Fulton, and Retallack, 9 each; Wheeler, 7; Swensen, 3.

14. Wright uses her initials as her name, and consequently most of her published work does not put a space after the C. Although neither her own publications nor the criticism concerning them is consistent on this matter, I have chosen to follow the example of her recent books and give her name as C.D. Wright.

15. Stephen Burt's identification in 1998 of a few of these poets and a number of others as a "post-avant-gardist" school he dubs "Ellipticism" seems to me arbitrary and without basis in the social formations, publishing networks, and poetic manifestos associated with genuine "schools" such as the original New York School or Black Mountain (Burt, Rev. of *Smokes*). In describing "Elliptical books," he may well be capturing some traits of what we might appropriately think of as a period style, but his claims for a school seem little more than a publicity stunt.

16. One interesting debate about the relation of women and minorities to literary conventions and experimental forms, conducted by Leslie Scalapino and Ron Silliman, can be found in Silliman and Scalapino, "What/Person: From an Exchange." Scalapino objects to claims Silliman made in a 1988 issue of *Socialist Review* that the historical position of people who are marginal means that they need to have their stories told so that their writing often appears more conventional.

17. Perloff, when considering the relation of innovation to theory and how for poststructuralist theorists "new" was an adjective applied from the outside, observes: "Accordingly—and this is an important aspect of the Language movement, which stands squarely behind so much of contemporary 'innovative' poetry—the 'new' rapprochement between poetry and theory that we find in the first issues of L=A=N=G=U=A=G=E (1978), and in such equally important journals as the San Francisco-based *This* and *Hills*, and the Canadian *Open Letter*—all these now a quarter-century old—had less to do with innovation per se than with the conviction on the part of a group of poets, themselves keenly interested in philosophy and poststructuralist theory, that poetics was an intellectual enterprise" (*Differentials* 157).

18. I could just as well have used as an example of theory-phobic rejection of intellectually challenging poetry the more recent "Advice for Graduating MFA Students in Writing: The Words & the Bees," published by the executive director of the AWP, D. W. Fenza, in the summer 2006 issue of the *Writer's Chronicle*. Among Fenza's nine directives, all couched in terms of the life of bees, the one given the most space is "3. Beware the Ichneumonids"—a section in which "literary theorists and cultural critics" (the "tenured class" of academics) and the Language poets are figured as deadly parasitic wasps who undermine poetry's chief task, "the accurate description of our society" (3, 2). There Fenza characterizes Charles Bernstein's approach to poetics as "morally repugnant" and ends the section by warning new MFAs to avoid alliances with "the ichneumonids [who] have nested in your shire" (4). I chose not to discuss Fenza's essay in view of the buckets of ink already spilled arguing about it and Bernstein's parodic response, particularly in the long stream of comments following from Reginald Shepherd's criticism of Bernstein in his blog. Anyone interested can track this exchange in Shepherd's blog and his entries in the Poetry Foundation blog,

Harriet, beginning with and following "AWP, Communazis, and Me" (28 Jan. 2008 in *Harriet*, <http://poetryfoundation.org/harriet/2008/01/awp_communazis_and_ me_1.html#more>).

19. Kirsch's view of proper allusion as drawing upon a common literary tradition is one that T. S. Eliot, for instance, would certainly have shared, but the need for extensive glosses on Eliot's references suggests its anachronism. Many of my undergraduate students would find the allusions that "deepen" Kirsch's understanding to be instead baffling and exclusive, indeed discourteous. Although those of us who teach may hope to expand the younger generations' knowledge of the literary traditions we know and thereby make allusions to them more accessible, the constant change that our "common" traditions are undergoing surely complicates an argument like his.

20. Kirsch makes complexity synonymous with a willful difficulty, seeing that difficulty as motivated largely by a self-indulgent desire to stand out. As I hope is clear, I believe he misrepresents the motivation for the kinds of complexity found in the work examined in this book. (And complexity, which sometimes overlaps with difficulty but should be distinguished from it, has long been a fundamental value in poetry.) However, there are different kinds of difficulty, and he and I would agree that there exists contemporary writing in which the difficulty seems gratuitous or motivated only by a desire to seem fashionable.

21. One of the important books launching this recent scholarly trend, though without a particular gender focus, was *Experimental—Visual—Concrete: Avant-Garde Poetry Since the 1960s*, edited by K. David Jackson, Eric Vos, and Johanna Drucker in 1996. Kathleen Fraser's essay of the same year, "Translating the Unspeakable: Visual Poetics, as Projected through Olson's 'Field' into Current Female Writing Practice" carried on from the visual interests of her earlier essay "Line. On the Line. Lining Up. Lined With. Between the Lines. Bottom Line" (1988) and pointed toward specifically female writers' uses of the visual page (collected in *Translating the Unspeakable*). Rachel Blau DuPlessis, Craig Dworkin, Elisabeth Frost, Alan Golding, and I are among those who have recently written about visual poetics and contemporary female poets. There has also been a revival of critical interest in ekphrastic writing, prompted in part by the work of W. J. T. Mitchell, particularly in *Iconology* (1986).

22. See Swensen, "Against the Limits of Language: The Geometries of Anne-Marie Albiach and Susan Howe." Prompted by Swensen's essay, I have discussed her volume *Oh* using a fractal model in "Singing Spaces: Fractal Geometries in Cole Swensen's *Oh*." Fractal form is something that both Retallack and Fulton have frequently discussed in their prose, though their understandings of how this mathematical concept translates into poetry diverge. Fulton's two essays on that subject are included in *Feeling as a Foreign Language*. Retallack's frequent references to the fractal (and fractal poetics, our fractal brains, etc.) are more scattered; for her, "Deterministic chaos, fractal geometries give us new images by redefining relationships between order and disorder, pattern and unpredictability, the finite and the infinite" (*Poethical Wager* 27). In chapter 4, I discuss Retallack's "Icarus FFFFFalling" in terms of fractal form.

23. The dissertation Waldrop wrote for the doctorate she received from the University of Michigan in 1966 was, as its subtitle announces, a study of "dissatisfaction

with language as theme and as impulse towards experiments in twentieth century poetry" (Waldrop, *Against Language?*).

24. A key date would be the 1984 publication in *American Poetry Review* of Perloff's "The Word as Such: L=A=N=G=U=A=G=E Poetry in the Eighties."

2. Ink of Eyes and Veins and Phonemes

1. This statement is one Wright tinkered with over the years so that it has appeared in slightly differing versions. The excerpt reproduced here is from *Cooling Time* (2005). The earlier version collected in Peter Baker's *Onward* (1996) is more terse: it does not include, for instance, "of one's own faith in the word" or the sentence "I believe words are golden as goodness is golden." One significant change in the *Cooling Time* version is the substitution of the word "finality" for what had initially been "closure." As noted below, the earlier use of "closure" suggests that Wright may have been drawing upon Lyn Hejinian's essay "Rejection of Closure."

2. The quotations from Hirsch are taken from my own transcriptions of a tape made by a Breadloaf student who attended the talk and the question period that followed. His vehemence reflects the high political stakes within the poetry scene (publishing opportunities, critical attention, awards and fellowships, teaching positions, etc.) of establishing affinities and oppositions.

3. For instance, Language writers at the Barnard conference "Where Lyric Tradition Meets Language Poetry: Innovation in Contemporary American Poetry by Women" in the spring of 1999 were uncomfortable with Brenda Hillman's presentation of her poems in *Loose Sugar* as combining lyric in the top portion of the page with Language writing at the bottom. While the Language writers themselves have recently been attacked for assimilating into the academy, they have at the same time been distressed to see aspects of their own politically motivated work appropriated into writing that seems fundamentally aligned with the literary conventions they so vehemently rejected. Language writers have not to my knowledge criticized C.D. Wright or perceived her as one of those superficially adopting some Language techniques, perhaps to obtain cultural cachet; Ron Silliman, for one, has admired her work for years.

4. The essays collected by Mark Wallace and Steven Marks in *Telling It Slant: Avant-Garde Poetries of the 1990s* suggest that a number of younger experimentalists in that decade are also interested in combining the resources of multiple traditions of which Language writing and the tradition it claims (of Stein, Zukofsky, etc.) is only one. See, for instance, the contributions by Mark Wallace and Juliana Spahr. That young poets training in mainstream AWP programs also appear to be moving away from the personal lyric norms reflects the pervasive influence of Language writing, but not necessarily their firsthand knowledge of Language work.

5. In an interview from 2001, Wright declared, "[O]f all the Language poets Silliman's express-line writing was and is the one that stuck to my ribs. It was so thingy, so specific, so formally radical, so hard-headed, yet witty, and now and then, in spite of itself, lyric. I liked his post-industrial music. I loved *Ketjak* and *Tjanting* and *Para-*

dise. . . . And the reach—the compulsion to pull everything in. What attracted me most about the Language poets was their big-headed endeavor to overhaul the language. What most repelled me was, by my lights, their collective snobbishness." She subsequently resists listing other San Francisco poets to whom her work is indebted, claiming her list "wouldn't make sense to anyone else" ("Looking").

6. Michael Greer, for one, has criticized Silliman's monolithic rendering of capitalism in this early essay: "The commodification of language is nearly total or thoroughgoing; popular culture, most notably, is wholly co-opted or colonized. *Only* certain avant-garde texts, in Silliman's view, offer spaces of possible resistance" (Greer 348).

7. Silliman's relation to realism is complicated. In "Disappearance of the Word, Appearance of the World," he asserts that the most complete expression of "the increasing transparency of language" that took place over a period of 400 years is "in the genre of fictional realism," adding that "it is the disappearance of the word that lies at the heart of the invention of the illusion of realism and the breakdown of gestural poetic form" (*New Sentence* 11, 12). However, his strong interest in exploring nonnaive, nonnaturalized approaches to realism is apparent in his work, and is also suggested by his giving the title "REALISM" to the anthology of Language writing he assembled for *Ironwood* and by his subtitling *In the American Tree: Language, Realism, Poetry.*

8. In a 1994 interview Wright claims that her Arkansas "homeplace" "protects me from being assimilated as a person and a writer. In a way, that's my signature—that I come from an unassimilable place" ("Bedrock" 1).

9. One way to characterize the difference between a poem like "The Lesson" and *Tjanting* would be via Wright's interest in documentary. James Agee is another influence on her work, and of course the documentary tradition in America has, until quite recently, concentrated on the rural life and folk traditions that are so fundamental for her. Thus, she admires Philip Booth's writing as "a poetry made without exaggeration, without distortion of the life being lived or the utterance it supports. It is writing for the record. And a part of it" ("Reading Relations" 207). As noted above, many of her early poems in particular document the emotional hardships—the loneliness, violence, entrapment—of particular Ozark lives. *One Big Self* is her most evidently documentary work to date, though documentary elements figure also in *Deepstep Come Shining* (to my mind, her greatest work to date) and *Rising, Falling, Hovering.*

10. In "Arguments with the Gestapo Continued: Literary Resistance" (1984) Wright criticizes the "literary sectarianism" of a passage from Silliman's introduction to this anthology, showing that she was acquainted with this issue of *Ironwood* (33), a journal in which she herself had published in 1981. Fraser directed the Poetry Center at San Francisco State from 1972 to 1975; when Wright worked there, the director was Frances Mayes.

11. The version of this essay printed in Fraser's collection of essays, *Translating the Unspeakable,* revises this passage.

12. Jenny Goodman's *Dictionary of Literary Biography* entry on Wright and her essay "Politics and the Personal Lyric in the Poetry of Joy Harjo and C.D. Wright"

have contributed importantly to my understanding of Wright's poetry. In the latter essay, Goodman argues that the personal poetry of Harjo and Wright "is not circumscribed by the limits of the private poem as we commonly know it: the recounting of a personal experience authenticated by the poet's 'I,' with its isolated individual voice, its grief for a closed-off past that can no longer be reached, and its limited range of diction and form" (40). Her valuable essay examines their "innovative combinations of experimental poetics, political statement, and autobiographical lyric" (40). The chapter at hand complements her work by elaborating further on the experimental dimensions of Wright's poetry and by showing the extent to which Wright draws upon Language aesthetics.

13. Wright has explained her not contributing to Fraser's journal *HOW(ever)*, which "was started in part as a response to what some saw as a feminist isolation for the inner circle of L=A=N=G=U=A=G=E poetry. I didn't attempt to contribute to *HOW(ever)* not because I didn't feel outside, or because I didn't identify with feminism, but because I preferred finished work, and they were committed to more provisional stages of publication" ("Looking").

14. I take the figure of grafting from Wright's "Like Peaches," a poem that seems to me key to the aesthetics of the volume in which it appears, *Tremble*. In that collection, which followed *Just Whistle*, Wright focused on innovation in the context of specifically lyric tradition. However, the notion of the poet as gardener-inventor, deliberately bringing together diverse types to generate new species—artificial products of human ingenuity, but still recognizably trees—applies as well to the artist of *Just Whistle*.

15. The following, from "Provisional Remarks On Being / A Poet / Of Arkansas," is typical of Wright's numerous statements about the importance of narrative for poetry: "Narrative is. You have to know when to enter in, when to egress, when to provoke, when to let be, be. However, narrative is overly identified with southern poetry; it is a global condition not a literary convention. Poets should be willing to exploit the rind of narrativity, and be more than willing to be lost at the heart" (810).

16. Wright's quest for new understandings of the body and body-centered understandings of subjectivity is evident not only in *Just Whistle* (in which the opening words are "The body") but also in her subsequent volumes, *Tremble* (as I discussed in a paper delivered at the 1999 Twentieth-Century Literature Conference at the University of Louisville) and *Deepstep Come Shining*.

17. Because the text of *Just Whistle* is most easily available in Wright's book of selected poems, *Steal Away*, page numbers refer to that edition. The original Kelsey Street edition is well worth seeking out, however, because of its inclusion of photographs created by Deborah Luster specifically for the poem. Moreover, the visual effects of the small press text are quite different, since there is more space between lines and many passages that appear with ragged right-hand margins in *Steal Away* have right-justified margins in the Kelsey Street version. That is to say, the later version respects the lineation of the earlier one, even though the page space no longer appears to determine that arrangement. Wright has assured me, however (e-mail dated 28 July 2008), that the passages that appear as right-justified prose in the Kelsey

Street version are indeed prose, though printed in *Steal Away* without right justification. The visual impression of dense blocks of text created by the later version is not created in the original edition. In quoting prose passages from *Just Whistle* in this chapter, I have not attempted to reproduce their visual appearance in either edition.

18. In *Tremble* (1996), Wright similarly interrogates conventions surrounding lyric voice and, particularly in poems with titles beginning "Like," simile.

19. I use *piece* to designate a unit of text in this extended poem, which is organized with one piece per page; in the original printing the pieces are formatted to be clearly distinguished as prose or lineated poetry.

20. In "Politics and the Personal Lyric in the Poetry of Joy Harjo and C.D. Wright," Goodman, also noting that the reader of the conventional personal poem is "a kind of voyeur" (35), argues similarly using a poem from *String Light* that it "challenges readers who expect the poem to be a window onto the poet's life; it continually calls attention to poetry itself, including its own presentation, as a construct" (45). In that earlier collection, the extreme heterogeneity of diction evident in *Just Whistle* and subsequent volumes was not among Wright's reflexive techniques.

21. My reading of *Just Whistle* may impose a false narrative coherence, insufficiently respecting the nonlinearity of this text that overlays multiple sorts of sexual wounds and multiple heterosexual relationships, and in which a number of sections do not advance the narrative. My perception of a strong narrative shape to the whole seems, however, confirmed by Wright's published comment that by the time she wrote *Just Whistle*, she had realized, "I didn't have to tell a story per se: I could fracture it, I could dump a whole lot of stuff into it and it would still be there. The telling itself stays partly in my head but the poetry evidences a trace of a tale" (Holman, "Trace of a Tale" 20). Elsewhere in the same "investigative poem" assembled by Bob Holman, she characterizes her writing as "anchored by narrativity," which remains "intact" even while being "[t]otally mutable" (17).

22. Seventeen sections use page space and margins in ways that say "poetry," while twenty are prose. The poetry and prose sections are not as easy to distinguish from one another in the *Steal Away* printing; the latter appear in the original Kelsey Street publication as blocks with right and left margins justified. That Wright felt no need to maintain a sharp visual distinction in *Steal Away* further supports my point about the suppleness of genre distinctions here.

23. Communion is not stressed by Language writers, except to the extent that it might occur in the activity shared by reader and writer of constructing the poem's meaning. Earlier in her career, Wright made starker distinctions, seeing only her prose—that is, her essays—as being primarily "about language." In "Hills" she said of her own writing, "the prose serves language first and the poem [serves] story" (*Further Adventures* 12). "I've been held to that statement from 'Hills' longer than I could uphold it in practice or spirit," she declared in written correspondence with the author (28 February 1999).

24. Of course, Language writing varies considerably in the manner and extent of its reliance on conventional intelligibilities. Bob Perelman, for instance, made considerable use of narrative in his fake dream poems, published in *The Future of Memory*.

25. In Elizabeth Grosz's *Volatile Bodies*, this is the project of the concluding chapter, "Sexed Bodies."

26. When asked by Fraser about whether *crow* suggested either a male or a female presence, Wright replied, "I thought of it as maybe neither. It was very graphic and very dirty, yet totally ambiguous. It was a word to express strong feelings, very sexual feelings, negative but more importantly strong, naked feelings" (Wright, "Bedrock" 8).

27. The folk song tells of a woman who takes pleasure in kissing boys she happens to encounter. The lyrics' suggestion of sexual liaisons kept secret perhaps lends a more cynical cast to this allusion: "Gin a body meet a body / Comin frae the well; / Gin a body kiss a body, / Need a body tell? / Ilka lassie has her laddie, / Ne'er a ane ha'e I, / But a' te lads they smile at me, / When comin' thro' the rye" (*Scottish* 65).

28. The Gestapo of the title (adapted from Thomas Merton's 1940 novel *My Argument with the Gestapo*) is not Language writing or Silliman. The piece wrestles with the problematically limited cultural and social power granted the poet in American society, including its academic institutions, and meditates on how to take "politically responsive action . . . effective against our essential removal from American life" (87).

29. There's humor here as well, since an earlier section, "Desk Cuts"—in part a send-up of self-pitying, guitar-playing blues writers—contains the following: "If love is blind / And God is love / And Ray Charles is blind / Is Ray Charles The One" (113).

30. According to Bedient, members of the "soft avant-garde" tend to fall into "a language of gutted abstractions" as they "perform . . . disenchantment" (58). Their popular style involves "wits flayed, the mirror of representation splintered, the language jazzed," as they "[go] too intently for the peculiar" (59). "Hard-core avant-garde writing" today, Bedient says, is still associated with Language writing, which he characterizes (reductively) as "earnest with didacticism" and "mostly about its own assumptions and intentions" (58).

3. The Then Some inBetween

1. Rachel Blau DuPlessis usefully discusses the need for female poets to write "otherhow" in order to transform the gender narrative implicit in poetry in *The Pink Guitar* and "Manifests." The radical experimentalism of DuPlessis's own poems, like the exploratory poetics of the poets examined in this book, is bound up with the refusal of conventional inscriptions or configurations of gender.

2. The persistence of these defining categories is evident, for instance, in Christopher Beach's chapter in *Poetic Culture* (1999) comparing Stephen Dobyns and Lyn Hejinian as poets who "operate within poetic subcultures often viewed as diametrically opposed" (55)—those being "mainstream or 'workshop'" poetry and the experimental avant-garde of Language poetry. Beach asserts he does "not mean to suggest, by counterposing Dobyns and Hejinian in this way, that the entire contemporary scene falls into such a binary opposition" (56), but he explains, as justification for his approach, that at least since the anthology wars of the 1960s "the demarcation between a poetic practice of mainstream, usually academic orientation and one of alternative, experimental, and largely countercultural orientation has been firmly in place" (57).

3. The difficulty of situating feminist poetry within the mainstream/Language binary at this time is evident, for instance, when Jed Rasula's attempt to map the contemporary scene in *The American Poetry Wax Museum* (1996) ends in his awkwardly setting aside "various coalitions of interest-oriented or community-based poets" producing work defined by "identity politics" in a category apart from either AWP writing or Language poetry (440, 443).

4. Edward Hirsch, Mark Jarman, and Joy Katz are among the reviewers who use the word "excess" or "excessive" in describing Fulton's work. Jarman's comment (in reviewing *Dance Script*) that "intellect, if it were really on its toes, would make for some restraint and restraint is rarely present in her poems" is fairly typical of those who feel Fulton goes too far ("Acts of Will" 84). William Zander claims that "all too often the language is *too* rich, the metaphors are *too* packed" (151). My point, of course, is that what constitutes "excess" is an ideologically constructed standard.

5. This passage from "Her Moment of Brocade" was cut from the version of the essay printed in *Feeling as a Foreign Language*.

6. The essay, "To Organize a Waterfall," was first published in 1991.

7. Reviewers of more recent volumes, *Felt* (2001) and *Cascade Experiment: Selected Poems* (2004), have generally been less personal and less negative, though some still complain that Fulton's quirky style is annoying, stagy, and so forth; *Publishers Weekly* of November 20, 2000, criticizes the writing in *Felt* for being "less composed than performed"—still invoking a standard of naturalness that fits the conventions of expressive lyric and is unsuited to experimental poetics (Rev. of *Felt* 65). The generally less vituperative tone of more recent reviewers probably reflects much more widespread acceptance of hybrid poetics, or, as Jed Rasula puts it, the extent to which "the beneficial legacy of language poetry . . . [has been] disseminated now into the environment of poetic innovation at large" (*Syncopations* 209). One consequence of Language poetry to which Rasula draws particular attention is "its erosion of the complacency with which the lyrical ego hoists its banner" (210); I have been suggesting that earlier reviewers failed to grasp the distance Fulton was establishing between her speakers and that conventional lyrical subject.

8. This is much less true now, and even in the mid-1990s there were notable exceptions, for instance in the critical treatments of Susan Howe's work. Anthologies of women's innovative writing edited by Maggie O'Sullivan and by Mary Margaret Sloan published in the years immediately following the release of *Sensual Math* helped increase recognition of the feminist dimensions and contexts of women's experimental writing.

9. Fulton's essay "Her Moment of Brocade" reveals the depth of her involvement with Dickinson's work, and numerous poems in *Sensual Math* contain allusions to Dickinson's poems. Cristanne Miller discusses the resemblances between Fulton's poetry and that of Moore (who is quoted several times in *Sensual Math*) in *Marianne Moore: Questions of Authority* (225–31).

10. Fulton explains her belief that "a truly engaged and contemporary poetry" must reflect the knowledge of quantum physics in "Of Formal, Free, and Fractal Verse" (*Feeling as a Foreign Language* 53). As discussed in chapter 4, her belief is

shared by Joan Retallack; I am not suggesting that Fulton is alone in wanting to keep poetry abreast of current science. For an ingenious example of post-Language poetry informed—and given form—by science, see Christian Bök's *Crystallography*.

11. For Fulton's own testimony to this effect, see "Interview" 599.

12. Reviewers who equate Fulton with her speakers often miss this intellectual complexity. For example, Katz, assuming that the speaker of "Echo Location" voices the poet's longings, scolds, "By desiring to know someone through a kind of flagrant violation, an invasive physical possession, Fulton unnerves us. . . . Fulton wants to mark her ownership in scrollwork, but this is a longing to shave and tattoo, more intimate, and much more painful, than spray-painting a name onto an overpass. It becomes clear by the middle of the piece that Fulton is talking about the writing process, and that the 'other' she wants to know and own is life's experience" (298–99). Here, in contrast, is a comment Fulton offered in her interview with Miller as part of a discussion of her use of gendered speakers: "I made 'Echo Location' ungendered because I didn't want either sex or gender to be burdened with the sadistic power the speaker wields at the poem's beginning. I didn't want either sex to be blamed. I used 'it' as the pronoun because 'Echo Location' thinks about dominance—and reciprocity. The poem describes the dominance of one person over another, of artist over art object, and religion over the aspirant" ("Interview" 589).

13. For example, in a largely positive review of *Powers of Congress*, Diane Wakoski is unhappy with "Point of Purchase" because she reads it as a "satire on postmodernist criticism" that "mock[s] the various techniques critics use to try to approach difficult poetry" (24). Apparently assuming that Fulton sides with her pool-shark speaker, Wakoski seems blind to the possibility that the poem is more than parodic—that what Fulton has called the poem's "contrapuntal structure" might also invite sympathy with the various reader/critics in her poem and validate (as well as make fun of) multiple reading strategies (*Feeling as a Foreign Language* 202). Fulton's work, which invites multiple simultaneous readings, requires a more actively creative reader than does most contemporary lyric, though Fulton maintains more control over interpretive options than do most Language poets.

14. For discussion of differing views within the Language avant-garde concerning the legitimacy of a "postindividualistic version of personal style" (Kalaidjian 192), see Walter Kalaidjian, *American Culture between the Wars*, 191–94.

15. In "The Erogenous Cusp" Miller insightfully discusses Fulton's deliberate refusal of gender specificity in *Powers of Congress*.

16. In correspondence with the author, Fulton stated that the use of the equal sign is unrelated to its use in the journal title *L=A=N=G=U=A=G=E*, one source for the label *Language writing*.

17. "Drills" exemplifies Fulton's treatment of personal material, where again she differs from both Language writers and mainstream lyricists. Like several other poems in the volume, "Drills" responds to the sudden death of Fulton's niece Laura at the age of twenty-one. The poems that allude to this personal tragedy are very moving, but they do not represent grief confessionally. In "Drills," the immersion in grief experienced by Fulton's sister, Laura's mother, becomes a key intellectual concept

that is woven into ruminations—at once abstract and deeply compassionate—on the boundaries and permeabilities of individual experience, on how human beings bear what is unbearable.

18. That Fulton's understanding of the denaturalizing function of poetic devices corresponds with the views of Language writers is suggested, for instance, by Ron Silliman's presentation of the "new sentence" used in much Language writing as redeploying the "torquing which is normally triggered by linebreaks, the function of which is to enhance ambiguity and polysemy" (*New Sentence* 90).

19. Several reviewers have noted that Dickinson's em dashes are an important precedent for Fulton's bride mark. In correspondence with the author, Fulton also mentioned the colon-strewn poems of her former teacher, A. R. Ammons, as a significant example.

4. Fields of Pattern-Bounded Unpredictability

1. When Retallack republished this essay in *The Poethical Wager* (2003), she revised this passage (as well as the one I quote next). Her omission in the later version of reference to the ego expressions of the writer suggests a less oppositional poetic climate in which experimental or exploratory poets feel less need to define their aesthetics via critique of the expressive personal lyric.

2. See "Conversation" 359–63 for a discussion between Retallack and Waldrop of masculine and feminine modes of writing. Both avoid essentialist identification of masculine and feminine with male and female person; both see language as woven from masculine and feminine elements; and both signal a desire to use their own work to awaken readers to the intuitive logics, the "polyphonic associations and resonances" associated with the feminine and (though they don't use this phrase) the Kristevan semiotic.

3. It is significant for later parts of this chapter that Retallack goes on to invoke fractals in the next sentence of this passage from "The Experimental Feminine": "Dynamic system models like fractal (cultural) coastlines or cultural DNA shift attention from narrow defensible borders to broad interactions among material, formal principles and possibility" (*Poethical Wager* 97).

4. Steven R. Evans's excellent entry on Waldrop in the *Dictionary of Literary Biography* pointed me to her sources. Evans refers with slight inaccuracy to "a textbook of quantum physics from the 1930s" (295); Eddington's book was published in 1929.

5. Discussing the similar construction of *Reproduction of Profiles*, Evans notes that the sources seem at first glance "diametrically opposed" and that "by tracing two cognate structures, the logical (Wittgenstein) and the erotic (Kafka), to their common fulcrum in the subject's desire to know, Waldrop throws a communicating wire between two areas of human endeavor that are often kept at a tidy distance" ("Rosmarie Waldrop" 294).

6. Biographical similarities may also fuel Waldrop's attraction to the work of Musil, who is among her favorite authors, and Wittgenstein. For instance, it seems likely that Wittgenstein and Musil, being Austrians who often thought of themselves

as Germans or Europeans (Luft 15), experienced something close to Waldrop's expatriate's sense of living between languages and cultures.

7. According to biographer Brian McGuinness, Wittgenstein "hardly knew the names of the writers Ficker selected for his benefaction in 1914: Musil with whom he has often been compared he probably never read" (37).

8. Evans sensibly links Waldrop's rejection of "the concept of a full and homogeneous center" and her interest in the "empty middle" to her experience growing up in Germany during World War II, to the fact of the concentration camps and their discrediting of the metaphysical concepts used to legitimate fascism ("Rosmarie Waldrop" 287).

9. *Lawn of Excluded Middle* was originally a separate publication, but Waldrop always intended the volume to be the second (middle) one in a loose trilogy; the trilogy, *Curves to the Apple*, appeared in 2006, and my parenthetic page citations are to that edition.

10. Waldrop's attribution is not quite accurate; Eddington, in making this statement, attributes it originally to Sir William Bragg (Eddington 194).

11. Eddington, writing with characteristic humor, explains: "The classical conception of gravitation is based on Newton's account of what happened; but it is time to hear what the apple had to say. The apple with the usual egotism of an observer deemed itself to be at rest; looking down it saw the various terrestrial objects including Newton rushing upwards with accelerated velocity to meet it. Does it invent a mysterious agency or tug to account for their conduct? No; it points out that the cause of their acceleration is quite evident. Newton is being hammered by the molecules of the ground underneath him. . . . Newton had to postulate a mysterious invisible force pulling the apple down; the apple can point to an evident cause propelling Newton up" (115).

12. The dynamic I am outlining is similar to the one Marjorie Perloff observes: noting that Waldrop in *Reproduction of Profiles* shows a greater interest than Wittgenstein of *Philosophical Investigations* in "the interactive deployment of these language games, in the way language games are related to gender and power," Perloff asserts that "[t]he quest is to escape the imposition of someone else's logic, even someone as close to her own sensibility as Wittgenstein" (*Wittgenstein's Ladder* 208–9). I would shift the emphasis to claim that such an escape has been achieved in a relationship of fruitfully ambivalent intimacy. While Perloff characterizes the poems of *Reproduction* as "Wittgenstein parodies" written from a feminist perspective, Monroe's more qualified assertion that Waldrop is in "seriously parodic dialogue with Wittgenstein" seems to me more accurate (133).

13. The phrase appears in Jonathan Monroe's excellent essay "Syntextural Investigations" (133) as part of his nuanced analysis of Waldrop's stance toward Wittgenstein in *The Reproduction of Profiles*.

14. In characterizing an "erotics of syntax" in Waldrop's *Profiles*, Monroe calls attention to Waldrop's "staging of binaries for the purpose of undoing them in a provisional union that (happily) dissolves into reassertion of difference and back again" (135).

15. Although its palimpsestic character is not uniform, the volume gains formal unification through the similar construction of its parts—series of brief prose poems written in complete propositional sentences—which in turn reflects their common project. That cohering project (in *Reproduction of Profiles* as well as *Lawn of Excluded Middle*) developed partly in response to Wittgenstein, since Waldrop experienced the extreme closure of his propositional writing as a challenge to her usual practice of open forms and grammatically incomplete units: "I tried to work with this challenge, accept the complete sentence (most of the time) and try to subvert its closure and logic from the inside, by constantly sliding between frames of reference. I especially brought the female body in and set into play the old gender archetypes of logic and mind being 'male,' whereas 'female' designates the illogical: emotion, body, matter. Again, I hope the constant sliding challenges these categories" ("Thinking of Follows" 613).

16. Entries from *Philosophical Investigations* that appear elsewhere in the palimpsest of the title series include, in section 3, number 439; in section 4, number 414; in section 5, number 435; in section 8, number 474; in section 9, number 543; in section 13, number 546; in section 14, number 549; in section 15, number 548; in section 16, notes on the page containing numbers 548–51; in section 20, numbers 618 and 621; in section 21, number 589; in section 22, entries 435 and 673; and in section 25, numbers 454–57. If I've not overlooked text from individual entries in the final sections of *Lawn*, that would mean the series replicates the structure I see in the volume as a whole (introduced below) wherein palimpsestic traces of preexistent texts diminish toward the end.

17. Even the title "The Perplexing Habit of Falling," which refers in part to the misogynist biblical tale of the fall and to early conceptions of a flat world sailors might fall off, alludes most directly to Eddington's discussion of the law of gravity and the inadequacy of Newtonian physics. The titles of the three series contained there, "The Attraction of the Ground," "Mass, Momentum, Stress," and "Accelerating Frame," also refer to physics.

18. I mean this in the context of the volume and am not suggesting that Waldrop has moved away from using source texts in her oeuvre as a whole. This continues to be one among many available strategies for her. For example, her 1994 *A Key into the Language of America* makes extensive use of Roger Williams's dictionary of the same name, while "Holderlin Hybrids" in her 2003 volume *Blindsight* "resonates against the German poet's twisted syntax" (back cover). I discuss Waldrop's use of Williams's book in "'Nothing, for a Woman, Is Worth Trying.'"

19. I have followed Retallack in adding an extra *r* when referring to the afterrimages constructed in the text; I hope such suggestively distorting repetition (evoking terra, terror, err, etc.) will signal the complex and multiple relations to what came before evident in what comes after.

20. In an analysis complementary to my own (and published as this chapter first went to press as an essay in *Contemporary Literature* [2000]), Ann Vickery also considers Retallack's use of fragments from *The Canterbury Tales* in the title sequence (Vickery 175–76).

21. This is not to suggest that Retallack devalues emotional responsiveness or unsentimentalized passion—quite the contrary.

22. This quotation derives from one of two epigraphs to "The Experimental Feminine." However, both epigraphs are Retallack's own creation, as is signaled by the playful links between Retallack's name and the names of the purported authors. This passage is attributed to K. Callater, which is *Retallack* spelled backward.

23. The later version of this essay that appears in *Poethical Wager* is somewhat less sanguine, reading "the currently unintelligible in which some sense of our future may be detected" (126).

24. The numbers of lines per half page are as follows: 11, 10, 9, 9, 8, 8, 7, 7, 7, 5, 5, 4, 3, 3, 3, 3, 2, 1, and on the last page a truncated line of text appears below the dividing line with nothing above.

5. Poems Living with Paintings

1. W. J. T. Mitchell observes, "Insofar as art history is a verbal representation of visual representation, it is an elevation of ekphrasis to a disciplinary principle" (*Picture Theory* 157).

2. As noted above, Foucault sees the central absence of the sovereign as pointing to the absence of a concept of man, a lacuna that will be filled in the modern episteme.

3. See, for instance, Joel Snyder and Ted Cohen, "Reflexions on *Las Meninas:* Paradox Lost," which establishes that Foucault was mistaken in seeing the mirror as reflecting the painter's model; instead it reflects the image on the canvas.

4. Quotations from this essay are taken from the version formerly posted at <http://www.du.edu/~cswensen/writewithize.html>. The version published in *American Letters and Commentary*, though largely the same, is not identical to the one quoted here.

5. Swensen offers works by Carol Snow, Laura Moriarty, and Mei-mei Burssenbrugge as examples of the first mode. Her examples of the second mode include works by Susan Howe and Johanna Drucker. I would place Myung Mi Kim's *River Antes*, discussed in chapter 7, in this second category, along with Swensen's own *Oh*, published the same year as *Try*; see Lynn Keller, "Singing Spaces: Fractal Geometries in Cole Swensen's *Oh*." Practitioners Swensen lists for the third mode include Robert Rauschenberg, Jasper Johns, Cy Twombly, Philip Guston, Barbara Kruger, and Ed Ruscha, among others.

6. In addition to *Try*, which also won the 2000 Poetry Center Book Award from the Poetry Center/American Poetry Archives, Swensen's books and chapbooks of poetry include *It's Alive, She Says* (1984); *New Math* (1988), which won the National Poetry Series Competition; *Noon* (1988), which won the New American Poetry Series Award; *Park* (1991); *Numen* (1995); *Oh* (2000); *Such Rich Hour* (2001); *Goest* (2004); *The Glass Age* (2007); and *Ours* (2008). She has also published translations of several books of contemporary French poetry. A number of poems in *Such Rich Hour* also respond to visual images; that book is based on a fifteenth-century book of hours, *Tres Riches Heures du Duc de Berry*, including the manuscript's monthly calendar illustrations.

7. Ashbery's "Self-Portrait in a Convex Mirror" certainly anticipates some of the traits of Swensen's first mode of ekphrasis, so that his extended poem might be said to "live with the [art] work and its disturbances" ("To Writewithize"). While Ashbery often "stands back" from Parmigianino's convex self-portrait, his perspective frequently shifts so the painting is subject to changing interpretations, and the boundaries between the writer and the painter represented in the convex mannerist portrait sometimes blur. The destabilizing techniques of Swensen's writing are more extreme, however, and its motion more vertiginous; in particular, her quicker swerves from one syntactic construction to another and her highly elliptical constructions produce the more open or indeterminate spaces and the rapidly mobile intersubjectivity of what I am calling her lacework aesthetic.

8. This harmony may render Mitchell's notions of ekphrastic hope, fear, and indifference largely inapplicable to Swensen's work. Reading ekphrasis as fundamentally about the overcoming of otherness—and offering fascinating readings that highlight its gendered dynamics—Mitchell draws upon analogies to race relations to propose that ekphrasis "thematiz[es] the 'visual' as other to language, 'a threat to be reduced' (ekphrastic fear), 'a potential same-to-be' (ekphrastic hope), 'a yet-not-same' (ekphrastic indifference)" (*Picture Theory* 163). Mitchell sees ekphrastic fear and ekphrastic hope as expressing our anxieties about merging with others; as we will see, these anxieties are thematized in some of the paintings Swensen considers in *Try*, but, both thematically and in its mode of ekphrasis, the volume proposes the possibility of transcending those anxieties.

9. Perspective derives from triangulation, and its development was part of a more general fascination with geometric proportion in the Renaissance, in which the number three figured importantly. For their arithmetic calculations, Italian commercial people relied on a proportional series called the Rule of Three, also known as the Golden Rule and the Merchant's Key (see Baxandall 95–101).

10. Swensen's emphasis on number also undermines received ideas of the word/image opposition. Number, after all, is at once a purely abstract concept and a material reality, and it is a site where aural, visual, and verbal apprehension commonly mix. One can experience number through sounded repetition, as when a word is repeated three times, and one can recognize number when observing three-line groupings in triplet stanzas; one can comprehend the numeral 3 or III as a visual symbol without sounding it, and one can translate it into an English word to be sounded as a one-syllable combination of a soft consonant cluster and a long *e* vowel; similarly, one can read the alphabetic signifier *t-h-r-e-e* and grasp the concept it signifies. Because number can exist as pure concept, it reinforces, too, Swensen's fascination in the volume with what is (or is imagined) beyond sensory apprehension.

11. In the chapter on Dante's *Purgatorio* where Heffernan considers the "envoicing of the silent image," he emphasizes the competition between verbal and visual renditions and the way in which the image is mastered by Dante's word. This does not seem to me the case with Swensen's envoicings throughout *Try* since they are so provisional and so constantly undergoing transformation. I see here neither mastery nor the attempt to achieve it.

12. While the Virgin Mary is most often represented in blue, nearly a quarter of van Eyck's painting on the cover of *Try* is occupied by the red robes of this particular Mary. In the passage quoted, the blues and greens into which the speaker is "splayed" are not just painter's pigments but also the colors of the natural world, of earth, water, and sky.

13. Heffernan presents as distinctly postmodern the self-referentiality of John Ashbery's "Self-Portrait in a Convex Mirror" and regards the focus on a mirror painting as enabling this reflectivity: "To write a poem about a self-portrait in a convex mirror is inevitably to find oneself—or imagine oneself—mirrored by it" (174). Swensen's observation that all representational art acts on us in ways that make the art self-referential might imply that all ekphrasis is more self-reflective than Heffernan acknowledges.

14. Swensen may also be alluding and responding to Jacques Derrida's extensive play on lacing in the fourth essay of *The Truth in Painting* ("try," we might note, is one meaning of *essay*). In the process of examining the flaws of Heidegger's and Meyer Schapiro's readings of Van Gogh's *Old Shoes with Laces*, Derrida makes a good deal of the "trajectory of the *lace*: a stricture by alternate and reversible passage from inside to outside, from under to over" (321). The lacing he highlights is a movement from inside the painting to outside, and from outside in, which has notable similarities to the binding of external world to painted world invoked in Swensen's lines. The lacework I have in mind, however, is not so much the one associated with shoes that involves piercing and stricture as the (female) art in which open space visible between intertwined threads is essential to the form.

15. Swensen's concern with the importance of the reader in producing the poem is no doubt informed by the extensive discussion of this topic in the critical prose of Language writers. Perhaps comparable to Susan Howe's engagements with archival documents, Swensen's ways of "living with" medieval and Renaissance art make clear that this principle can apply not just to the reader's making sense of the markedly elliptical and disjunctive texts of contemporary experimentalists but also to the reader/viewer's interactions with earlier, more canonical works in which the spaces left for the reader to inhabit may not be so deliberate or obvious.

16. Again Swensen's "Working Notes" is helpful since it announces her interest not simply in highlighting the ways in which representational art operates by confusing the viewer's identity with that of the figures depicted, but also in disrupting that ideologically weighted process:

> "One question I was exploring in writing on these works and on my viewing of them was the relationship of writing to this initiatory process—could writing disrupt in an interesting way, at the very least creating a self-consciousness that complicates the overlap and reintroduces elements of 'personal' decision—in quotes because the question of what 'personal' might, can, does mean is one of the underlying considerations."

17. A complementary reading of these lines might take them as alluding to Auden's "Musée des Beaux Arts," in which the vanishing figure—those "white legs disappearing into the green / Water"—is the mythic hero. What comes to life is, again, the background and the ordinary lives lived there. The Christian reading, however,

seems to me primary, since I take Swensen to be interested in discerning the consequences of a transformation in faith via changes in painting.

18. In Bellini's time, moreover, the place of the body and bodily sensation in salvation was being debated by theologians who argued about the sensible qualities of paradise or the spiritual information that may be contained in ordinary mortal sight (Baxandall 103–5).

19. Swensen's "disarm," indicating that the painter usually defends himself against such fleshly additions as if against an attack, would suggest wariness and active resistance. Essays in Caroline Walker Bynum's *Fragmentation and Redemption* suggest that medieval attitudes toward the body were not necessarily so defensive. Associating the body with suffering and generativity, medieval people—far less likely than people currently are to eroticize the body—emphasized the "humanation" of God, the enfleshment of Christ, as the source of salvation. In *Holy Feast and Holy Fast*, Bynum emphasizes, however, woman's association with the physical, lustful, and appetitive part of human nature and notes that the flesh of Christ is often associated with Mary and therefore with women (262, 267). Of course, Swensen's readings of medieval work—not those of Bynum or other scholars—are my primary concern here.

20. As Swensen recognizes, Christian attitudes toward women and toward sensory experience vary greatly, depending on the era, the region, the denomination, and so forth. Medieval attitudes toward the body and bodily sensation were complex since the body was the locus both of temptation and of encounter with the divine (Bynum, *Fragmentation* 258). Bynum points out that in medieval European thought, allegorically speaking, woman is to man as matter is to spirit; this means that "*woman* or *the feminine* symbolizes the physical, lustful, material, appetitive part of human nature. . . . When combined with the negative view of marriage and sexuality that characterized much early Christian thought, such views could and did encourage misogyny" (*Holy* 262). She also cautions, however, that modern attitudes may distort the evidence: "The recent outpouring of work on the history of the body, especially the female body, has largely equated body with sexuality and understood discipline or control of body as the rejection of sex or of woman. We must wipe away such assumptions before we come to medieval source material. Medieval images of the body have less to do with sexuality than with fertility and decay. Control, discipline, even torture of the flesh is, in medieval devotion, not so much the rejection of physicality as the elevation of it—a horrible yet delicious elevation—into a means of access to the divine" (*Fragmentation* 182). *Try*'s focusing on representations of the former prostitute, Mary Magdalene, rather than the adored and sinless Virgin, brings to the fore aspects of Christianity that associate woman with sexual depravity. Yet by considering over the course of the volume numerous representations of the *Noli Me Tangere* scene, Swensen acknowledges varied attitudes toward the body and woman's touch. This chapter argues that *Try* as a whole brings into focus a transition registered in Renaissance Christian painting from the primacy of spiritual purity and the life hereafter to an increasingly positive emphasis on physical experience in and of this world.

21. Heffernan, in tracing the evolution of ekphrasis, identifies as a distinctive trait of modern ekphrasis its springing from the museum and the apparatus of institutionalized art (138). Ekphrastic poetry of our time, he says, represents individual works of art within the context of the museum, a context that includes all the words that surround the paintings, even their titles. That certainly applies to *Try*, in which truncated bits from art historians appear. Swensen's work is unusual, however, not just in the extent to which it foregrounds the museum context, but in the fluidity with which these poems, in their "living with" paintings, move in and out of the museum and the institutions that "inform and regulate our experience" of visual art (139).

22. Here is the story, as summarized on the Getty Museum Web site, in connection with a late fifteenth-century representation of the flight into Egypt by George Trubert: "The Holy Family passed a newly sown field of wheat while fleeing, and it miraculously grew to full height. Later, soldiers pursuing the family asked a farmer when the travelers had passed; though now harvesting the same wheat, he truthfully replied that he saw them when the wheat was planted. Discouraged, the soldiers turned back" ("Flight").

23. This line alludes to the theologically controversial directive in John 2:15, "Do not love the world or anything in the world. If anyone loves the world, the love of the Father is not in him."

6. Resisting the Cultural Steamroller

1. Wheeler's reference to talk-show host Geraldo Rivera, like the essay's comparison of talk-show host Rosie O'Donnell with innovative poet Susan Howe, links her claims to those Marjorie Perloff makes in "The Changing Face of Common Intercourse" in *Radical Artifice*, which Wheeler cites in a footnote. Pointing to the crucial role "natural" or "authentic" speech previously played in poetry, Perloff argues that talk shows have transformed speech into spectacle and emptied speech of its particularity of reference. Perloff champions poetries whose deliberate artifice counters the illusion of "direct speech, direct feeling" (45).

2. Wheeler's essay title responds most obviously to Dana Gioia's "Can Poetry Matter?" first published in the *Atlantic* in 1991. In contrast to Wheeler's sophisticated cultural critique via complexity and a brash mixing of modes and tones, Gioia champions a return of verse narrative in an accessible plain style while he rejects "avant-garde posturing" and heralds the restoration of "direct, unironic emotion" (Gioia 251). Vernon Shetley's *After the Death of Poetry* is another example of a recent publication whose title calls attention to widespread doubts about poetry's current vitality or significance.

3. Thanks to Susan Bernstein for calling my attention to the sound-bite quality of the essay's construction.

4. Like Wheeler's earlier volumes, *Source Codes* contains a number of poems that employ regular stanzaic structures or set forms such as the sonnet and at least flirt with regular rhyme patterns. Typically, the lines have a rich musicality often involving internal rhyme, although the rapid shifts in diction, the overlapping deployments of sometimes distorted clichés, and the density of syntax may mask the work's skillful formalism.

5. Wheeler's use of the term "crossover," which usually evokes the crossing by musical performers of boundaries between audiences of different races, is itself a bold assimilation that signals how rigidly divided the audiences for "experimental" and "mainstream" poetries have tended to be.

6. In "Reading, Raiding, and Anodyne Eclecticism," Wheeler observes that "wrong assimilation—or appropriation—has been roiling the radical seas" (149). She cites attacks on the editors of *Fence*, who were accused of "'trendifying' difficult ideas" (149); for the text of one such critique see Steve Evans's *Third Factory: Notes to Poetry* from January 2001.

7. The essay's subtitle, "Word without World," points to Language poet Ron Silliman's early programmatic essay, "Disappearance of the Word, Appearance of the World," which concerns "the subjection of writing (and through writing, language) to the social dynamics of capitalism" (*New Sentence* 8).

8. Wheeler's essay does not argue about sophistication but demonstrates it self-mockingly by keeping count of the intellectually prestigious "brand names" she quotes, including Bourdieu, Baudrillard, and a handful of Language writers.

9. For an overview of this eclecticism in Wheeler's first four collections, see Keller, "Susan Wheeler's Open Source Poetics."

10. Mobilio 14; Burt, Rev. of *Smokes*; Burt, "Shearing" 6; Yenser 156; Stefans, "Little Reviews," Rev. of *Smokes*; Burt, Rev. of *Smokes*; Hass 56; Belitt.

11. Burt's attempt to group poets in a "school" on the basis of some common devices—being "good at describing information overload," telling "almost-stories," creating "protagonists who know they are only symbols in poems," and so on—is problematic. The term "school" conveys collaboration, interaction, community, whereas the poets Burt labels Ellipticals have no significant connection to each other. Moreover, the commonalities he sees do not seem necessarily more significant than the differences that separate the writers in question. His understanding of Wheeler's poetry in particular is weakened by a tendency to regard the speakers in her poems as versions of Wheeler herself. Burt's claims have sparked controversy, some of which is published as "Special Feature: Elliptical Poets" in *American Letters and Commentary*. Although his recent labeling of "The New Thing" poets (Burt, "New Thing") is surely at least partly tongue-in-cheek, it exhibits similar weaknesses.

12. In an earlier review of *Smokes*, Stefans had also discerned there "an important . . . rapprochement of the indeterminate, militantly ironic stance of the postmodern with the comforting, bourgeois closure of the sentimental lyric" ("Little Reviews," Rev. of *Smokes*).

13. Wheeler observes in "What Outside?" that race is for Americans "our paradigm 'Outside'" (195); given her opposition to any "codification of boundaries that turns what is 'outside' into what cannot be admitted 'inside'" (193), it follows logically that both the visual images she constructs and the idioms she evokes should—in defiance of those who would fault such aesthetic miscegenation as cultural appropriation—bring racial outsiders inside.

14. The passage is a single sentence from partition 3, section 2, memb. 3 of Burton's treatise.

15. Her thinking here may resemble that of Gilles Lipovetsky and others who have argued that the variety of consumer products in fact encourages variation in individual expression.

16. Surveying the relation of innovative poetry to lyric conventions, especially challenges to the lyric "I," Linda Kinnahan rightly observes that although early Language writing dismissed the lyric subject, some feminist experimentalists at least since the early 1990s have wrestled with that model as too closed, and that within the Language community reconsiderations of the lyric have changed over time (Kinnahan 9–23). I am not claiming that all linguistically innovative writers take a thoroughly iconoclastic stance toward lyric subjectivity.

17. The passage from Gertrude Stein, on the final page of *Picasso*, reads: "[W]hen I looked at the earth I saw all the lines of cubism made at a time when not any painter had ever gone up in an airplane. I saw there on the earth the mingling lines of Picasso, coming and going, developing and destroying themselves, I saw the simple solutions of Braque, I saw the wandering lines of Masson, yes I saw and once more I knew that a creator is contemporary, he understands what is contemporary when the contemporaries do not yet know it" (50). I am grateful to Adalaide Morris, who called my attention to this source.

18. The allusions are minimalistic, but "suffice" and "shores" are distinctive enough to evoke Stevens's description of modern poetry as "The poem of the mind in the act of finding / What will suffice" and Eliot's "These fragments I have shored against my ruins." Wheeler also evokes Robert Frost's "Fire and Ice," which concludes: "I think I know enough of hate / To say that for destruction ice / Is also great / And would suffice."

19. HTML is not technically a source code but a markup language. Unaware of this, Wheeler was thinking of HTML as a source code ("Interview" 587).

20. Many of those involved in digital poetics see their work as both leading and extending experimental poetic practice; see, for instance, the epilogue to Loss Pequeño Glazier, *Digital Poetics*, or, in a less direct presentation, the notes in Brian Kim Stefans, "Stops and Rebels: A Critique of Hypertext" (*Fashionable Noise* 61–169).

21. I would like to thank Albert Sheen, who provided this kind of translation for me and talked helpfully with me about these pages.

22. Wheeler did not know this piece of code was flawed when she put it into the volume ("Interview" 586).

7. The Thing Seen Together with the Whole Space

1. In the interview titled "Generosity as Method," Kim talks of using "Meridian" in the classroom; she expresses her admiration for the work of Celan, along with that of Theresa Hak Kyung Cha, as follows: "With these writers we are in the company of language that has been met with potential erasure; what happens in that kind of collaboration between the impossibility of utterance and finding the means by which to utter? That space is never a decided, resolved, fixed point, and part of the exquisiteness is that it is constantly in motion, constantly reshaping itself. . . . For me those

works that keep re-invigorating that space of silence and erasure, the space of the seemingly untranslatable, are the ones in which you really feel some sort of endurance and power."

2. Similar understandings have been voiced at least since the rise of modernism; think, for instance, of William Carlos Williams's hostility to such forms as the sonnet. For a discussion of Kim's adaptation of modernist poetics, particularly via Ezra Pound, see Josephine Park's "'Composed of Many Lengths of Bone.'"

3. Warren Liu provides an excellent reading of *Commons* that develops from his perception that in the notes at the end of the volume, rather than in fact providing "an interpretive framework through which a reader might understand the text, Kim asserts that the text itself is in fact more concerned with all that the text is not" (Liu 252). Focusing on elision and illegibility, and attending to language as a potential commons, Liu explores how *Commons* "reframes the negative—by negating it" (253). Though our readings approach the text from very different perspectives, he and I agree on a number of points, including that Kim's "exploration of how language functions to mask or suppress the fundamental power relations among *generalized* forms of knowledge production . . . is intimately linked to the recognition that we must use that same language to define, understand, and uncover *specific* iterations of power (or powerlessness)" (253). Liu offers strong arguments for the importance of reading Kim specifically as an Asian American poet.

4. A focus of "Generosity as Method" is Kim's belief that real change is not generated through opposition. For example, she states early in the interview, "Something I'm trying to work out in my own writing is this idea that change is neither strictly 'oppositional' nor does it occur as a natural, linear progression. Even in the way we talk about how radicalization or change happens, we begin by bifurcating: does change happen this way or that way—even the [*sic*] in our desire to participate in that radicalizing process we can't begin to actually figure out the complexity of it; immediately we come to this either-or proposition. I'm interested in augmenting or complicating that model of change by opposition, by friction, by overthrowing the law of the father, in order to embrace a model of radicalization that doesn't solely rely on that kind of direct opposition." Much of that interview concerns her understanding of how poetry is and isn't political.

5. There are, of course, nonvisual modes of attention that also foster awareness of complexity. Joseph Jonghyun Jeon's skillful analysis in "Speaking in Tongues" of Kim's remarkable use of sound would easily support an argument that the aural provides Kim with another such resource. Kim tends to privilege the visual in *Commons*, however, as is suggested by the shift in the following passage from all "the senses" to the eye.

P: Of what use are the senses to us—tell me that
E: To indicate, to make known, to testify in part

Burning eye seen
Of that
One eye seen
(13)

6. My thanks to Joseph Jonghyun Jeon, who pointed out the usefulness of this definition for my argument, and whose generous response to a draft of this chapter included several other valuable insights I have incorporated.

7. Sometimes Kim omits the quotation marks, counting on readers' ears to recognize the language of journalistic reportage without visual cues, as on the page that conveys worldwide ecological disaster with text that seems to quote news reports about crop failure and plagues of pests in Afghanistan, Africa, the United States, and Bolivia—for example, "At least 250,000 acres of cotton and fruit crops are under immediate threat from the huge / swarm of locusts which have invaded the southern plain from the Pamir Mountains" (42).

8. Cartesian perspectivalism is characterized by, among other things, "[t]he abstract coldness of the perspectival gaze," "the withdrawal of the painter's emotional entanglement with the objects depicted in geometricalized space" (Jay 8). According to Martin Jay, scholars have noted that the invention of perspective and the "emergence of the oil painting detached from its context and available for buying and selling" both occurred at the time when "the natural world was transformed through the technological world view into a 'standing reserve' for the surveillance and manipulation of a dominating subject" (9–10). The point of "Scopic Regimes of Modernity," however, is to complicate the widespread notion of a single hegemonic visual mode in the modern era. Jay argues that the "dominant . . . visual model of the modern era, that which we can identify with Renaissance notions of perspective in the visual arts and Cartesian ideas of subjective rationality in philosophy," was in fact a contested domain involving several visual subcultures (4).

9. The reduction of woman to body is clearly encoded in the page of "Lamenta" titled "Mask Play," where the closest female analogs to "Man Mask" are "Vagina Mask" and "Hemorrhage Mask" (26).

10. In a later passage a speaker recounts an experience of burning, perhaps from a weapon like napalm: "It burn skin to bone / Scar tissue on top of nerve ending / Ugly power of military / I scream too hot too hot / Naked where clothes were a second before" (78).

11. My thanks to Eun Jung Anderton, who discussed with me these and other bits of Korean in *Commons*.

12. Excellent discussions of Kim's work with transliteration and translation (as well as many other aspects of Kim's poetry) are provided by Joseph Jonghyun Jeon in "Speaking in Tongues" and Xiaojing Zhou in her chapter of *The Ethics and Poetics of Alterity in Asian American Poetry* titled "Myung Mi Kim: Speak and It Is Sound in Time." Our understandings are often similar. Jeon's essay examines especially Kim's uses of sound, demonstrating that "Kim's poetry attempts to dramatize not how a foreign speaker learns to speak the native language of a new place but how the languages themselves learn to speak each other" (127). Zhou attends, as I do, to the way in which Kim's poetics "enacts her sense of the poet's ethical responsibility" (230); Zhou sees in Kim's experimentation, and particularly in her "practice of plurality of language," a "Levinasian ethics of alterity" (266). In the part of her essay devoted to *Commons*, Zhou identifies as a major concern of Kim's poetics challenging "the cen-

trality of the lyric I/eye, whose vision or observation serves as the ground of knowledge" (268); according to Zhou, Kim "undermines . . . the subject's mastery of the
visible as complete knowledge to be possessed" (271). Her take on the visual, then,
diverges from mine, since I emphasize Kim's reclaiming of the visual for alternative
ways of knowing.

13. Shelley Sunn Wong has observed that the frontispiece to *Dictée*—an image of
Korean phrases etched on the wall of a coal mine in Japan—contains the only Hangul script in the entire work; Wong argues that this opening gesture cracks open a
"discourse of wholeness" that has historically framed the narrative of American life
(Wong 107–8). Kim's more extensive use of Hangul might be seen as expanding upon
Cha's and continuing that fracture. In addition to sharing an interest in issues surrounding translation and transliteration, Cha and Kim incorporate into their work
some of the same concerns about an ethics of seeing. Park and Jeon, among others,
have developed fruitful comparisons between the work of these two Korean American experimental artists.

14. Both Jeon and Zhou provide additional discussions of Hangul and Kim's use of
that alphabet.

15. Kim makes this point herself in her interview with the author, conducted in
October 2006 (Kim, "Interview"). She also discusses this passage in "Pollen Fossil
Record": "being compelled to write down as exactly as possible the words of Olga
Kim, speaking about her forty years of living in Siberia, and knowing fully that an
atrophied, arrested, third grade Korean writing is what was available. What was
missing? What was forgotten? What was never learned in the first place? What was
and was not written 'correctly'?" (110).

16. Kim's changing approach to page space may well reflect the influence of Susan
Howe, who was Kim's colleague for several years at SUNY Buffalo prior to Howe's
retirement. The page duplicated in Figure 7 is especially evocative of Howe's distinctive play with type on the page.

17. In some sense this chapbook is a collaborative work that is the joint production
of Cross and Kim. For the purposes of this chapter, however, it is important that Kim
had all the design elements in mind before Cross became involved. Responding to
my inquiry specifically about the black inner cover but also about the design generally, Kim wrote in an e-mail on July 10, 2007, "[A]lmost everything about the book's
design was Michael's response to something I'd 'requested.' I paid a great deal of
attention to the placement of each element on the page—e.g., the 'three-fold' pages
had to read across (and back) as a 'scroll' potentially. . . . Generally, then, every design
element (not the cover itself) was something I presented to Michael Cross" (quoted
with Kim's permission).

WORKS CITED

"Aggregate." *Shorter Oxford English Dictionary.* 3rd ed. 1970.

Altieri, Charles. "Avant-Garde or Arrière-Garde in Recent American Poetry." *Poetics Today* 20.4 (1999): 629–53.

———. *Self and Sensibility in Contemporary American Poetry.* Cambridge: Cambridge UP, 1984.

———. "Some Problems about Agency in the Theories of Radical Poetics." *Postmodernisms Now: Essays on Contemporaneity in the Arts.* University Park: Pennsylvania State UP, 1998. 166–92.

Andrews, Bruce, and Charles Bernstein, eds. *The L=A=N=G=U=A=G=E Book.* Carbondale: Southern Illinois UP, 1984.

Armantrout, Rae. *Collected Prose.* San Diego: Singing Horse, 2007.

Auden, W. H. "Musée des Beaux Arts." *Collected Poems.* Ed. Edward Mendelson. New York: Random House, 1976. 146–47.

Baxandall, Michael. *Painting and Experience in Fifteenth-Century Italy: A Primer in the Social History of Pictorial Style.* 2nd ed. Oxford: Oxford UP, 1988.

Beach, Christopher. *Poetic Culture: Contemporary American Poetry between Community and Institution.* Evanston: Northwestern UP, 1999.

Bedient, Calvin. Poetry reviews. *Boston Review* 27.2 (Apr.–May 2002): 58–60.

Belitt, Ben. Cover blurb. *Bag 'o' Diamonds.* By Susan Wheeler. Athens: U of Georgia P, 1993.

Bernstein, Charles. *A Poetics.* Cambridge: Harvard UP, 1992.

———. "Response: Every Which Way but Loose." *Reimagining Textuality: Textual Studies in the Late Age of Print.* Ed. Elizabeth Bergmann Loizeaux and Neil Fraistat. Madison: U of Wisconsin P, 2002. 178–85.

Bök, Christian. *Crystallography.* Rev. ed. Toronto: Coach House, 2003.

Burt, Stephen. "The New Thing: The Object Lessons of Recent American Poetry." *Boston Review* 34.3 (May/June 2009). 11 June 2009 <http://bostonreview.net/BR34.3/burt.php>.

———. "Shearing Away." *Poetry Review* 88.1 (1998): 4–7.

———. Rev. of *Smokes*, by Susan Wheeler. *Boston Review* 23.3 (Summer 1998). 11 June 2009 <http://bostonreview.net/BR23.3/burt.html>.

Bynum, Caroline Walker. *Fragmentation and Redemption: Essays on Gender and the Human Body in Medieval Religion*. New York: Zone, 1991.

———. *Holy Feast and Holy Fast: The Religious Significance of Food to Medieval Women*. Berkeley: U of California P, 1987.

Celan, Paul. "The Meridian." *Paul Celan: Selections*. Ed. Pierre Joris. Berkeley: U of California P, 2005. 154–69.

Chaucer, Geoffrey. *Troilus and Criseyde*. Trans. Barry Windeatt. Oxford: Oxford UP, 1998.

"Commons." *Shorter Oxford English Dictionary*. 3rd ed. 1970.

Conte, Joseph. *Unending Design: The Forms of Postmodern Poetry*. Ithaca: Cornell UP, 1991.

Davidson, Michael. *Ghostlier Demarcations: Modern Poetry and the Material Word*. Berkeley: U of California P, 1997.

Derrida, Jacques. *The Truth in Painting*. Trans. Geoff Bennington and Ian McLeod. Chicago: U of Chicago P, 1987.

Drucker, Johanna. "Intimations of Immateriality: Graphical Form, Textual Sense, and the Electronic Environment." *Reimagining Textuality: Textual Studies in the Late Age of Print*. Ed. Elizabeth Bergmann Loizeaux and Neil Fraistat. Madison: U of Wisconsin P, 2002. 152–77.

DuPlessis, Rachel Blau. *Blue Studios: Poetry and Its Cultural Work*. Tuscaloosa: U of Alabama P, 2006.

———. "Manifests." *Diacritics* 26 (Fall–Winter 1996): 31–53.

———. *The Pink Guitar: Writing as Feminist Practice*. New York: Routledge, 1990.

Eddington, A. S. *The Nature of the Physical World*. New York: Macmillan, 1929.

Eliot, T. S. *Selected Prose of T. S. Eliot*. Ed. Frank Kermode. New York: Harcourt, 1975.

Evans, Steve, ed. *After Patriarchal Poetry: Feminism and the Contemporary Avant-Garde*. Spec. issue of *differences: A Journal of Feminist Cultural Studies* 12 (Summer 2001). i–v, 1–168.

———. "The Resistible Rise of Fence Enterprises." *The Third Factory: Notes to Poetry* (2004). 11 June 2009 <http://www.thirdfactory.net/resistible.html>.

———. "Rosmarie Waldrop." *American Poets Since World War II*. Ed. Joseph Conte. Vol. 169. Dictionary of Literary Biography. Detroit: Gale Research, 1996. 284–96.

———. *Third Factory: Notes to Poetry* (2001). 11 June 2009 <http://www.umit.maine.edu/~steven.evans/3F-index.htm>.

Rev. of *Felt*, by Alice Fulton. *Publishers Weekly* 247.47 (20 Nov. 2000): 64–65.

Fenza, D. W. "Advice for Graduating MFA Students in Writing: The Words & the Bees." *Writer's Chronicle* 38.6 (2006): 1–8.

"Flense." *Shorter Oxford English Dictionary*. 3rd ed. 1970.

"The Flight into Egypt." *The Getty Museum*. The J. Paul Getty Trust. 11 June 2009 <http://www.getty.edu/art/gettyguide/artObjectDetails?artobj=1847>.

Foucault, Michel. *The Order of Things: An Archeology of the Human Sciences*. New York: Pantheon, 1971. Trans. of *Les Mots et les choses*. Editions Gallimard, 1966.

Fraser, Kathleen. "An Interview with Kathleen Fraser." By Cynthia Hogue. *Contemporary Literature* 30.1 (Spring 1998): 1–26.

———. "Partial Local Coherence: Some Notes on Language Writing." *Ironwood* 20 (1982): 122–42.

———. *Translating the Unspeakable: Poetry and Innovative Necessity.* Tuscaloosa: U of Alabama P, 2000.

Frost, Elisabeth. *The Feminist Avant-Garde in American Poetry.* Iowa City: U of Iowa P, 2003.

Frost, Elisabeth, and Cynthia Hogue, eds. *Innovative Women Poets: An Anthology of Contemporary Poetry and Interviews.* Iowa City: U of Iowa P, 2006.

Fulton, Alice. "Alice Fulton." *The Poet's Notebook: Excerpts from the Notebooks of Contemporary American Poets.* Ed. Stephen Kuusisto, Deborah Tall, and David Weiss. New York: Norton, 1995. 43–64.

———. *Cascade Experiment: Selected Poems.* New York: Norton, 2004.

———. *Dance Script with Electric Ballerina.* Philadelphia: U of Pennsylvania P, 1983.

———. *Feeling as a Foreign Language: The Good Strangeness of Poetry.* St. Paul: Graywolf, 1999.

———. *Felt.* New York: Norton, 2001.

———. "Her Moment of Brocade." *Parnassus* 15.1 (1989): 9–44.

———. "An Interview with Alice Fulton." By Cristanne Miller. *Contemporary Literature* 38.4 (1997): 586–615.

———. *Palladium.* Urbana: U of Illinois P, 1986.

———. *Powers of Congress.* Boston: Godine, 1990.

———. *Sensual Math.* New York: Norton, 1995.

———. "The Wick That Is the White between the Ink: An Interview with Alice Fulton." By Linden Ontjes. *Seattle Review* 27.2 (2005): 24–44. 11 June 2009 <http://people.cornell.edu/pages/af89/interviews/sr.html>.

Gilbert, Sandra. "Looks of Memory and Desire." *Poetry* 168 (Aug. 1996): 281–302.

Gioia, Dana. *Can Poetry Matter? Essays on Poetry and American Culture.* St. Paul: Graywolf, 1992.

Glazier, Loss Pequeño. *Digital Poetics: The Making of E-Poetries.* Tuscaloosa: U of Alabama P, 2002.

Golding, Alan. "Visual Materiality in Bruce Andrews." *Jacket* 22 (May 2003). 11 June 2009 <http://jacketmagazine.com/22/and-gold.html>.

Goodman, Jenny. "C. D. Wright." *American Poets Since World War II.* Ed. R. S. Gwynn. Vol. 120. Dictionary of Literary Biography 5. Detroit: Gale Research, 1992. 329–33.

———. "Politics and the Personal Lyric in the Poetry of Joy Harjo and C.D. Wright." *MELUS* 19.2 (1994): 33–56.

Greer, Michael. "Ideology and Theory in Recent Experimental Writing or, The Naming of 'Language Poetry.'" *boundary 2* 16 (1989): 335–55.

Grosz, Elizabeth. *Volatile Bodies: Toward a Corporeal Feminism.* Bloomington: Indiana UP, 1994.

Hartley, George. *Textual Politics and the Language Poets.* Bloomington: Indiana UP, 1989.

Hass, Robert. Afterword. *Smokes*. By Susan Wheeler. Marshfield: Four Way, 1998.

Hayles, N. Katherine. "Chance Operations: Cagean Paradox and Contemporary Science." *John Cage: Composed in America*. Ed. Marjorie Perloff and Charles Junkerman. Chicago: U of Chicago P, 1994. 226–41.

Healy, Randolph. "The Eighteenth Letter." *Lynx: Poetry from Bath* 13 (Dec. 1999). Ed. Douglas Clark. 11 June 2009 <http://www.dgdclynx.plus.com/lynx/lynx138.html>.

Heffernan, James A. W. *Museum of Words: The Poetics of Ekphrasis from Homer to Ashbery*. Chicago: U of Chicago P, 1993.

Hejinian, Lyn. *The Language of Inquiry*. Berkeley: U of California P, 2000.

Hinton, Laura, and Cynthia Hogue, eds. *We Who Love to Be Astonished: Experimental Women's Writing and Performance Poetics*. Tuscaloosa: U of Alabama P, 2002.

Hirsch, Edward. "The Body's Stubborn Limits." *Metropolitan Detroit* (July 1984): 41–42.

Holman, Bob. "Trace of a Tale: C.D. Wright: An Investigative Poem." *Poets & Writers Magazine* 30 (May/June 2002): 12–23.

Howe, Susan. *The Birth-mark: Unsettling the Wilderness in American Literary History*. Hanover: Wesleyan UP, 1993.

———. *The Midnight*. New York: New Directions, 2003.

Izenberg, Oren. "Language Poetry and Collective Life." *Critical Inquiry* 30.1 (2003): 132–59.

Jackson, K. David, Eric Vos, and Johanna Drucker, eds. *Experimental—Visual—Concrete: Avant-Garde Poetry Since the 1960s*. Amsterdam: Rodopi, 1996.

Jameson, Fredric. *Postmodernism, or, The Cultural Logic of Late Capitalism*. Durham: Duke UP, 1991.

Jarman, Mark. "Acts of Will." *Missouri Review* 7.3 (1994): 83–94.

Jay, Martin. "Scopic Regimes of Modernity." *Vision and Visuality*. Ed. Hal Foster. Seattle: Bay, 1988. 3–23. Discussions in Contemporary Culture 2.

Jeon, Joseph Jonghyun. "Speaking in Tongues: Myung Mi Kim's Stylized Mouths." *Studies in the Literary Imagination* 37 (2004): 125, 127–48.

Kalaidjian, Walter. *American Culture between the Wars: Revisionary Modernism and Postmodern Critique*. New York: Columbia UP, 1993.

Katz, Joy. "What Are We Doing in This Carwash?" *Parnassus* 22.1–2 (1997): 296–316.

Keller, Lynn. "'The New Syntax of Love': Lyricism as Experiment in C.D. Wright's *Tremble*." Twentieth-Century Literature Conference. University of Louisville. Feb. 1999.

———. "'Nothing, for a Woman, Is Worth Trying': A Key into the Rule of Rosmarie Waldrop's Experimentalism." *We Who Love to Be Astonished: Experimental Women's Writing and Performance Poetics*. Ed. Laura Hinton and Cynthia Hogue. Tuscaloosa: U of Alabama P, 2001. 103–15.

———. "Singing Spaces: Fractal Geometries in Cole Swensen's *Oh*." *Journal of Modern Literature* 31.1 (Fall 2007): 136–60.

———. "Susan Wheeler's Open Source Poetics." *American Poets in the 21st Century: The New Poetics*. Ed. Claudia Rankine and Lisa Sewell. Middletown: Wesleyan UP, 2007. 304–19.

Kim, Myung Mi. "Anacrusis." *HOW2* 1.2 (1999). 11 June 2009 <http://www.asu
.edu/pipercwcenter/how2journal/archive/online_archive/v1_2_1999/current/
readings/kim.html>.

———. *Commons.* Berkeley: U of California P, 2002.

———. "Convolutions: The Precision, the Wild." *American Poets of the 21st Century:
The New Poetics.* Ed. Claudia Rankine and Lisa Sewell. Middletown: Wesleyan
UP, 2007. 251.

———. "Generosity as Method: An Interview with Myung Mi Kim." By Yedda Mor-
rison. *Tripwire: A Journal of Poetics* 1 (Spring 1998). *Electronic Poetry Center.* Oct.
2008. University of Buffalo. 11 June 2009 <http://epc.buffalo.edu/authors/kim/
generosity.html>.

———. "An Interview with Myung Mi Kim." By Lynn Keller. *Contemporary Literature* 49.3 (Fall 2008): 335–56.

———. "Myung Mi Kim." Interview by James Kyung-Jin Lee. *Words Matter: Conversations with Asian American Writers.* Ed. King-Kok Cheung. Honolulu: U of
Hawai'i Press, 2000. 92–104.

———. *River Antes.* Buffalo: Atticus/Finch Chapbooks, 2006.

———. *Under Flag.* 1991. Berkeley: Kelsey Street, 1998.

Kinnahan, Linda A. *Lyric Interventions: Feminism, Experimental Poetry, and Contemporary Discourse.* Iowa City: U of Iowa P, 2004.

Kirsch, Adam. "Discourtesies." *New Republic* 21 Oct. 2002: 32–36.

Krieger, Murray. "The Ekphrastic Principle and the Still Movement of Poetry; or
Laokoön Revisited." *The Play and Place of Criticism.* Baltimore: Johns Hopkins
UP, 1967. 105–28.

Kristeva, Julia. *Desire in Language: A Semiotic Approach to Literature and Art.* Ed.
Leon Roudiez. Trans. Alice Jardine, Thomas Gora, and Leon S. Roudiez. New
York: Columbia UP, 1980.

Lehman, David, ed. *Ecstatic Occasions, Expedient Forms: 65 Leading Contemporary
Poets Select and Comment on Their Poems.* New York: Macmillan, 1987.

Lipovetsky, Gilles. *The Empire of Fashion: Dressing Modern Democracy.* Trans. Cath-
erine Porter. Princeton: Princeton UP, 1994.

Liu, Warren. "Making Common the Commons: Myung Mi Kim's Ideal Subject."
American Poets of the 21st Century: The New Poetics. Ed. Claudia Rankine and
Lisa Sewell. Middletown: Wesleyan UP, 2007. 252–66.

Logan, William. "Morphing Apollo." *New York Times Book Review* 10 Dec. 1995: 37.

Lowe, Lisa. "Unfaithful to the Original: The Subject of *Dictée.*" *Writing Self, Writing
Nation.* Ed. Elaine H. Kim and Norma Alarcón. Berkeley: Third Woman, 1994. 35–69.

Luft, David F. *Robert Musil and the Crisis of European Culture.* Berkeley: U of California P, 1980.

Major, Clarence, ed. *Juba to Jive: A Dictionary of African-American Slang.* New York:
Viking Penguin, 1994.

McCaffery, Steve. "The Death of the Subject: The Implications of Counter-Commu-
nication in Recent Language-Centered Writing." *L=A=N=G=U=A=G=E* Supplement 1 (June 1980). *Eclipse.* University of Utah. 11 June 2009 <http://english.utah
.edu/eclipse/projects/LANGUAGEsupp1/LanguageSupp1.pdf>.

McGuinness, Brian. *Wittgenstein: A Life, Young Ludwig 1889–1921*. Berkeley: U of California P, 1988.

Messerli, Douglas, ed. *"Language" Poetries: An Anthology*. New York: New Directions, 1987.

Miller, Cristanne. "'The Erogenous Cusp,' or Intersections of Science and Gender in Alice Fulton's Poetry." *Feminist Measures: Soundings in Poetry and Theory*. Ed. Lynn Keller and Cristanne Miller. Ann Arbor: U of Michigan P, 1994. 317–43.

———. *Marianne Moore: Questions of Authority*. Cambridge: Harvard UP, 1995.

Mitchell, W. J. T. *Iconology: Image, Text, Ideology*. Chicago: U of Chicago P, 1986.

———. *Picture Theory*. Chicago: U of Chicago P, 1994.

Mix, Deborah. *A Vocabulary of Thinking: Gertrude Stein and Contemporary North American Women's Innovative Writing*. Iowa City: U of Iowa P, 2007.

Mobilio, Albert. Rev. of *Bag 'o' Diamonds*, by Susan Wheeler. *Voice Literary Supplement* Apr. 1994: 14.

Monroe, Jonathan. "Syntextural Investigations." *Diacritics* 26.3–4 (1996): 126–41.

Mullen, Harryette. *Muse & Drudge*. San Diego: Singing Horse, 1995.

———. "Solo Mysterioso Blues: An Interview with Harryette Mullen." By Calvin Bedient. *Callaloo* 19.3 (1996): 651–69.

Musil, Robert. "The Perfecting of a Love." Trans. Eithne Wilkins and Ernst Kaiser. *Selected Writings*. Ed. Burton Pike. New York: Continuum, 1986. 179–222.

Nemerov, Howard. *Reflexions on Poetry and Poetics*. New Brunswick: Rutgers UP, 1972.

Nielsen, Aldon Lynn, and Lauri Ramey, eds. *Every Goodbye Ain't Gone: An Anthology of Innovative Poetry by African Americans*. Tuscaloosa: U of Alabama P, 2006.

O'Connor, Flannery. "Some Aspects of the Grotesque in Southern Fiction." *Mystery and Manners: Occasional Prose*. Ed. Sally Fitzgerald and Robert Fitzgerald. New York: Macmillan, 1969. 36–50.

Olson, Charles. "Projective Verse." 1950. *Collected Prose*. Ed. Donald Allen and Benjamin Friedlander. Berkeley: U of California P, 1997. 239–49.

O'Sullivan, Maggie, ed. *Out of Everywhere: Linguistically Innovative Poetry by Women in North America and the UK*. London: Reality Street, 1996.

Park, Josephine Nock-Hee. "'Composed of Many Lengths of Bone': Myung Mi Kim's Reimagination of Image and Epic." *Transnational Asian American Literature: Sites and Transits*. Ed. Shirley Geok-lin Lim, John Blair Gamber, Stephen Hong Sohn, and Gina Valentino. Philadelphia: Temple UP, 2005. 235–56.

Perelman, Bob. *The Future of Memory*. New York: Roof Books. 1998.

———. *The Marginalization of Poetry: Language Poetry and Literary History*. Princeton: Princeton UP, 1996.

———. "Ten to Ten: Bob Perelman Interviewed by Nagy Rashway and Nicholas Zurbrugg." *Electronic Poetry Review* 4 (2002). 11 June 2009 <http://www.epoetry.org/issues/issue4/text/prose/perelman1.htm>.

Perloff, Marjorie. *The Dance of the Intellect: Studies in the Poetry of the Pound Tradition*. New York: Cambridge UP, 1985.

———. *Differentials: Poetry, Politics, Pedagogy*. Tuscaloosa: U of Alabama P, 2004.

———. *Radical Artifice: Writing Poetry in the Age of Media*. Chicago: U of Chicago P, 1991.

———. *21st-Century Modernism: The "New" Poetics*. Malden: Blackwell, 2002.

———. *Wittgenstein's Ladder: Poetic Language and the Strangeness of the Ordinary*. Chicago: U of Chicago P, 1996.

———. "The Word as Such: L=A=N=G=U=A=G=E Poetry in the Eighties." *American Poetry Review* 13.3 (May–June 1984): 15–22.

Rankine, Claudia, and Lisa Sewell. *American Poets in the 21st Century: The New Poetics*. Middletown: Wesleyan UP, 2007.

Rankine, Claudia, and Juliana Spahr. *American Women Poets in the 21st Century: Where Lyric Meets Language*. Middletown: Wesleyan UP, 2002.

Rasula, Jed. *The American Poetry Wax Museum: Reality Effects, 1940–1990*. Urbana: NCTE, 1996.

———. *Syncopations: The Stress of Innovation in Recent American Poetry*. Tuscaloosa: U of Alabama P, 2004.

Retallack, Joan. *AFTERRIMAGES*. Hanover: Wesleyan UP, 1995.

———. *The Poethical Wager*. Berkeley: U of California P, 2003.

———. "Poethics of a Complex Realism." *John Cage: Composed in America*. Ed. Marjorie Perloff and Charles Junkerman. Chicago: U of Chicago P, 1994. 242–73.

———. ":RE:THINKING:LITERARY:FEMINISM:" *Feminist Measures: Soundings in Poetry and Theory*. Ed. Lynn Keller and Cristanne Miller. Ann Arbor: U of Michigan P, 1994. 344–77.

———. "What Is Experimental Poetry & Why Do We Need It?" *Jacket* 32 (Apr. 2007). 11 June 2009 <http://jacketmagazine.com/32/p-retallack.shtml>.

Rukeyser, Muriel. "The Book of the Dead." *The Collected Poems of Muriel Rukeyser*. Ed. Janet Kaufman and Anne Herzog. Pittsburgh: U of Pittsburgh P, 2005. 73–110.

Scottish Songs. London: Bayley & Ferguson, n.d.

Shepherd, Reginald. *Lyric Postmodernisms: An Anthology of Contemporary Innovative Poetries*. Denver: Counterpath, 2008.

Shetley, Vernon. *After the Death of Poetry: Poet and Audience in Contemporary America*. Durham: Duke UP, 1993.

Silliman, Ron, ed. *In the American Tree: Language, Realism, Poetry*. 1986. Orono: Natl. Poetry Foundation, 2001.

———. *The New Sentence*. New York: Roof, 1987.

———, ed. "REALISM: An Anthology of 'Language' Writing." *Ironwood* 20 (1982). 61–139.

———. *Tjanting*. Berkeley: The Figures, 1981.

Silliman, Ron, Carla Harryman, Lyn Hejinian, Steve Benson, Bob Perelman, and Barrett Watten. "Aesthetic Tendency and the Politics of Poetry: A Manifesto." *Social Text* 19/20 (1988): 261–75.

Silliman, Ron, and Leslie Scalapino. "What/Person: From an Exchange." *Poetics Journal* 9 (1991): 51–68.

Simpson, Megan. *Poetic Epistemologies: Gender and Knowing in Women's Language-Oriented Writing*. Albany: State U of New York P, 2000.

Slavitt, David. "The Year in Poetry." *Dictionary of Literary Biography Yearbook 1995*. Detroit: Gale Research, 1996. 28.

Sloan, Mary Margaret, ed. *Moving Borders: Three Decades of Innovative Writing by Women*. Jersey City: Talisman, 1998.

Smitherman, Geneva. *Black Talk: Words and Phrases from the Hood to the Amen Corner*. Rev. ed. Boston: Houghton, 2000.

Snyder, Joel, and Ted Cohen. "Reflections on *Las Meninas*: Paradox Lost." *Critical Inquiry* 7.2 (Winter 1980): 429–47.

"Special Feature: Elliptical Poets." *American Letters and Commentary* 11 (1999): 45–76.

Stefans, Brian Kim. *Fashionable Noise: On Digital Poetics*. [Berkeley]: Atelos, 2003.

———. "Little Reviews." Rev. of *Smokes*, by Susan Wheeler. *Arras: New Media Poetry and Poetics*. 11 June 2009 <http://www.arras.net/the_franks/wheeler_smokes.htm>.

———. "Little Reviews." Rev. of *Source Codes*, by Susan Wheeler. *Arras: New Media Poetry and Poetics*. 11 June 2009 <http://www.arras.net/the_franks/wheeler_source_code.htm>.

Stein, Gertrude. *Picasso*. 1938. Boston: Beacon, 1959.

Swensen, Cole. "Against the Limits of Language: The Geometries of Anne-Marie Albiach and Susan Howe." *Moving Borders: Three Decades of Innovative Writing by Women*. Ed. Mary Margaret Sloan. Jersey City: Talisman, 1998. 630–41.

———. *The Glass Age*. Farmington: Alice James, 2007.

———. "Interview with Cole Swensen." *Jubilat* 10 (Summer 2005): 81–94.

———. "To Writewithize." 2000. 4 Nov. 2002 <http://www.du.edu/~cswensen/writewithize.html>. [The page that contained this version is no longer available.]

———. "To Writewithize." *American Letters and Commentary* 13 (Winter 2001): 122–27.

———. *Try*. Iowa City: U of Iowa P, 1999.

———. "Working Notes on *Try*." *HOW2* 1.1 (Mar. 1999). 11 June 2009 <http://www.asu.edu/pipercwcenter/how2journal/archive/online_archive/v1_1_1999/csnoli.html>.

Swensen, Cole, and David St. John. *American Hybrid: A Norton Anthology of New Poetry*. New York: Norton, 2008.

Taylor, Linda. "'A Seizure of Voice': Language Innovation and a Feminist Poetics in the Works of Kathleen Fraser." *Contemporary Literature* 33.2 (1992): 337–72.

Taylor, Mark C. *The Moment of Complexity: Emerging Network Culture*. Chicago: U of Chicago P, 2002.

Tejada, Roberto. Rev. of *Sensual Math*, by Alice Fulton. *Sulfur: A Literary Bi-Annual of the Whole Art* 38 (Spring 1996): 155–56.

Vickery, Ann. *Leaving Lines of Gender: A Feminist Genealogy of Language Writing*. Hanover: Wesleyan UP, 2000.

Wakoski, Diane. "Words of Power." *Women's Review of Books* 8.9 (June 1991): 24–25.

Waldrop, Rosmarie. *Against Language? Dissatisfaction with Language as Theme and as Impulse towards Experiments in Twentieth Century Poetry*. The Hague: Mouton, 1971.

———. "Alarms & Excursions." *The Politics of Poetic Form: Poetry and Public Policy*. Ed. Charles Bernstein. New York: ROOF, 1990. 45–72.

———. *Blindsight*. New York: New Directions, 2003.

———. "A Conversation with Rosmarie Waldrop." Interview by Joan Retallack. *Contemporary Literature* 40 (1999): 329–77.

———. *Curves to the Apple: The Reproduction of Profiles, Lawn of Excluded Middle, Reluctant Gravities*. New York: New Directions, 2006.

———. "Form and Discontent." *Diacritics* 26.3–4 (1996): 54–62.

———. "An Interview with Rosmarie Waldrop." By Edward Foster. *Talisman* 6 (Spring 1991): 27–39.

———. *A Key into the Language of America*. New York: New Directions, 1994.

———. *Lawn of Excluded Middle*. Providence: Tender Buttons, 1993.

———. "Rosmarie Waldrop." *Contemporary Authors Autobiographical Series*. Vol. 30. Detroit: Gale Research, 1999: 297–314.

———. "Rosmarie Waldrop." *L=A=N=G=U=A=G=E* 1.3 (1978). *Eclipse*. University of Utah. 11 June 2009 <http://english.utah.edu/eclipse/projects/LANGUAGEn3/Language3.pdf>.

———. "Thinking of Follows." *Moving Borders: Three Decades of Innovative Writing by Women*. Ed. Mary Margaret Sloan. Jersey City: Talisman, 1998. 609–17.

Wallace, Mark, and Steven Marks, eds. *Telling It Slant: Avant-Garde Poetics of the 1990s*. Tuscaloosa: U of Alabama P, 2002.

Wasserberg, Charles. "Reprieve from Plainness." *Borders Review of Books* 6.8 (Sept. 1986): 1–3.

Watten, Barrett. *The Constructivist Moment: From Material Text to Cultural Poetics*. Middletown: Wesleyan UP, 2003.

Wheeler, Susan. *Bag 'o' Diamonds*. Athens: U of Georgia P, 1993.

———. "An Interview with Susan Wheeler." By Lynn Keller. *Contemporary Literature* 45 (2004): 573–96.

———. *Ledger*. Iowa City: U of Iowa P, 2005.

———. "Poetry, Mattering?" *By Herself: Women Reclaim Poetry*. Ed. Molly McQuade. St. Paul: Graywolf, 2000. 317–27.

———. "Reading, Raiding, and Anodyne Eclecticism: Word without World." *Antioch Review* 62 (Winter 2004): 148–55.

———. *Smokes*. Marshfield: Four Way, 1998.

———. *Source Codes*. Applecross: Salt, 2001.

———. "A Tag Without a Chit." <http://english.rutgers.edu/atag/htm>. [The page that contained this copyrighted statement from 4 Apr. 1997 at Rutgers University, "Poetry and the Public Sphere," is no longer available.]

———. "What Outside?" *Talisman* 19 (Winter 1998–1999): 192–95.

Wiegman, Robyn. *American Anomalies: Theorizing Race and Gender*. Durham: Duke UP, 1995.

Wittgenstein, Ludwig. *Philosophical Investigations*. 1953. Trans. G. E. M. Anscombe. New York: Macmillan, 1968.

Wong, Shelley Sunn. "Unnaming the Same: Theresa Hak Kyung Cha's *Dictée*." *Writing Self, Writing Nation*. Ed. Elaine H. Kim and Norma Alarcón. Berkeley: Third Woman, 1994. 103–40.

Wright, C.D. "The Adamantine Practice of Poetry." *Brick* 35 (Spring 1989): 55–59.

———. "Argument with the Gestapo Continued: II." *Five Fingers Review* 5 (1987): 79–89.

———. "Arguments with the Gestapo Continued: Literary Resistance." *Five Fingers Review* (1984): 30–34.

———. "Bedrock, Roots and Veins: A Talk with C.D. Wright." Interview by Kathleen Fraser. *Poetry Flash: A Poetry Review and Literary Calendar for the West* 259 (Mar. 1995): 1, 6–8, 10.

———. *Cooling Time: An American Poetry Vigil.* Port Townsend: Copper Canyon, 2005.

———. *Deepstep Come Shining.* Port Townsend: Copper Canyon, 1998.

———. *Further Adventures with You.* Pittsburgh: Carnegie Mellon UP, 1986.

———. "Infamous Liberties & Uncommon Restraints." *AWP Chronicle* 23.6 (1991): 1–4.

———. *Just Whistle: A Valentine.* Photographs by Deborah Luster. Berkeley: Kelsey Street, 1993.

———. "Looking for 'one untranslatable song': An Interview with C.D. Wright." By Kent Johnson. *Jacket* 15 (Dec. 2001). 11 June 2009 <http://jacketmagazine.com/15/cdwright-iv.html>.

———. *The Lost Roads Project: A Walk-in Book of Arkansas.* Photographs by Deborah Luster. Fayetteville: U of Arkansas P, 1994.

———. "Op-Ed." *Onward: Contemporary Poetry and Poetics.* Ed. Peter Baker. New York: Peter Lang, 1996. 167.

———. "Provisional Remarks On Being / A Poet / Of Arkansas." *Southern Review* 30.4 (1994): 809–11.

———. "Reading Relations." *Ironwood* 15 (Fall 1987): 207–10.

———. *Rising, Falling, Hovering.* Port Townsend: Copper Canyon, 2008.

———. *Room Rented by a Single Woman.* Fayetteville: Lost Roads, 1977.

———. *Steal Away: Selected and New Poems.* Port Townsend: Copper Canyon, 2002.

———. "A Taxable Matter." *Field* 40 (Spring 1989): 24–26.

———. *Tremble.* Hopewell: Ecco, 1996.

Wright, C.D., and Deborah Luster. *One Big Self: Prisoners of Louisiana.* Santa Fe: Twin Palms, 2003.

Yenser, Stephen. "Poetry in Review." *Yale Review* 87.1 (1999): 149–62.

Zander, William. "Wit in Poetry." *Literary Review* 28.1 (Fall 1984): 149–53.

Zhou, Xiaojing. *The Ethics and Poetics of Alterity in Asian American Poetry.* Iowa City: U of Iowa P, 2006.

INDEX

academia. *See* institutions

Academy of American Poets, 5, 124, 184n6

"Accelerating Frame" (Waldrop), 83

"Aesthetic Tendency and the Politics of Poetry," 11

African Americans, 14–15, 61, 65, 67. *See also* racial oppression

AFTERRIMAGES (Retallack), 10–11, 19, 73, 85–95

Agee, James, 42, 189n9

aggregation, 156, 163–64, 166, 170, 171, 176, 178

Akerman, Chantal, 123

"Alarms & Excursions" (Waldrop), 74–75

Albers, Joseph, 114

allusions: in "courteous" poetry, 12, 13; Creeley's, 18; Fulton's, 57–63, 68; Mullen's, 15; Swensen's, 120; Wheeler's, 138, 139–40; Wright's, 24, 34–35, 42. *See also* collage techniques; source texts

Altieri, Charles, 36–37, 49, 129, 134, 185n8

American Academy of Arts and Sciences, 124

American Hybrid (Swensen and St. John), 4, 6

American Poets in the 21st Century (Rankine and Sewell), 4

American Women Poets in the 21st Century (Rankine and Spahr), 4

Ammons, A. R., 47, 50, 195n19

"Anacrusis" (Kim), 154

Andrews, Bruce, 170

Apollo. *See* Daphne and Apollo myth

"Appendix II" (Wheeler), 145, 146–51

"Appendix III" (Wheeler), 145

Armantrout, Rae, 3, 10, 185n12

Arras (journal), 129

Ashbery, John, 48, 70, 100, 126, 200n13

assimilation (crossover poetics), 25, 124–52. *See also* hybridity; iconoplasm

Assorted Poems (Wheeler), 128

astronauts, 131–32, 147

atomic weapons, 86–87, 90, 93, 122, 160, 162

Atticus/Finch Press, 170

"The Attraction of the Ground" (Waldrop), 83

Auden, W. H., 92, 100, 127, 200n17

authenticity, 42, 49, 54, 56

"Avant-Garde or Arrière-Garde in Recent American Poetry" (Altieri), 129

awards: for exploratory poetry, 7, 11; for Fulton's poetry, 11, 47; for Swensen's poetry, 11, 100, 198n6; for Wheeler's poetry, 11, 128

AWP (Association of Writers and Writing Programs) writing programs, 5, 28, 47, 186n18, 188n4, 193n3

Bag 'o' Diamonds (Wheeler), 128, 145

Beach, Christopher, 3, 192n2

Bedient, Calvin, 14, 45, 48

Benson, Steve, 11

Bernstein, Charles, 3, 47, 149, 186n18

Berryman, John, 126
The Best American Poetry, 128
"betweenness." *See* hybridity
binaries (dichotomies): Cartesian, 23,
    29–30, 35, 41; exploratory poetry as
    breaking down, 10, 13–14, 46, 57–60,
    69, 71–72, 79, 87, 96, 137, 150, 196n14,
    205n4; prose/poetry, 35–36, 181, 191n23;
    in recent contemporary poetry scene, 7,
    46, 126; and Wright's works, 23, 29–30,
    35, 37–42
Black Talk (Smitherman), 15
bodies (female): anatomical experiments
    on, 160–64; Burton on, 136; Christian-
    ity's views of, 110–12, 121, 136, 201n19,
    201n20; Waldrop on, 77–80, 81, 83–85,
    197n15; Wright on, 29–45, 190n16. *See
    also* gender; sexuality
Bohr, Niels, 82
*Book of Mediaeval Lore from Bartholomew
    Anglicus*, 159
"The Book of the Dead" (Rukeyser), 160
Bosch, Hieronymus, 116–17
"bride mark" (Fulton's invented punctua-
    tion mark), 10–11, 58–62, 69, 195n19
"A BRIEF AND BLAMELESS OUTLINE
    OF THE ONTOGENY OF CROW"
    (Wright), 38–39
Burning Deck Press, 19
Burt, Stephen, 129, 186n15, 203n11
Burton, Robert, 136

Cage, John, 19, 70, 71, 72, 87, 90, 154, 182
Canterbury Tales (Chaucer), 88
Capilla del Rosaria, 136
capitalism, 24, 52–54, 132, 137, 181, 189n6,
    203n7
Carroll, Lewis, 126
Cartesian perspectivalism, 161, 162
Cascade Experiment (Fulton), 47
"Cascade Experiment" (Fulton), 50, 193n7
Celan, Paul, 154, 204n1
Cha, Theresa Hak Kyung, 136, 166–67,
    204n1
chaos theory, 18, 71–72, 128
Chaucer, Geoffrey, 87–89
childbirth, 30, 31, 37, 40, 41, 43, 44
Chinese language, 166, 167

Christianity and the Bible, 42; flight into
    Egypt, 109–10, 117–19, 120; misogyny
    in, 110–13, 121, 136, 201n19, 201n20; and
    Wright, 22, 24, 42–43. *See also* Jesus;
    Mary (Madonna); Mary Magdalene
closure (poetic): Fulton's use of, 53, 55;
    Hejinian on, 13–14, 18, 22, 34, 188n1;
    narrative and, 29, 55; Retallack's use
    of, 95; Swensen's resistance to, 119;
    traditional poetic forms' association
    with, 70; Waldrop's resistance to,
    197n15; Wright's resistance to, 21–22,
    33, 45
Coleridge, Samuel Taylor, 16, 126, 138
collage techniques, 181; in Retallack
    and Waldrop's poetry, 72, 73, 85–90,
    94–95; in Swensen's poetry, 101, 119;
    in Wheeler's works, 124–28, 130–37,
    145, 149, 150, 151–52. *See also* allusions;
    genres (hybridity of); source texts
colors: Kim's use of, 163, 164; Swensen's
    use of, 104, 110–11, 114–16
Commons (Kim), 19, 155, 156–69, 170, 171,
    177, 181, 205n3
complexity (intellectuality): as discourte-
    ous, 12–13; poetry that exhibits, 1–2,
    8–9, 11–20, 52–53, 71, 93, 128, 135, 144–51,
    179, 181–82, 187n20, 194n12, 202n1;
    resistance to, in U.S., 1–2, 11–13, 128, 180.
    See also allusions; "exploratory poems";
    intelligibility; knowledge
complexity theory, 50
constraints (poetic), 70–74, 83, 85, 102, 135,
    170
contracts of (contracted) intelligibility, 2,
    29, 37–38
"Convolutions" (Kim), 154
courtesy (poetic), 12–13, 14
Creeley, Robert, 18
Cross, Michael, 170, 176
Cupid, 61, 64

Dance Script with Electric Ballerina (Ful-
    ton), 47
Daphne and Apollo myth, 51, 61–68
"dark matter," 64, 65, 67
De Fabrica Humani Corporis (Vesalius),
    161

"The Death of the Subject" (McCaffery), 13

Debré, Olivier, 115–16, 119, 121

Deepstep Come Shining (Wright), 189n9, 190n16

defamiliarization, 8; Fulton's use of, 59, 64; Kim's use of, 153; Retallack's use of, 93; Swensen's use of, 102, 105; Waldrop's use of, 79–80; Wheeler's use of, 127, 132, 144; Wright's use of, 26, 34, 36–37, 43. *See also* disjunctions

"Dejection" (Coleridge), 138

destruction and creation, 85–87. *See also* atomic weapons

Devore, Sy, 61, 63

Dickinson, Emily, 50, 55, 57–58, 59–60, 68, 127

Dictée (Cha), 136, 166–67

digital technology, 7, 130, 145, 180–81

"Disappearance of the Word, Appearance of the World" (Silliman), 23–24, 189n7, 203n7

disjunctions: in Howe's poetry, 16; in Kim's poetry, 154–55; in Language writers' poetry, 24, 35, 45, 46, 50; in Retallack's poetry, 10, 90–92; in Swensen's poetry, 16, 101; in Wheeler's poetry, 127, 130–37, 144, 146, 149–51; in Wright's poetry, 28, 29. *See also* defamiliarization

documentary impulses, 160–65, 167, 181, 189n9

"The Dog Track" (Wheeler), 145

"Drills" (Fulton), 59, 194n17

Drucker, Johanna, 142, 146, 149

Duncan, Robert, 136

DuPlessis, Rachel Blau, 9, 154, 192n1

"Echo Location" (Fulton), 194n12

ecopoetics (journal), 182

Eddington, A. S., 73, 74–78, 81, 82, 84, 87, 197n17

"Eight" (Wheeler), 136

ekphrasis: definition and history of, 99, 187n21; Swensen's use of, 7, 97–123

"The Ekphrastic Principle and the Still Movement of Poetry" (Krieger), 99

electrons, 46, 63, 67, 82, 84

Eliot, T. S., 9, 87, 89, 107, 143, 187n19

"Ellipticism," 129, 186n15, 203n11

English language, 8, 166–68

environmental issues, 128, 174, 177, 178, 181–82

"Eolian Harp" (Coleridge), 138

"Epilogue" (Swensen), 123

epistemes, 97–98, 106, 110, 112, 121, 122, 123

equal signs, 10–11, 58–62, 69, 168–70

error (cultivation of), 130–37, 144, 146, 149–51

ethics (ideologies; morality; politics), 181–82; Fulton's, 52, 53; Kim's, 154–79; Retallack's, 17, 72, 90, 154, 181–82; Silliman's, 24, 42, 189n6, 203n7; Waldrop's, 72, 74–75; Wheeler's, 127, 129, 130, 137, 139–43, 150; Wright's, 21, 24, 28, 29, 42–45, 181

Evans, Steven, 184n7, 195n4, 195n5, 196n8, 203n6

Eve (Biblical figure), 113

Every Goodbye Ain't Gone (Nielsen and Ramey), 4

excess (in Fulton's poetry), 47–48, 50, 193n4

"Exordium" (Kim), 157–58, 159

"The Experimental Feminine" (Retallack), 88–89, 95–96, 198n22

exploratory poems: characteristics of, 8, 9, 20; defined, 2, 7; demands placed on readers by, 13, 18–19, 32–34, 52, 128, 134, 142, 150, 155, 159, 174, 194n13, 200n15; female poets' search for alternative poetic practices through, 2, 3, 5–10, 19, 180–82; Fulton's alternative poetic practices in her, 47, 50, 56, 58–62; institutional recognition of, 7; Kim's alternative poetic practices in her, 153, 156, 163–64, 167–71, 178–79; Language poetry's influence on, 4–5, 6, 7, 11, 16, 19–20, 22–24, 26–29, 33, 36, 37, 42, 45, 69, 127, 129, 145, 188n4, 188n5; Swensen's alternative poetic practices in her, 105, 107, 111; Waldrop's and Retallack's alternative poetic practices in her, 73, 79, 82, 89, 93; Wheeler's alternative poetic practices in her, 124, 128, 141; Wright's alternative poetic practices in her, 23, 27–28, 47, 50, 56, 58–62

poetry, 6–7, 181; creolization, 137; of Fulton's work, 46, 50–69; of genres, 35–36, 68, 70, 124, 125, 181, 191n23; of languages, 167; and Mullen, 14–15, 23; reactions to, 22, 23, 193n7; of Retallack's work, 89, 94; of Wheeler's work, 124–52; of Wright's work, 22–23, 29–45

"I cannot dance upon my Toes" (Dickinson), 59
"Icarus FFFFFalling" (Retallack), 73, 91–95
iconoplasm, 2, 126–52
identity: African American, 14–15; Asian American, 205n3; constructedness of, 10, 22, 28, 57–58, 82, 95, 137–39, 148–49; cultural obsession with personal, 94, 127, 151–52; Language poets' resistance to personal, 125; Musil's concept of, 75; slippage of, in Swensen's poems, 103–106. *See also* gender; nationalism; racial oppression; self-referentiality; subjectivity
Iliad (Homer), 99
imagery, 48, 71, 141–42
"Immersion" (Fulton), 60–61
imperialism (colonialism), 8, 93, 132, 133, 140, 156, 160–64, 166–67, 170, 177, 181
In the Name of the Father (film), 140
"In the Old Days" (Wright), 39–40
institutions: Language poetry not initially recognized by, 22, 183n1; poetry's home in, 4–5, 124–25; political stakes of poetry, 188n2; recognition of exploratory poetry by, 7, 11, 47. *See also* awards; AWP writing programs; publication
intelligibility: "contracts of (contracted)," 2, 29, 37–38; narrative, in Wright's works, 29–45; transgressing limits of, 8, 16, 18, 47, 191n24; transgressing limits of, as discourteous, 12–13, 14; transgressing limits of, in Kim's works, 154, 168, 173–74; transgressing limits of, in Retallack's works, 17, 72, 75, 83–85, 90–91, 96, 128; transgressing limits of, in Wheeler's works, 127, 145–51. *See also* narrative
intertextuality. *See* palimtexts

ionization, 100, 101, 103, 112–13, 122, 123
Ironwood, 3, 27, 189n10

Jakobson, Roman, 8
Jameson, Fredric, 61, 125
Jay, Martin, 156, 161, 162, 206n8
Jeon, Joseph Jonghyun, 12, 205n5, 206n6, 207n13
Jesus, 101, 102–103, 105, 108, 109–11, 114, 117, 119–22, 133. *See also* Christianity
Joyce, James, 72
Juba to Jive (Major), 15
Just Whistle (Wright), 19, 29–45

Katz, Joy, 50–51, 193n4, 194n12
Keats, John, 63, 99, 102–103
Kim, Myung Mi, 7, 8, 16, 19, 153–79, 181
King, Martin Luther, Jr., 15
Kinnahan, Linda A. Taylor, 6, 50, 204n16
Kirsch, Adam, 12–13, 14, 16, 17
knowledge: exploratory poets' "rage" for, 14–18, 20; Kim's concerns about, 157–58, 160–64, 175, 207n12; Mullen on acquisition of, 14; and storytelling, 29. *See also* epistemes; error; science
Korean language, 165, 166–68. *See also* Hangul
Krieger, Murray, 99, 102

lace and lacing: Fulton's use of metaphor of, 11, 58–60; Swensen's aesthetic of, 106, 107, 110, 112, 117, 199n7, 200n14
"Lamenta" (Kim), 158–64, 166, 168
Landscape with Rest in Flight to Egypt (Lorrain), 118
landscapes: paintings of, 117–19; secularization and, 106–108, 111, 115, 121; in Wheeler's poetry, 142–43
language(s) (words): broken, 16; as commodities, 24, 36, 124–25, 189n6; constructing the world through, 22; denaturalizing, 59; facing, as political, 42; as instrument of thought, 77, 180; mixing kinds of, 144–51, 154–55; multiple, used by exploratory poets, 7, 15, 87, 89, 92, 159, 165–69, 181, 182; as nontransparent medium of constructing poetry, 5, 7, 35, 47, 72; as previously

"My Last TV Campaign" (Fulton), 53–58, 69

My Life (Hejinian), 34

narrative: closure's association with, 29; in Fulton's works, 54–55; in Kim's work, 176; in Musil's work, 75–76; by repetition, 122; in Retallack's work, 88, 92–93; in Swensen's work, 98, 102, 109, 191n23; in Wheeler's work, 127; in Wright's work, 29–45

National Poetry Series, 47, 198n6

nationalism, 93, 140, 151, 153. *See also* imperialism

The Nature of the Physical World (Eddington), 74

New American poets, 18, 198n6

"New Formalists," 2

"A New Release" (Fulton), 66–67

New Republic, 12

"new sentence," 26, 27, 36

New York Times Book Review, 47

"Nine" (Wheeler), 136

"Nineteen" (Wheeler), 136

Noli Me Tangere (anonymous Spanish painter), 104, 110–15, 117, 118, 119, 120

North (Heaney), 140

"Ode on a Grecian Urn" (Keats), 63, 99, 102

"Of Modern Poetry" (Stevens), 143

Olson, Charles, 36, 100, 136

"On *Lawn of Excluded Middle*" (Waldrop), 73, 76

"On the Eve of Their Mutually Assured Destruction" (Wright), 43

"On the Morn Of" (Wright), 43

"One" (Swensen), 114

"One" (Wheeler), 136, 137–39

One Big Self (Wright), 181, 189n9

"Op-Ed" (Wright), 21–22

Orcagna (artist), 105, 106

The Order of Things (Foucault), 97, 117

Orpheus, 113

Ovid, 61, 62, 63, 66, 92–93, 94

page space: in exploratory poetry, 7, 18; Fulton's use of, 64; Kim's use of, 153–54, 156–59, 164–79; Language writers' use of, 125; Retallack's use of, 90–92, 95; Swensen's use of, 16–17, 100, 107, 191n22; Wheeler's use of, 147; Wright's use of, 35–36. *See also* punctuation marks; visual elements

paintings (and words), 18, 97–123, 199n10. *See also* collage techniques

palimpsests, 73–74, 75, 78, 82, 83, 84, 89, 104, 110. *See also* source texts

palimtexts, 73, 74, 76, 77, 78, 83, 87–90, 93

Palladium (Fulton), 47, 48

"Paper House" (Wheeler), 136

Parks, Rosa, 15

"Partial Local Coherence" (Fraser), 27–28, 184n2

"Passport" (Fulton), 54–55, 57

patriarchy, 16, 58, 60, 62, 63, 69, 73, 77–81, 88, 94, 95–96, 136–37, 167, 176; in Christianity, 110–12, 121, 136, 201n19, 201n20. *See also* feminism; gender: oppression on basis of

pattern-bounded unpredictability, 2, 70–96

Penury (Kim), 170

Perelman, Bob, 11, 183n2, 191n24

"The Perfecting of a Love" (Musil), 74, 77, 82

Perloff, Marjorie: on exploratory poetry, 7, 8; on Language poetry, 5–6, 52–53, 183n1, 186n17; on natural speech, 202n1; on postmodern storytelling, 29, 31, 42; on resources for poetry, 141–42; on Wittgenstein's influence on poets, 84, 196n12

Philosophical Investigations, Part I (Wittgenstein), 74, 76–78, 81, 83, 196n12

physics, 50, 71, 73, 76, 77, 80, 81, 83, 85, 193n10, 197n17. *See also* fractals; gravity

Picasso (Stein), 143

Picture Theory (Mitchell), 101

Pictures from Brueghel (Williams), 100

Poetic Culture (Beach), 3, 192n2

poetics: defined, 3; fractal, 93; as intellectual exercise, 186n17; "of reciprocal alterity," 182; pleasures of, 20; Waldrop's, 82; Wright's, 21–45. *See also* "exploratory poems" poetry: as living with art, 97–123, 202n21; question of continuing significance of, 124, 152, 180, 202n2; transformative possibilities of, 24, 43–44, 136. *See also* "exploratory poems"; institutions; Language poetry; "mainstream poetry"; poetry scene; *specific poets, poems, and critics*

"Poetry, Mattering?" (Wheeler), 124–27, 132, 147, 150–52

Poetry Center (San Francisco State), 22, 27, 189n10, 198n6

poetry scene, 2–7, 10, 19, 46, 68, 126, 188n2; among Language poets, 7, 19, 22, 23, 25, 26, 27, 183n2

"Pollen Fossil Record" (Kim), 155, 157, 207n15

polysemy: in Fulton's poetry, 10, 47, 51, 55, 65; in Kim's poetry, 164–65, 167; in Language poets' writings, 13; in Mullen's poetry, 14–15; in Swensen's poetry, 104–105; in Waldrop's poetry, 77, 85; in Wheeler's essay, 126; in Wright's poetry, 33

polyvocality: of Fulton's poetry, 47, 51–52, 65; of recent poetry scene, 6–7, 10; in Swensen's poetry, 103

pop culture (mass culture): exploratory poets' use of, 7, 14–15, 84, 94; Fulton's use of, 50, 52–58, 61–68; Wheeler's use of, 127, 130–37, 139–42, 144–45

postmodernism: characteristics of, 22, 29, 61, 68, 70, 125, 129, 142, 144, 200n13; feminist poets linked to, 50–51, 100; and identity, 138

poststructuralism: and authenticity, 42; as influence on exploratory poetry, 8, 18, 37, 50, 127; as influence on Language poetry, 3, 11, 22, 28, 186n17; and lyric poetry's viability, 181

Powers of Congress (Fulton), 47, 49, 52, 53

Presley, Elvis, 61, 63, 64, 65

"The Priming Is a Negligee" (Fulton), 59

procedures (chance; process), 181; in Retallack's poetry, 10, 71, 73, 87, 88, 90–92, 128, 181, 182; in Swensen's poetry, 102

"The Profit in the Sell" (Fulton), 54

"Projective Verse" (Olson), 100

"Prologue" (Swensen), 102–109, 110, 115, 117–18

prose vs. poetry, 35–36, 181, 191n23

"Provide, Provide" (Frost), 151

publication (of poetry), 5, 7, 11, 128

punctuation marks: Fulton's invented, 10–11, 58–62, 69, 195n19; Kim's use of, 159–60, 164, 168–69, 170, 171–73; Wright's use of, 35

quotation marks, 159–60, 164, 195n19

racial oppression, 8, 9, 14–15, 61, 156, 181, 199n8, 203n13. *See also* African Americans

Rasula, Jed, 9–13, 20, 53, 193n3, 193n7

readers (audiences): "courtesy" toward, 12–13, 14, 15; critical, for exploratory poetry, 11; demands placed on, by exploratory poets, 13, 18–19, 32–34, 52, 128, 134, 142, 150, 155, 159, 174, 194n13, 200n15; for poetry, 4, 21, 68, 75, 180–81; Wright's "contract" with, 2, 29, 37–38

"Reading, Raiding, and Anodyne Eclecticism" (Wheeler), 127

"REALISM: An Anthology of 'Language' Writing" (Silliman), 27, 42

refugees, 164–65

"The Rejection of Closure" (Hejinian), 13–14, 15, 188n1

Reluctant Gravities (Waldrop), 96

Renaissance, 97, 98, 101, 108, 121, 122, 160–64, 200n20

repetition: Mullen's use of, 14; narrative by, 122; Wright's use of, 34, 41

representation, 97–123, 149

Reproduction of Profiles (Waldrop), 195n5, 196n12, 197n15

Retallack, Joan, 7–11, 19, 70–74, 83–96, 187n22, 194n10, 198n22; on complexity, 1, 128; ethics of, 17, 20, 72, 90, 154, 180–82

":RE:THINKING:LITERARY:FEMINISM:" (Retallack), 72

Riley, Bridget, 136, 143

Rising, Falling, Hovering (Wright), 181, 189n9

Williams, William Carlos, 50, 92, 100, 205n2
Wittgenstein, Ludwig, 8, 18, 72–81, 83, 84, 87, 195n5, 196n12, 197n15
Wittgenstein's Ladder (Perloff), 84
women: alternative poetic practices of exploratory poets among, 2, 3, 6, 7–10, 19, 23, 27–28, 47, 50, 56, 58–62, 73, 79, 82, 89, 93, 105, 107, 111, 124, 128, 141, 153, 156, 163–64, 167–71, 178–79, 181–82; and Christian misogyny, 110–12, 121, 136, 201n19, 201n20. *See also* "exploratory poems"; feminism; gender; patriarchy; *specific women poets*
"Women, Innovation, and 'Improbable Evidence" (Rasula), 12
"Wonder Bread" (Fulton), 57–58
words. *See* language(s)
Wordsworth, William, 138
"Works" (Kim), 166
Wright, C.D., 7, 11–13, 19, 21–45, 69, 181

Yeats, William Butler, 58, 63, 158